"Lappé and Du Bois are chroniclers of change—in the way we think about ourselves and the world in which we live . . . a convincing and refreshing reaffirmation of the democratic process."
—PATRICK J. LEAHY, SENATOR, STATE OF VERMONT

"This book provides inspiration to all of us who want to make our communities better places in which to live and work. It shows what can happen when citizens and governments roll up their sleeves and work together."
—DONALD BORUT, EXECUTIVE DIRECTOR, NATIONAL LEAGUE OF CITIES

"After years of listening to regular women and men at the grassroots, the authors have distilled hundreds of inspiring success stories into a unique 'how-to' book, infusing the concepts of 'democracy,' 'power,' and 'public life' with vibrant new meaning and challenging us to profoundly rethink our lives."
—FRITJOF CAPRA, FOUNDER AND PRESIDENT, THE ELMWOOD INSTITUTE, AND AUTHOR OF THE TAO OF PHYSICS AND THE TURNING POINT

"A remarkable book. Its lessons are essential and ground-breaking."
—PETER YARROW, PETER, PAUL & MARY

"*Quickening* is an invaluable toolkit for all Americans concerned with reviving our democratic vitality. . . . The book is immensely heartening, drawing on what real people are doing now to help us, as individuals and groups, contribute to making our country (and the world) come closer to the ideals most of us profess."
—ROBERT N. BELLAH, PROFESSOR OF SOCIOLOGY, UNIVERSITY OF CALIFORNIA, BERKELEY, AND COAUTHOR OF HABITS OF THE HEART

"Americans are not apathetic, but either feel they cannot or do not know how to participate effectively. *The Quickening of America* gives every American an extremely practical tool for learning how to effectively take charge—not alone but in full partnership with others."
—JOHN PARR, PRESIDENT, NATIONAL CIVIC LEAGUE

"Lappé and Du Bois have written an invaluable guide to democracy as a living practice from which those who wish not just to read about, or talk about, but to live democracy can draw inspiration and guidance."
—BENJAMIN BARBER, WHITMAN PROFESSOR OF POLITICAL SCIENCE, RUTGERS UNIVERSITY, AND AUTHOR OF STRONG DEMOCRACY

"This book is so refreshing! It is not only thought-provoking, it's action-provoking. Lappé and Du Bois guide readers toward the rewards and excitement that come from using power to change our schools, our communities, and places of work—our lives."

"This book encourages the dream of making a difference and provides the practical steps for making it come true."

The Quickening of America reads like a conversation with an old and trusted friend. *Quickening* is as accessible as it is empowering, a refreshing manual that builds confidence and purpose with anecdotes, empathy, and plain common sense."

"Lappé and Du Bois convincingly and practically show how democracy can be an effective, efficient, and ennobling means of solving problems throughout our society. This is a user's manual on citizenship everyone should read."

"In *The Quickening of America* I learned how to move—with power, effectiveness, and good humor—beyond self-imposed limits . . . we regular people can and must make history."

The Quickening of America is one of the most engaging, hopeful, and useful books you'll ever find. It's full of real life stories that will inspire you and new ideas and resources that will challenge you to think about—and *do*—democracy in a whole new way.

"*The Quickening of America* offers proof that remedies for the nation's most pressing social problems reside in the collective imagination of its populace."

—SHARON E. SUTTON, ASSOCIATE PROFESSOR,
PROGRAM ON CONFLICT MANAGEMENT ALTERNATIVES,
COLLEGE OF ARCHITECTURE AND URBAN PLANNING, UNIVERSITY OF MICHIGAN

"As an elected official who longs for more empowered citizens, I hope thousands of people will read this book, where they will discover again what hard work, but also what satisfying work, democracy can be."

—DANIEL KEMMIS, MAYOR, CITY OF MISSOULA, MONTANA, AND CHAIR,
NATIONAL LEAGUE OF CITIES' LEADERSHIP TRAINING COUNCIL

"Lappé and Du Bois remind us that the future is aborning in the present, that the democracy we want and need most is already present in communities all over America, and that ordinary people are the teachers of the living democracy we must turn to. *The Quickening of America* is a curriculum and a degree program to be widely read and studied. Like all good education, its greatest strength is that it reminds you—us—of all we already know."

—COLIN GREER, PRESIDENT, NEW WORLD FOUNDATION

"The liveliness of their presentation, the vividness of their stories, and the clarity of their charts and questions make this an important book for anyone who cares about democracy in America."

—MIKE MILLER, EXECUTIVE DIRECTOR, ORGANIZE TRAINING CENTER

"*The Quickening of America* is a wonderful book—clear, inspiring, and very accessible. Anchoring the points in real examples from real people makes the conclusions undeniable."

—MARTIN TEITEL, PH.D., C.S. FUND

THE
Quickening
OF
America

*Quickening . . . the first signs
of life, entering a phase of
active growth and development*

THE

Quickening

OF

America

Rebuilding our nation,
Remaking our lives

Frances Moore Lappé • Paul Martin Du Bois

JOSSEY-BASS, INC. PUBLISHERS
SAN FRANCISCO

Substantial discounts on bulk quantities of Jossey-Bass books are available to corporations, professional associations, and other organizations. For details and discount information, contact the special sales department at Jossey-Bass Inc., Publishers. (415) 433-1740; Fax (415) 433-0499.

For sales outside the United States, contact Maxwell Macmillan International Publishing Group, 866 Third Avenue, New York, New York 10022.

Manufactured in the United States of America. Nearly all Jossey-Bass books and jackets are printed on recycled paper containing at least 10 percent postconsumer waste, and many are printed with either soy- or vegetable-based ink, which emits fewer volatile organic compounds during the printing process than petroleum-based ink.

Library of Congress Cataloging-in-Publication Data

Lappé, Frances Moore.
    The quickening of America : rebuilding our nation, remaking our lives / Frances Moore Lappé, Paul Martin Du Bois.
      p. cm.
    Includes bibliographical references and index.
    ISBN 1-55542-605-0
    1. Political participation—United States. 2. Democracy—United States. 3. Social participation—United States. I. Du Bois, Paul Martin, date. II. Title.
JK1764.L36 1994   93–35547
323'.042'0973—dc20   CIP

FIRST EDITION
PB Printing   10 9 8 7 6 5 4 3 2 1   *Code* 9413

To our special partner, Linda Pritzker, with our admiration, gratitude, and love.

And to our "children," who have so often guided our lives:
Carl Campbell, Jon Dixon, Aaron Du Bois, Caleb Du Bois,
Joshua Du Bois, Kara Du Bois, Rangell Du Bois, Anna Lappé,
Anthony Lappé, Charlene Owens, Willie Stubbs,
Cynthia West, and Nate West.

Contents

Acknowledgments

WRITING THIS BOOK KEPT US BUSY learning the very lessons it conveys to others. We've come to value teamwork even more highly, and to appreciate the benefit of diverse perspectives working toward a common purpose. The hundreds of generous people who have made this book possible fall into several clusters.

First are our "teachers." When we conceived of this book, we hoped we would find a dozen, perhaps two dozen, exemplary stories of people who are moving from despair to practical problem solving. Instead, we found hundreds, and eventually thousands, of people and programs that are, quite literally, reframing the way Americans understand our democracy. They taught us more than we ever dared to imagine. The millions of Americans who are transforming themselves, their schools, their workplaces, and their communities are responsible for the strengths of this book.

Next, we thank those who make possible the Center for Living Democracy. Most especially, we thank our beautifully supportive friend and mentor Linda Pritzker. Your wisdom and enthusiasm for our vision have touched us deeply and nourish us daily. We have also been deeply honored by Frank Roosevelt's faith in the importance of our work. We greatly appreciate the friendship and generosity of Bill and Bea Beddor. Several other individuals have also been especially generous. Thank you Steve

Chessin, Martin Rudy Haase, Mollie Katzen, John Moore, and Nancy Roberts.

The Center for Living Democracy enjoys a distinguished Board of Trustees, from whom we have learned a great deal. Thank you Dr. Benjamin Barber of the Walt Whitman Center at Rutgers University, John Parr of the National Civic League, Dr. George Wood of the Institute for Democracy in Education, Dr. Sharon Sutton of the Program on Conflict Management Alternatives at the University of Michigan, and Lisa Richter of Shorebank Advisory Services.

The staff of the Center for Living Democracy has contributed to this book in ways too numerous to mention. We thank Nancy Lon, executive coordinator, and Molly Roth Hamaker, former director of the center's Learning Annex, not only for your excellent assistance in research and production of this book, but for your delightful good cheer and encouragement. You make it possible to live up to the Center's founding motto: "It's gotta be fun!"

During the final stages, we were privileged to work with three highly skilled editors, each contributing his or her special insight: Alan Shrader, Jude Berman, and Carl Rogers. We appreciate your contributions under very tight deadlines!

Others helped shape the book's content and message during monthly center "seminars." Still others assisted with research, fact-checking, and administrative support. Thank you:

John Abbe	Robin Everest	Cynthia McDermott
Tom Atlee	Nancy Friedman	Kate Melby
Zillah Bahar	Tamara Gould	Eric Reed
Terry Barker	Scott Greenberg	Mara Rose
Sarah Benson	Jason Gribling	Craig Slater
Glen Berger	Charles Hamaker	Ben Smith
Jen Chapin	Richard Heinberg	Jory Thein
Judy Clark	Rhonda Holmes	Alita Van Hee
Trena Cleland	William Kramer	Dawn Van Hee
Fred Cook	Anna Lappé	Susan Vaughan
Ken Ehrlich	Robin Laurence	Michael Young
Kathy Emmons	Jeannette Lim	

Vitally important are those who have given freely of their time and talent to make this book happen. For feedback on the initial draft, we are especially grateful to Sue Bumagin, Susan Kanaan, Paul Korn, Mike Miller, Terry O'Connell, John Parr and his colleagues at the National Civic League, Jim Rubens, and Carol Wilson. Our thanks also go to the Industrial Areas Foundation for your invaluable assistance in the research for this book and your insights into public life from which we have learned a great deal. Many citizen organizers helped us develop some of the concepts presented in this book, and our friends in the IAF stand out for your special contribution of time and wisdom.

And finally, we want to express our gratitude to our gifted and dedicated colleagues at Jossey-Bass Publishers who have worked so hard on this book, as well as to Rentsch Associates for your work in promoting it. You've turned hard work into something pleasurable and effective, again confirming our belief in the power of teamwork. Thanks for all you are doing to help spread the message of Living Democracy.

We thank all of these friends and colleagues and hope that this book lives up to your hopes for it.

Make This Book Yours

PLEASE USE THIS BOOK. We hope you see this book as a lever to uproot long-held habits of thought and action that have limited your life. So, make it yours. Write in it. Challenge it. Test it out. Work with it.

This book can be used in any order that suits you. You can begin with Part One, Two, or Three. Each part is very different, so you might want to try one, leave it midway, and move to another. Here's what you'll find in each part:

Part One distills the key insights of successful Americans. Through their voices, you'll understand why rethinking self-interest, power, and public life is the key to bringing new meaning and effectiveness into our lives.

Part Two takes you on a tour of real changes taking place throughout America—what amounts to a quickening in the evolution of our democracy. The word *quickening* means new life. It suggests a new stage in the growth and development of our democracy—when democracy becomes not simply what we have, but what we *do*, with excitement and satisfaction. We call this new stage *Living Democracy*. In Part Two you'll meet effective citizens who are successfully tackling America's biggest problems—from education and government to human services and jobs and the media. How are they succeeding in changing their lives and improving their futures? From a factory in Massachusetts to a classroom in Ohio and a radio station in Texas, regular Americans are applying the lessons we all need in order to create the lives we want . . . and a country that works.

Part Three looks at the quickening of democracy's development through another lens. Here we ask, what are the *skills* we Americans need in order to be effective? How can we become problem solvers ourselves? You'll have an opportunity to reflect on your own skills as you read about the ten *democratic arts* that successful Americans are developing. You'll also be encouraged to focus on your own development and the qualities you can build through a deliberate process of growth.

This book is full of questions. Enjoy them. Pick up a pad of paper and a pencil and record your answers to the writing exercises included in each chapter. Remember: no one but you has to see your responses. If you wish, this book can become your personal record, a diary, of the growth in your thinking about how to move yourself (and your community) into successful, hope-filled action.

This book takes you along on an exciting journey. But to work for you, it must become *your* journey. In whatever order you dive into these chapters, we hope you'll dive deeply.

PART ONE

Overcoming the Myths That Limit Us

THIS BOOK IS BUILT on the experience, insights, and voices of everyday people who have something to teach us all.

In Chapter One we invite you to let go of the negative messages hitting you daily about the sad shape of our society. We highlight little-known but very promising developments that suggest a key message of this book: Our society may be on the edge of a critical breakthrough in appreciating the contributions of everyday people to solving public problems. Some Americans are breaking free of old assumptions in order to discover democracy as a rewarding practice, one central to our happiness and our effectiveness. In Chapter One we also tell you something about ourselves—the path that led us to write this book.

In Chapter Two we tackle the myths about public life that are blocking Americans' growth and effectiveness in every aspect of our lives, from workplaces and schools to our communities. Then in Chapter Three we probe the touchy subject of self-interest, encouraging you to rethink its importance for healthy public lives. In Chapter Four, the final chapter of Part One, we ask you to reflect on your own notions of power—and the power you yourself have—as we explore the power being developed by those who are successfully changing their communities, their states, and our country . . . and also their lives.

1

A Powerful New Concept for Effective Living

WELCOME TO A FRESH WAY OF THINKING about our lives. Millions of Americans are discarding old assumptions in order to discover a rewarding practice, one central to our happiness, well-being, and effectiveness.

It's democracy. Yes, democracy! But not the textbook version we all learned in school. It's democracy *as a way of life* that meets the deep human need to know that our voices count, to shape the decisions that most affect our well-being. We call it *Living Democracy*.

Across virtually every dimension of our society—from the classroom to the community, from the workplace to city hall—Americans are giving shape to a profound new understanding of the role of everyday people in solving public problems.

Most of us haven't yet perceived this development. That's not surprising. We're bombarded daily with bad news that undermines our sense of hope: news of war, famine, AIDS, drive-by shootings, and more. In a land of abundance, nearly a quarter of our children are born into poverty. One in five teens carries a weapon. We have more citizens locked behind bars than any country in the world. And while the number of billionaires doubles in only a decade, homelessness swells to stunt the lives of over a million Americans.

3

How Do You Feel About It?

What words best describe the emotions you feel when hit with all of today's negative news?

And in the face of all this distress, what can we do? Typically, our culture communicates that there are only three ways we can respond:

- Give up! Just focus on doing well for ourselves because the world is going to hell. Or,

- Protest! Make demands. Fight for the right choice—on the environment, the homeless, abortion. And at least get a few rewards from feeling righteous. Or,

- Sacrifice! Give up any notion of going to the roots of the suffering. Deny your own self-interests in order to relieve the suffering of others.

These three are the only choices Americans often perceive—resignation, protest, or self-sacrifice. But this book offers another option. Here the regular Americans you'll be learning from demonstrate the possibility of a more satisfying set of responses. They teach us that something else is happening. Something positive. Something hopeful. Some Americans are joining together to further a quiet revolution, one beginning to touch every arena of American life.

Joe Caldwell works at GM's Saturn plant in Spring Hill, Tennessee. Joe told us that in his previous job he felt just like a "body on the line doing the same thing day after day." Joe now calls that life the "old world." Of his current job, Joe says, "You're not bored to death like in the old world. I've grown a lot because I've had the opportunity to get involved with a lot of segments of the business." At Saturn, Joe is part of a team set up like its own business. He and his co-workers are responsible for their own purchasing, budgeting, and maintenance. "The team leader is elected, not a boss, just a resource to give direction. And employees are self-hiring. The final decision is ours," Joe told us. "Here you see your accomplishment. When I first got here, it was strange, an eye-opener. But it's very, very rewarding." Joe's plant is now outperforming most others in the industry.

In Chicago, in 1977, Mimi Kaplan learned she had breast cancer. The doctors couldn't answer her questions. They couldn't address her fears, particularly her main concern, "How can I cope with chemotherapy while holding down a job?" So Mimi reached out to women facing similar problems. Their first support meeting led to a national organization, Y-ME, in which clients turn the tables on the medical professionals. Today Y-ME supports women cancer patients throughout the country and even guides doctors in improving their patients' care.

Theresa Francis, sixty-four, is a widow and mother of three grown children. For twenty-five years she worked for Century Brass in Scoville, Connecticut. When her company threatened to move, she feared for her job. For as many years, Theresa sang in her church choir but had a limited public life beyond that. Then, she says, "I got involved with the Naugatuck Valley Project because of the sense that I could do something to save my own job." Once she became connected to this community-church-union organization, Theresa's life changed. "I learned so much for myself. I met with presidents of companies. I investigated city plans for land use and ownership. I met with the mayor. Now I'm high for anything I want to do, making myself stretch. That feels so good, I can't *tell* you."

We invite you to meet these people, and many others like them. Neither Joe, Mimi, nor Theresa fits the "activist" stereotype. Yet they experienced changes in their own views of themselves and what they could do. They are taking charge of their own futures. They are among the hundreds of people we've talked with who are successfully addressing the problems that concern us all.

Come join our journey. For three years we've travelled across America to find the stories that don't get reported in the daily press, the stories of *what's working.* Along the way, we've learned a lot about some successful people: people who are learning the skills each of us needs to become effective; people who are transforming themselves and the way they think about their lives; people who are learning the key lessons about remaking America and remaking ourselves.

Here are the two key questions that have guided our journey:

- How do each of us, like Joe, Mimi, and Theresa, gain meaning and joy in our lives?

- How do we bring day-to-day democracy to life, moving America toward a more effective form of democracy—a Living Democracy—that changes the way decisions get made in our jobs, our schools, and our communities?

Our answer: by hearing the stories of regular people who are charting new paths in a journey of historic proportions, by learning the practical concepts they are developing, and by trying them out in our own lives and becoming public problem solvers ourselves.

In this book you'll meet people discovering four hope-instilling, practical tools: public life, relational self-interest, relational power, and what we call the Arts of Democracy. These regular Americans will share with you the tools that are transforming their lives and communities in five areas: economics, the media, human services, government, and education.

To fully enjoy (and learn from) this journey, we invite you to *use this book* to the fullest. Write in it. Mark it up and make it your own road map to a special kind of meaning in your life and to the rewards that come from solving public problems. And don't be inhibited by the questions we ask. They are there to help you understand yourself—and your opportunities. This book is like a personal diary. You can make it work for you. You can use it to build hope in your life.

WHAT GIVES US HOPE

Our lives have been recharged by the people you'll meet in this book and by the breakthroughs they're making in addressing problems that have long stumped our country's "experts" and "higher authorities." Here are just a few of the developments—little known across America—that provide a solid foundation for hope:

Classrooms. In two thousand schools nationwide, youngsters are learning mediation skills. They're helping to settle disputes, reducing violence and injuries among their classmates.

Law Enforcement. In four hundred cities, police departments are moving officers out of squad cars and onto the streets. They are working with citizens to solve neighborhood problems, and crime rates are beginning to drop.

Child Welfare. In thirteen states, welfare officials no longer automatically remove a child from an abusive family. A counselor enters the daily life of the family, coaching its members in how to build love and avoid violence. Families are saved and the cost of intervention is halved.

Workplaces. In four major industries, businesses owned by their workers now rank in the top ten. Stocks in worker-owned companies are now out-performing all major market averages.

City Governance. In Birmingham, Alabama, citizens elect neighborhood councils that negotiate regularly with city hall. For the first time, African-American neighborhoods are getting their share of much-needed capital improvements.

Banking. In 1991, poor and moderate-income citizens stopped the highly financed banking lobby from gutting a federal law that requires banks to invest in low-income neighborhoods. The law, which low-income people themselves had helped to pass, has brought billions of dollars into poor communities.

Public Housing. In at least twenty public housing projects nationwide, tenants are now the managers. Results include dramatic reductions in drug activity and other crimes.

School Governance. In dozens of school districts, schools are now run not only by the school board and administrators but also by school-based teams that include teachers and parents.

What Would You Do?

Suppose you have the power to make one of these stories happen in your community. Which one would it be?

Why does this matter to you? What's happened in your own life that makes you choose this particular issue?

What's striking to us about these diverse developments is this: Regular people—not public officials or so-called experts—are assuming power. More than that, they are *redefining power*.

They have much to teach us—about making decisions, about solving problems, and about power.

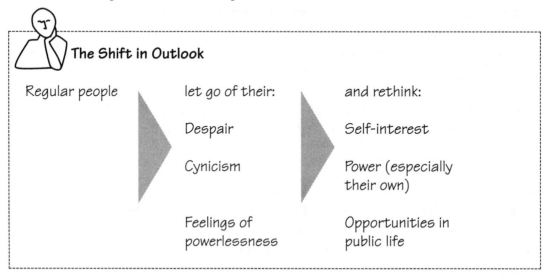

The Shift in Outlook

Regular people	let go of their:	and rethink:
	Despair	Self-interest
	Cynicism	Power (especially their own)
	Feelings of powerlessness	Opportunities in public life

After the civil disturbances in Los Angeles in 1992, the majority of Americans agreed in a *New York Times* survey that the biggest barrier to addressing our social problems is that we simply don't know how.[1] But the people you will meet in these pages prove this widespread belief is wrong. They are discovering practical solutions, freed from dogma.

These people are not seeking *more* government. Nor are they seeking *less* government. Instead, they are developing effective roles for government, made accountable to citizens' real concerns. Similarly, those moving our society toward a truly Living Democracy see neither the marketplace nor corporations as the enemy. They don't view them as the panacea, either. Instead, these citizens are asking, how can the market and business serve our community's needs and values? Finally, those building Living Democracy are letting go of the notion that there is one formula to fit all communities. They are experimenting with *what works,* changing as they learn new lessons.

So it is an extraordinary era—one marked by the possibility of new life, by a quickening in the development of our democracy. In the face of widespread despair about America's problems, this book celebrates the fact that we are alive in such an era of possibility.

But, first, here's the single realization that motivates our life's work and compelled us to write this book.

By the time the two of us met, began to work together, fell in love, and married, we'd each had more than twenty years of experience searching for answers to America's deepening social and environmental problems.

Coming from very different paths, we had both arrived at one critical conclusion. The biggest problem facing Americans is not those issues that bombard us daily, from homelessness and failing schools to environmental devastation and the federal deficit. Underlying each is a deeper crisis. Some see that deeper problem in the form of obstacles that block problem solving: the tightening concentration of wealth, the influence of money in politics, discrimination, and bureaucratic rigidity, to name a few. These *are* powerful barriers. But for us the crisis is deeper still. The crisis is that *we as a people don't know how to come together to solve these problems.* We lack the capacities to address the issues or remove the obstacles that stand in the way of public deliberation. Too many Americans feel powerless.

By our mid forties, we realized that none of the particular concerns on which we and many others had focused our energies can be addressed without tackling this deeper crisis—the crisis of our capacity to solve our problems. To work out solutions to any of these far-reaching problems, we as a people first have to ask:

- How can we Americans learn the concepts and practices that make us effective public problem solvers?

- How can we Americans gain the capacity to make our engagement in public life rewarding and sustaining?

Trying to answer these questions forced the two of us to recognize that something essential has been missing, even in societies that call themselves democracies—even in the world's preeminent democracy, our very own. Let us use our own experiences for a few moments to explain what has been missing from America's democracy.

BENEATH ALL THE ISSUES LIES THE REAL CRISIS

A LIMITING VISION OF OURSELVES IN SOCIETY
—

We were both born at the end of World War II—one black, one white; one male, one female. Our experiences growing up could hardly appear more different. Paul was born in Harlem but was raised on a New Jersey farm. Frances was born in rural Oregon and reared in Fort Worth, Texas. Yet beneath these and other differences, we grew up absorbing similar lessons about what it means to achieve the good life in America.

While our parents were involved in community activities, primarily through their churches, the larger culture gave us another message: satisfaction came in *personal* relationships and *private* achievement. Families and careers were most important. Rewards would accrue if we worked hard, if we applied ourselves competitively in the marketplace and were loyal spouses and responsible parents. Public life, on the other hand, was a drag.

We weren't unusual. Like other Americans from all walks of life, we absorbed negative messages about public life at school, through the media, and from the attitudes of those around us.

Your View of Public Life

Focus for a moment on your earliest impressions of public life. Was public life seen mainly as a burden? Or as a source of reward?

In school the two of us learned that what was required to achieve the good life was not to ask questions. In fact, I (Paul) was even kicked out of a seminary because, as the Rector told me, I asked too many questions in theology class. I was heartbroken. My dreams of a meaningful life of service as a missionary to Africa, or to my own country's poor, had been crushed because, I concluded, I hadn't been smart enough to keep my natural inquisitiveness shut up inside me.

We learned that preparing for real life meant breaking the world down into disconnected "subjects"—English at second period, math at third, music at sixth. If we memorized the material or mastered these subjects, we'd make the grade and eventually become successful adults. Family responsibility, in Paul's case, meant doing specific duties, not speaking out, and never, ever talking back. Pay attention! Show respect! Experts were in charge, whether teachers or parents.

In work life, too, the expectations, the lessons, weren't very different. We learned that success at work meant conforming to an employer's design. As a teenager and young adult trying to "make it" in the white world of business and commerce, I (Paul) dug graves at a cemetery, unloaded thousands of watermelons for a roadside stand, picked berries and grapes on a New Jersey farm, rolled coils in a Pittsburgh steel plant, and served as night watchman in a New York office building. In all this, the single most common statement I heard—probably hundreds of times—was what I came to call "The Big Order": "Do as you're told."

Here too, just as in school and family life, someone else—a boss or an expert—was in charge. The primary capacities we needed for success in all these arenas were the same: we had to be able to absorb, follow orders, compartmentalize, and defer to others because they were supposedly better qualified or simply had more authority.

We learned similar lessons about politics. For us it was distant, remote from our daily experience, what *professionals* do. We came to believe our task as citizens was to let professionals pick other professionals to run for office. Then we'd simply choose which of them would make the important public decisions for us.

Along with millions of young people, we learned to equate democracy with a set of formal institutions—constitutional government and the two-party system. Preparing for citizenship meant learning civics, memorizing how a bill becomes law, or reciting the articles of the Constitution.

We came to believe we were lucky enough to be born with democratic institutions already in place, with precious little for ordinary citizens like us to create. Sure, there were rough edges to be smoothed—the legacies of racism and poverty and continuing political corruption, for example. Nonetheless, we were taught, democracy is what we already have.

And in all of this, there was little expected from our "hearts"—little public recognition of any human need to express public concerns. We feared that our own innate desire to contribute to something bigger than ourselves made us oddballs. After all, the wider culture communicated that expressing compassion was not a need we feel, but simply another duty that we could meet annually through "one great hour of sharing" or a check to the United Way or the United Negro College Fund.

All these messages were coherent. And they required very little of us. Civic responsibility was for the second Tuesday in November when good citizens trudge to the polls. Charity was for whatever day we pay our bills.

What then is the problem? What's missing?

It was only later that we realized that most of us growing up in late twentieth-century America have absorbed ten damaging messages about public life, messages that we now call *myths*.

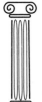

America's Top Ten Myths

Here are the top ten myths that the public culture taught us while we were growing up in modern America. Which of these have you learned?

MYTH ONE

Public life is what someone else— a celebrity or big shot— has.

MYTH TWO

If I'm not a celebrity, public life is unappealing and unrewarding.

MYTH THREE

Public life involves a lot of ugly conflict.

MYTH FOUR

Public life competes with—even detracts from—a satisfying private life.

MYTH FIVE

We must learn to squelch our self-interest for the common good.

MYTH SIX

For most people, public life is really about pursuing their own selfish interests.

MYTH SEVEN

Power is a dirty word.

MYTH EIGHT

There's only so much power to go around, so I have to fight for what's mine.

MYTH NINE

Power is a one-way force; if I've got it, I can make others do my bidding.

MYTH TEN

Power is about winning victories today, now!

We call them myths because these messages simply don't work. For more and more Americans, they do not create the good life, the meaningful life, the effective life. The failure of these assumptions creates consequences vastly more serious than in prior generations. The signs of public breakdown are too painfully obvious.

THE IMPORTANCE OF PUBLIC LIFE

What's missing from the messages we absorbed is an appreciation of the capacity and the need that regular people—almost all of us—have to connect to the larger world. To know that *our lives count beyond our immediate families.* The lives of those you'll meet in this book confirm this capacity and this need.

What's been missing, therefore, is the concept of *public life.* Not public life as fame and notoriety, like the flashy images of Hollywood stars, sports figures, and politicians. Not public life as mere voting. But public life as the roles we take at work, at school, and in our communities.

Narrowly conceiving of public life as what famous people have, or solely as our ties to government, carries a great price. We cheat ourselves of potential decision-making opportunities because the workplace and educational institutions—the places where we spend the bulk of our waking hours—aren't considered part of our democratic public lives. Neither are the media nor the human services we use. Each one of these institutions encourages little participation in decision making.

What's missing has been the core insight that democracy—whether it works or not—depends on how each of us lives our public life, our lives outside our families. Also missing has been any understanding that without meaningful public lives we can't protect and further the well-being of those we care about most in our private lives.

To make even clearer the contrast between these notions about democracy we've all grown up with and the Living Democracy we're introducing in this book, we've constructed an imaginary argument between two people with very different understandings of democracy.

Try reading this dialogue aloud with someone. Read it twice, changing voices so you can get a sense of which voice feels more true to your own thinking. Voice One represents the formal view of democracy, the view most of us inherited. Voice Two represents a newer view, one taking shape out of more and more Americans' actual experience today.

Formal Democracy Versus Living Democracy: An Argument

VOICE ONE: Democracy is one form of government, pure and simple. It depends on some key institutions: elected leadership; more than one party; a balance of power. In the case of the United States, that means three branches of government.

VOICE TWO: But lots of countries have impressive institutions of democracy, and still the majority of citizens live in misery. To work, democracy has to be more. It has to be a way of life—a way of life that involves the values and practices people engage in daily in all aspects of their public lives.

VOICE ONE: Sure, it depends on some practices. The citizen has to vote, for example; the public official has to be honest. But the great thing about democracy is precisely that it doesn't require very much from citizens, leaving them free to pursue their *private* lives. That's what really matters to people.

VOICE TWO: Citizenship is a lot more than voting. And our public lives are much more than just our ties to government. Politicians are not the only people who live in a public world. Every one of us lives in a public world. But our public lives are rewarding—for ourselves and our society—to the extent that we have a real say in the workplace, at school, in the community, in relation to the media, and to human services, as well as in government.

VOICE ONE: But democracy isn't about what goes on in the workplace or school. These institutions are *protected* by democratic government, but they certainly aren't the same thing as democracy. Furthermore, your ideas turn ordinary people into decision makers. Democracy works best when people elect *others* who are better qualified to keep the machinery of government running smoothly.

VOICE TWO: Citizens ought to determine the values upon which the decision makers act. It's these so-called experts—people who are supposed to be better qualified—who have gotten us into the mess we're in now! Experts don't have to be on *top* making the choices. Instead, they ought to be on *tap* to citizens who are choosing the directions our society ought to go in.

VOICE ONE: But most people don't want to be involved. Public life is no picnic. It's nasty and getting nastier all the time. In a democracy, public life is a necessary evil. We minimize the nuisance by minimizing government—and by assigning public roles to others, to officials, in order to protect our private freedom.

VOICE TWO: But in reality there are millions of regular people discovering the *rewards of public life* at school, at work, and in the community. They are discovering that their voices *do* count. They're building strengths they didn't know they had—to communicate, to make decisions, to solve problems. Some are even discovering the fun of power!

VOICE ONE: You've blurred some important distinctions. People you're talking about may be building their *character* through good works, but all that's required for *citizenship* is responsible voting—electing the best people to run our government.

VOICE TWO: Democracy requires a lot more of us than being intelligent voters. It requires that we learn to solve problems with others—that we learn to listen, to negotiate, and to evaluate. To think and speak effectively. To go beyond simple protest in order to wield power, becoming partners in problem solving. This isn't about so-called good work; it's about our vital interests. And it isn't about simply running our government; it's about running *our lives*.

VOICE ONE: But what you're saying about the way it *ought to be* is irrelevant. Americans are apathetic.

VOICE TWO: No, Americans aren't apathetic. Study after study shows they're angry. Angry about being shut out of decision making. Angry that their democracy's been stolen from them.

VOICE ONE: Our democracy hasn't been stolen. It's still in place. It's been in place for over two hundred years!

VOICE TWO: Democracy is never fully in place. It is always in flux, a work in progress. Democracy is dynamic. It evolves in response to the creative action of citizens. It's what we make of it.

This argument takes only four minutes to read through once. But here are three short questions that might keep you and a friend talking all night:

- *Think back over the last year. Where have you heard or read any of these arguments?*

- *Which voice in this dialogue best matches your own views?*

- *What are some of the influences in your life—people, institutions, or experiences—that have shaped your views?*

In this dialogue, the "voice" of Living Democracy values our formal democracy. But it argues that it alone can't solve our problems. Today's problems require much more. Why? Because they touch us all; our problems are interrelated. Second, they're complex; they involve our attitudes, our daily behavior, even such intangibles as hope itself.

This means that whether they relate to environmental degradation, poverty, racism, crime, drugs, or failing schools, these problems elude hierarchical and expert-driven strategies.

The Limits of Problem Solving by Authorities

In this column are ten big social problems.	List those in authority who are expected to solve these problems.	Now list some other people whose involvement is crucial if the problems are going to be solved someday.
Environmental degradation		
Poverty		
Crime		
Drug abuse		
Failing schools		
Homelessness		
Racism		
Widespread unemployment		
Violence in our media		
Inadequate health care		

Many people who complete this exercise conclude that our society's mounting problems will be solved only when more and more citizens perceive *themselves* as having a stake in solving our problems and believe in themselves as problem solvers. And invaluable lessons are being learned about how people everywhere are doing just that. These lessons are emerging especially at local, statewide, and regional levels. They are not widely visible. They don't make the evening news. Yet some findings are strikingly clear in the extraordinary range of settings you'll explore as you journey through this book. People in every walk of life, in every part of the country, tackling all the problems that plague our society, are teaching us that:

- The most effective decision making depends on the ingenuity and experience of those who are directly affected, from patients and welfare clients to students, teachers, and employees.

- The best decisions arise from the interplay of diverse experiences and viewpoints.

- The best decision making is an ongoing process, not an end point. It is always evolving in response to new information and new insights.

- To be successful, problem solving must actively involve those who must ultimately implement the decisions.

These simple discoveries add up to one core insight: democracy *can* work. Not democracy as we have known it—simply a set of formal institutions—but *democracy as a way of life* that involves us every day.

As this chapter opened, we suggested the limiting options that Americans feel we have in face of our society's distress. Basically, they boil down to three—resignation, protest, or self-sacrifice. But the people in this book offer a third set of responses.

They teach us that, despite the magnitude of our society's problems, we can choose not to bury our need to make a difference. That need is real. It is legitimate. We can claim it and let no one talk us out of it.

From this solid base, we can jump in. We can make an impact in our public lives, and not just through single-issue protest. Going deeper, we can help to transform the very *way* public decisions get made. We can help reshape decision making itself so that more and more of us have a voice, and have the opportunity to learn how to make sound judgments, whether this means the way decisions get made in our workplaces, classrooms, cities, or our nation. Only then are we tackling the real crisis, that crisis of democracy that lies beneath every issue.

But how? you ask. We can choose to learn how, and that is what this book is all about, people learning how to become creators of our future, creators of a democracy that works because it is alive with the insights and energy of us all.

What's to Come

- In the next chapter you'll have a chance to examine your public life. You may be surprised to find just how public it already is.

- In Chapter Three you'll analyze your self-interest. It may not be what you think it is, and it's not something to be ashamed of.

- In Chapter Four you'll be challenged to redefine power so you can discover lots more than you think you have.

- In Part Two—Chapters Five through Nine—you'll discover the compelling stories of regular Americans successfully attacking problems that concern each of us. We'll explore the important lessons they are learning to improve their lives and their communities—in the workplace, the media, human services, government, and education.

- In Part Three, you'll find practical ideas for applying these lessons to your life in order to become more effective.

2

We Each Have a Public Life

WALK INTO ANY BOOKSTORE and we immediately get hit with an array of books claiming to help us tackle any private problem, from grief to impotence, from home decorating to anorexia. Turn on the TV and we peek into the intimate details of other people's private struggles.

The message is clear: our private life, revolving around family and close friends, is what really matters. It's the source of our fulfillment, the secret to our happiness. And besides, what else is there? Surely not *public* life.

Public life is what someone *else* has: the president, the mayor, the Hollywood celebrity. Certainly *I* don't have a public life, and I want to keep it that way. Public life is brutal. It's nasty and mean-spirited. It's the world of big egos and cutthroat politics.

Americans learn to focus on private life and abhor public life, but at great cost. Ironically, that cost is paid both in our public lives—where our communities suffer—*and* in our private lives as we search for meaning and personal growth. So join us now as we tackle four myths we listed earlier. These are myths that debilitate us, leaving us passive onlookers while some of the most important decisions of our lives get made by others. We'll explore alternatives that can free each of us to discover the fulfilling rewards of public life.

The journey we'll take in this chapter explores these myths one by one. Where did they come from? Why do they *seem* to make sense? Why aren't

The Public Life of _____

(write your name here)

Here's an opportunity for you to go deeper into your attitudes toward public life. Rate yourself on a scale from one to five for each of the contrasting positions expressed below. Circle the appropriate number in each scale.

**My perception of my
public life**   1   2   3   4   5

I don't think I'm engaged in public life at all. I go through my days earning a living or going to school, attending to my friends and loved ones—pretty much just taking care of business.

I see myself as actively engaged in public life— in my workplace, in my school, in my place of worship, as a consumer, as a TV watcher, and so on.

The nature of public life   1   2   3   4   5

Public life repels me. It's cutthroat and driven by big egos.

I *like* the idea of partici- pating in public life. I see it as rewarding and positive.

Public life versus private life   1   2   3   4   5

Public life is too time- consuming. My public and private lives compete too often for my time and attention.

My public and private lives are mutually enhancing and actually contribute to each other.

How I view my role   1   2   3   4   5

There's not much of a role for me in public life. It's con- trolled by others—distant authorities and powerful figures.

I feel capable, empowered, in my public life. I know I can make things happen.

Now that you have evaluated your role in public life, here are two big questions only you can answer: (1) With which of the above responses are you most dissatisfied? (2) How could you shift to a more positive role in public life?

they useful any longer? What are the liberating insights that can replace them?

 ## Myth One: Public Life Is What Someone Else Has

The Limiting Myth

Officials and celebrities—people who want to be in the limelight—have public lives. Public life is for the educated and the experts. It's also for "activists"—people who like making waves.

The Empowering Insight

We each have a public life. Every day—at school, where we work, where we worship, within civic and social groups, as well as at the polls—our behavior shapes the public world. Public life draws on the strengths of all of us.

To the extent we buy the view that it's the other guy who has a public life, we defeat ourselves. We give our power to someone else. The truth is, we all live in a public world, like it or not, aware of it or not. It's the world of our workplace, our school, our religious community, our voluntary association. It's the world of the health services we need, the media that deliver thousands of messages into our living room, the government agency meant to serve us. And of course the elected official who is supposed to respond to our values.

Do you recall the three people who began this book—Joe, Mimi, and Theresa? Theresa is enlarging her impact in her community through an organization in Connecticut. Mimi transformed her ties to human services in Chicago. Joe is experiencing an eye-opening change in his auto plant in Tennessee.

In fact, we each play many roles in this public world, as worker, consumer, viewer, employer, supervisor, client, voter, opinion giver, student, service recipient, critic, contributor, leader, participant. Even many roles we think of as private—parent, for example—have vast public consequences. Personal choices we make daily—what we eat, where we shop, how much we drive—have far-ranging economic and societal and ecological consequences.

Why is it so difficult for many of us to imagine the possibility that public life can bring meaning and happiness to our lives?

One reason is that our concept of ourselves—what we think we're capable of and what brings us satisfaction—has simply not caught up with the changed reality of our modern lives. And much has changed.

A century ago, life *was* simpler. Think about your grandparents' lives. Did they grow up in the same small town or neighborhood in which they were born? Community life for many of our grandparents was an extension of their families and religious community. Work, too, was often a family affair.

Many people today yearn for this earlier simplicity. But nostalgia can blind us to the rich possibilities of our modern lives. In earlier days, relationships and roles were more limited, structured, and hierarchical. Today,

---

Just How Involved Are You?

Circle the areas in which you are most involved.

Underline the areas in which you are least involved.

Education   Religious life   Health care

Social services   Civic life

Cultural life   Voluntary organizations   Your job

Media   Community improvement

What can you learn about yourself?

• If you wanted to increase your involvement in one of these areas, which one would it be? _____

• Why? _____

• What are the rewards you expect from increased involvement? _____

_____

every one of us operates in a public world in which those fixed relationships, such as employer-employee, are being rethought. Let's look at a few examples.

At Work. In the last century, few women had work lives beyond the home and farm. For many men as well, earning a living didn't require relating to many other people. But stop a moment and estimate how many new people you meet or talk to in your work each week. Now multiply that number by two thousand and that's how many people you'll relate to during a forty-year work life. If your guess was five, that's ten thousand people—more than in most small towns in America. Not only do we come into contact with literally thousands of people, success in today's workplaces requires that we become decision makers with others.

At School. A century ago, a child could succeed at school by following the rules and keeping quiet. Schoolmates often came from homes similar to a child's own. Remember your own school days: the only teamwork was probably on the playing field. And we'll bet you never even heard the term *multiculturalism*. Today's urban schools bring together not only many backgrounds but even many languages. Some schools, those that are among the most successful, involve students in collaborative classwork and community life.

In the Community. In the last century, major community decisions—which companies came to town, where businesses located, which production technologies they used—were decided by a few people responding to the market. Today, with a greater population density, and with the growing awareness of the hazards of current technologies, more people are asking whether they feel safe leaving the future of their communities to chance, or in other people's hands.

In Religious Life. While many religious denominations keep a strict separation between their religious devotion and community engagement, more and more congregations are involving worshipers directly in public decisions to act on such values as compassion, social justice, and "stewardship of the earth."

In every core aspect of contemporary life we are engaged in complex public relationships. The world has changed to make us all much more connected to one another and to a common fate.

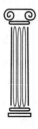 ## Myth Two: Public Life Is Unappealing and Unrewarding

The Limiting Myth

Public life is a necessary evil, a means of protecting our private lives. Public problems are just too big. It's too depressing to get involved against such odds. It's too easy to burn out.

The Empowering Insight

Public life serves a deep human need: to know that one's life counts and can make a difference in the larger world. Public life has its distinct rewards; there's much to be learned along with the chance for excitement, fun, and recognition. It is just as essential to our growth and happiness as is private life.

It's true, for many people public life is strictly defensive. People come together to try to protect themselves from the impact of decisions that others have made, whether related to the dumping of toxic wastes, the flight of American companies overseas, or the location of a highway through their neighborhood.

But as more and more regular people discover that they *do* have the capacity to speak out and make things happen, public life changes. Suddenly, it's no longer a dull, defensive duty. It becomes central to their well-being, to their very self-respect and dignity. "I'm hooked for life," is the way Pam Emigh of the Pennsylvania Environmental Network puts it.

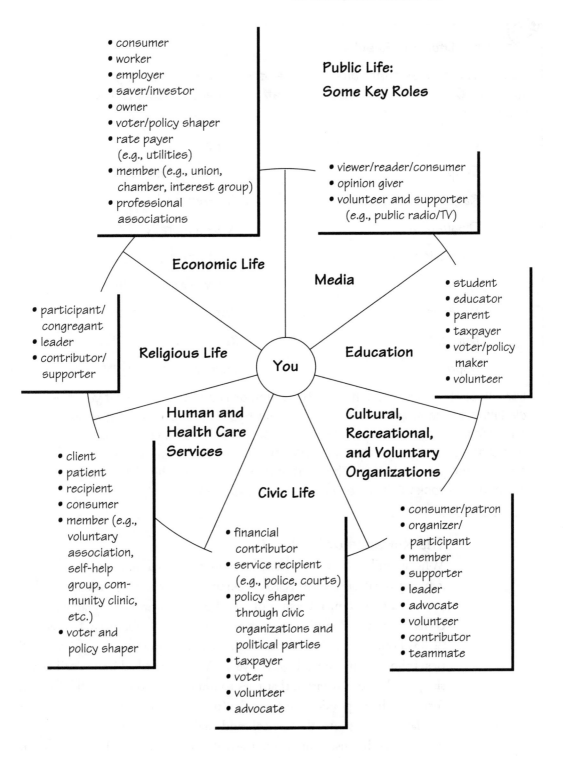

Public Life:
Some Key Roles

Economic Life

- consumer
- worker
- employer
- saver/investor
- owner
- voter/policy shaper
- rate payer
  (e.g., utilities)
- member (e.g., union,
  chamber, interest group)
- professional
  associations

Media

- viewer/reader/consumer
- opinion giver
- volunteer and supporter
  (e.g., public radio/TV)

Religious Life

- participant/
  congregant
- leader
- contributor/
  supporter

You

Education

- student
- educator
- parent
- taxpayer
- voter/policy
  maker
- volunteer

Human and
Health Care
Services

- client
- patient
- recipient
- consumer
- member (e.g.,
  voluntary
  association,
  self-help
  group, com-
  munity clinic,
  etc.)
- voter and
  policy shaper

Civic Life

- financial
  contributor
- service recipient
  (e.g., police, courts)
- policy shaper
  through civic
  organizations and
  political parties
- taxpayer
- voter
- volunteer
- advocate

Cultural,
Recreational,
and Voluntary
Organizations

- consumer/patron
- organizer/
  participant
- member
- supporter
- leader
- advocate
- volunteer
- contributor
- teammate

Public Life: Your Results

Think of three times that you've made a strong effort to invest yourself in public life. Circle the words that you most closely associate with these experiences.

Cynicism	Hope
Despair	Accomplishment
Rage	Connection
Disgust	Acting morally
Alienation	Excitement
Dread	Growth and learning
Boredom	Satisfaction
Burnout	Recognition
Depression	Energy

Did you circle more words in the left column or the right column? If you circled mostly the negative, discouraging feelings on the left, don't give up. These feelings are not inevitable. In the rest of this book, you'll be introduced to some important skills that can change your experiences. If you circled mostly the words on the right, congratulations! The skills you'll discover in this book will help you build on your experiences.

The Rewards of Public Life

Why are millions of Americans becoming involved in a new breed of citizen organizations, such as Kentuckians for the Commonwealth, which proudly boasts a membership of ten thousand who actively address concerns from toxic dumping to open government? Member Jean True admits, "I was home raising kids for ten years. I didn't know anything about politics. I thought my only job was to vote." When we asked Jean to tell us why she joined an organization that tries to improve the quality of life for Kentuckians, she responded, "It's just the fun! That you can get together some regular people, go to the capitol, and make changes in state policy. You meet others. It's just plain fun to learn about it all. . . . We have a great time doing what we do, going toe-to-toe and head-to-head with state legislators. We sometimes know more than they do! It's the fun of power—the ant knocking over the buffalo."

Wib Smith, a middle-aged professional in Memphis, had long been concerned about the quality of life in his city. For decades, he watched the city decay while racial tension intensified. He had participated in citizen protests to try to get more city resources directed to poor and black neighborhoods, but in the end the protests seemed fruitless. They never went anywhere, he told us.

"My righteous indignation was wearing thin," Wib admitted. Then he joined Shelby County Interfaith (SCI), a citizen organization that is successfully tackling school reform and designing innovative jobs programs. "Now I see if you are willing to work, to take small steps, you can do anything," Wib said. "It's exciting to see things happen. To plan . . . wait, and then find out, yeah, the mayor *did* come to our meeting! It tickles me. I never really believed I could make a difference. Now I do."

Gerald Taylor coordinates the network of citizen organizations (linked to the national Industrial Areas Foundation) in the Southeast that includes Wib Smith's SCI. Gerald has worked with citizen groups since he was a teenager. He knows Wib isn't unusual. In fact, he says, most people want to make a difference. "Why enter public life?" Gerald asked, then immediately answered his own question: "To tap the spirit in all of us, asking what is my mark, the imprint I want to create with my life?"

Sadly, this need to make our mark in the larger world gets buried for those who've lost hope for the possibility. Yet it is an almost universal human need, running as deep as our need for satisfying private lives. It is the need to know we're contributing to a purpose beyond ourselves.

Public Life: Your Rewards

Have you ever had the experience of not believing you could make a difference and then finding out you can?

What accomplishment outside of your family makes you most proud?

Why do you feel proud? What other rewards did you receive?

The Rewards of Learning and Growing

In Living Democracy, the human need to learn and grow flourishes. As we traveled across America to find success stories of citizens changing the way decisions get made on their jobs, in their schools, and throughout their communities, we've been impressed by how powerfully citizens receive the reward of learning. To many, it is as important as winning. Jan Wilbur of The Metropolitan Organization (TMO) in Houston, Texas put it this way: "It's not just the victories that make people feel powerful. This work is the highest form of citizen education. The individual development that takes place is incredible! The first time a person talks to a city official, they're shaking. The second or third time, they're talking to the official as an equal. Getting the street fixed is important, but more important is knowing that feeling of confidence will never be lost again."

Through TMO, thousands of Houston citizens are learning how to influence public decisions. They've succeeded, for example, in shifting millions of dollars of city revenue into long-neglected neighborhoods. When we asked Jan how getting involved with TMO had changed *her*, she answered, "It helped put a backbone in me."

The theme of overcoming fear runs through the lives of many we met who are deliberately developing a place for themselves in public life. Jean True of the influential, statewide Kentuckians for the Commonwealth (KFTC) described a similar feeling: "The first time I was supposed to speak at an EPA hearing, I couldn't even get up and read my statement. I thought I was going to throw up." But from that shaky beginning she rose to become co-chair of KFTC. The night we met her she was at ease standing before two hundred people offering a toast at KFTC's tenth anniversary celebration.

Public Life: Your Learning

Have you ever worried that you are no longer learning as much as you once did?

From what experiences are you presently learning the most?

What changes in your public life would help you to learn even more?

While many Americans typically perceive public life as a drag, one full-time citizen organizer in Fort Worth expressed the rewards of learning: "We have fun. It's all about growth and development—enjoying seeing people change, enjoying seeing myself change."

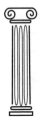 ## Myth Three: Public Life Means Ugly Conflict

The Limiting Myth

Public life is always nasty. It's cutthroat. Who wants to be part of that? It's all about conflict, while most people just want some peace and harmony in their lives.

The Empowering Insight

In public life we encounter differences, even more than in private life. But conflict doesn't have to be nasty or destructive. It can be healthy and informative, bringing insights about ourselves and new perspectives for solving problems.

As soon as we step beyond the bounds of immediate family and friends, we meet people who are different. Interests often collide. Tension occurs. Unfortunately, "we're told to run from tension in American culture," says Gerald Taylor, the citizen organizer in Tennessee who has spent most of his life learning these lessons. Then he adds, "If we're tense, the ads tell us to take an aspirin. But when you hold someone accountable in public life for what they know they ought to be doing, you *are* confronting them. There *is* tension. But we can learn to make that tension creative."

Conflict makes us visible. It brings us attention. For many people that's uncomfortable.

"People fear embarrassing themselves," notes Pam Emigh, who's joined with others to clean up toxic waste in Morrisdale, Pennsylvania. "In our communities there's a big 'authority thing.' Teacher is law. Minister is law. So if a corporation comes in and puts a toxic dump in your yard . . . they're right. It's embarrassing to challenge that authority. It's easy to feel that we just don't know enough."

What Are the Rewards of Developing Our Public Lives?

While talking with hundreds of Americans, we've heard people describe at least nine categories of rewards.

Put an X next to the rewards you have already received from public life.

Now circle the five rewards you would most like to receive from your public life.

Feeling better about myself

More personal power, less fear

A new pride in accomplishment

Satisfaction in helping, in making a contribution, in doing my share to make the world more like it "should be"

Feeling my actions are more in tune with my values

Feeling better physically

More energy

Greater calm and serenity

An overall feeling of happiness and well-being

Having more meaningful relationships

Caring interactions with those who share my concerns, hopes, and vision

Feelings of mutual respect among those with whom I regularly interact

Learning

Effective interaction skills, such as how to negotiate

Greater knowledge of how the world works

Discovering the difference between what is meaningful and what is trivial

More insight into myself

Discovering how much I have to contribute

Satisfaction in expressing care for loved ones

Knowing that my efforts will create a better future for those I love

Mentoring

Satisfaction from seeing those I've coached grow and succeed.

Receiving recognition

Respect from others

Appreciation

Public visibility

Feeling a sense of purpose in life, greater hope

Knowing my individual efforts are part of historic change

Enjoying improvements in the quality of life

Better jobs, schools, neighborhoods, housing, medical care, environment

What allows us to overcome our fears in order to make our voices heard? For many people the answer is anger. Healthy public action often begins when we experience our anger and put it to constructive use. Here's how Jean True described her initial feelings when she realized she couldn't learn what her Kentucky state legislators knew about toxic dumps near her home: "Yes, I was scared, but I began to see the closed hearings, the lack of access to information that citizens need. I thought, 'But this is America!' I was outraged. The driving force was that they made me so angry."

In South Texas, we talked with Elizabeth Valdez, a young citizen organizer who is working to get clean water and other amenities for her community. She explained that she has learned to see that "anger can be good. You just have to recognize it. Then you ask, *Why* am I angry? What is this about? You have to evaluate it. Then put it out there; use it." For Elizabeth, a feeling of anger was the first step toward positive change. Evaluating it—not avoiding it—was the second step. And deciding that anger was a source of power to *act* was the third crucial step toward changing both herself and her community.

Learning from the Uncomfortable

List three challenging encounters in public life you've experienced in the past year.

1. _____

2. _____

3. _____

Most people experience a mix of feelings in public life, some comfortable, some not so comfortable. If any uncomfortable feelings arose for you in these situations, how did you handle them? What could you have done?

Now imagine you are describing these events to several people much younger than yourself. What are the lessons you want them to learn from your behavior in each case? What will you suggest is the best way to handle each situation?

Disciplined Anger, Positive Conflict

Americans are learning that conflict does not have to be nasty. In Memphis, this is how Shelby County Interfaith member Wib Smith explained it to us: "I used to think confrontation was bad. You just don't *do* that. But my views are changing. It's OK to confront someone in public office, to say, 'I think you are wasting our tax dollars.' I don't have to foam at the mouth or call them names."

But, we wondered, how do people overcome their fear of confrontation so they can do it positively and effectively? "By practice, by little bitty steps," says Wib. And Gerald Taylor, who worked with Wib in Memphis, stressed one key insight that helped him: "In public life you accept the fact that some people will not like you and that you do not like some people with whom you have to deal. We don't care whether they [officials] like us. We can have a relationship with them—and respect them—and still not like them and not have them like us."

Wib and Gerald noted that being fully prepared also helps make conflict creative rather than destructive. Unprepared people, folks who don't know the arguments they are going to deliver and receive, more easily get "hot under the collar" from embarrassment or defensiveness. Being prepared for conflict helps people think through how they are going to handle it, giving them a greater sense of control—of themselves and the situation they will face. At Shelby County Interfaith, preparation means rehearsing before any public encounter. "At SCI, we usually have at least two rehearsals," Wib explained. "You rehearse. Get critiqued. Rehearse again." Practices like this can turn nasty conflict into creative confrontation.

Your Effective Anger

When was the last time you felt angry about something outside your family life?

Upon reflection, what is the best way to express your anger so that you can change things for the better? Is this what you've done in the past? What might you do to further strengthen your capacity to express your anger effectively?

Myth Four: Public Life Competes with a Satisfying Private Life

The Limiting Myth

Sometimes we enter public life to protect our private lives. Most of the time public life simply interferes with a healthy private life.

The Empowering Insight

Public life often enhances our private lives.

Public life—our job, our community involvement, our educational activity—is often seen as threatening to our family ties. Sometimes public commitments divert our attention and capture our time. And some of the indirect pluses for our family and friends are hard to see. But if public life develops essential aspects of our character and teaches us important skills, there's enormous potential for public life to *enhance* our private relationships.

Pauline Thompson, now in her sixties, has been involved with Kentuckians for the Commonwealth for only a few years. She talked with us about the positive effect a more active public life has had on her long marriage to Daniel: "Getting involved in KFTC made us a lot closer. He's come over to my way and I've come over to his. We go to meetings, and then we come home and hash it out. We have common interests now that we didn't have before."

Their public lives allowed Pauline and Daniel to make new discoveries about each other: "Seeing each other in action, we've learned to appreciate each other more. He's just plain *smart*," Pauline says of Daniel, whose formal education went only to the fifth grade.

Deepening one's public life through new roles at work can also spill over positively into private life. At the Polaroid company in Cambridge, Massachusetts, workers now take part in decision making much more than they did in the old, hierarchical firm. For Sheila Martel, a chemical purchasing agent, this expanded public role has affected the other aspects of her life. "I look at situations differently now. I am more open-minded, not as quick to judge. I understand more complexity now.

My Family and My Public Life

Here are three ways my involvement in public life has benefited my family and friends:

1._____

2._____

3._____

Are there any ways in which your involvement in public life has detracted from your relationship with family or friends? If so, how? Are there ways in which you feel the public life of a family member has detracted from your relationship with him or her?

_____

_____

_____

"One result is a lot more goal-setting at home and at work. I handle conflicts better because we are trained to be more sensitive to the person, trained to listen."

Many also talked to us of the positive effect of their public lives on their children. Fay McLain is a low-income mother in St. Paul, Minnesota. Before getting involved in the Joint Ministry Project, a congregation-based organization, Fay said that she watched her community go downhill. She sighed as she told us, "I ignored it. I thought I couldn't do anything. I felt powerless." Then Fay's face brightened as she described the morning she told her sixteen-year-old daughter that she was meeting with the mayor that day: "She looked so surprised! 'Mom, how did you do it? Can just anybody meet the mayor?'" We knew that becoming a positive role model for her daughter was a powerful motivator for Fay. A new public life was having a positive effect at home.

We've heard many Americans link their public and private commitments on an even deeper level. "I got involved in the community when I had my first child," a middle-class woman in California told us. "I realized then that I had to help solve our society's problems so my child would have a future." Many of those we interviewed see their involvement in their communities—whether for the environment, better schools, or preventing crime—as direct and meaningful expressions of concern for their loved ones.

Another Way to Show Your Love?

What could you do in your community that would benefit your family?

What specific benefits can you expect from doing this?

In all, the link between the public and private dimensions of our lives can be strongly positive. New ways of problem solving, better decision-making abilities, greater patience and tolerance, appreciation for differences—these are the skills people are developing in public lives that are improving their private lives as well. Most importantly, public life offers a rewarding means of furthering the well-being of those we love. It's a powerful way of building hope.

You Don't Need to Be a Member

Many of the examples we have used relate to people working with citizens' organizations. But don't think you have to be a member of a community organization in order to practice democracy the way these citizens do. In this book you'll meet many individuals who are not members of such organizations who have nonetheless become very effective in schools, workplaces, the media, political practice, and human services. The skills they use can be applied to any activity in public life. They are part of a Living Democracy.

3

Claiming Our Self-Interest (It's Not Selfishness)

IF PUBLIC LIFE IS ABOUT our daily lives—not just our ties to government or what public figures have—then what is the point of public life? What is its purpose? In answer, our culture carries two quite contrary messages. First, we're told that public life is about "getting what's ours"—about standing up for our rights. On the other hand, we're told that public life should really be about squelching our interests, that we should engage in public life on behalf of those less fortunate, or for the common good.

In both of those messages, self-interest really means selfishness—something we should either assert or suppress. But self-interest need not carry that narrow meaning.

Self-Interest: How Do You Score?

Think about your attitudes toward your self-interest. Rate yourself on a scale from one to five for each of the contrasting positions expressed below. Circle the appropriate number in each scale.

I should help others without thinking of my own selfish interests.	1 2 3 4 5	My needs are as legitimate as others'.
I can only afford to look out for my narrow interests in this competitive world.	1 2 3 4 5	I can easily see how my interests are linked to those of others.

Self-interest is what we legitimately bring to public life. Self-interests include our passions—all the things we care most about. For many people, this means one's family, security, health, faith, and professional development, as well as broader passions such as concern for the natural environment and our fellow human beings. With this understanding, distinguishing between one's self-interest and one's values becomes very difficult.

What Are Your Most Important Self-Interests?

Take a moment to consider your most crucial self-interests. For yourself and those you love, what matters most? (For example, when you turn on the TV, is your interest in good entertainment? Information and education? Connection to the worlds of others? What else?) Write them down.

When you are at work?

_____

When you are at school?

_____

When you seek health care?

_____

When you turn on your TV?

_____

When you drive through your neighborhood?

_____

When you think about your children's future?

_____

Are these interests of yours legitimate?   Yes _____   No _____

Do they feel selfish or mean-spirited?   Yes _____   No _____

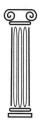 ## Myth Five: We Must Squelch Our Self-Interests for the Common Good

The Limiting Myth

We should enter public life to serve the common good, trying to leave our own interests behind.

The Empowering Insight

Trying only to serve others in public life can defeat the goal of creating healthy communities. Acting on our own interests, as well as those of others, can be legitimate as well as constructive.

Many people, understandably, want to help others, especially when suffering is spreading all around us. And helping can be satisfying. In fact, a recent study of over three thousand people uncovered a "helpers' high." Fully 95 percent of volunteers report that after helping others they feel better, both emotionally and physically. They have more energy and enjoy a feeling of serenity.[1]

Let there be no doubt about it, service has an important place in public life. But, we're learning, service alone cannot create strong communities. Healthy communities are not divided between givers and receivers. In healthy communities, *everyone* builds capacities at once.

Service to others is healthiest and most useful when it comprises only one of the reasons we act in public life.

The Problem with Simply Helping

Here's something else we learned from people who are successful, long-term public problem solvers: When we are trying to solve other people's problems, we might actually help them meet a particular pressing need. If so, we can justly feel accomplished. But if our goal is ongoing improvement—if we want to change what created the need in the first place—then a very different approach is called for. It requires *building people's capacities for problem solving* so problems can be addressed directly by the people most affected.

Learning from Helping

Think back to when you last helped someone outside your family.

What did you do?

How did it feel?

What were the results?

What did you learn from the experience?

Do you want to do it again?

The Industrial Areas Foundation (IAF) is among the most developed national networks of citizen organizations. Tens of thousands of Americans—including a number we've already quoted—have been drawn into satisfying public engagement through IAF organizations. Their credo, drummed home during intensive citizen training, includes an eleven-word injunction: "Never do anything for others that they can do for themselves."

Certainly for those brought up in religious communities, an admonition *against* helping someone is almost shocking. Reverend Terry Boggs, a minister now active with Allied Communities of Tarrant, an IAF affiliate in Fort Worth, had to take a hard look at himself: "I used to try to take care of everyone. I wanted to try to save them. In an IAF training session I saw that this couldn't work. And that realization has changed every aspect of my life—even my relationship with my son. I used to try to protect him and do things for him. But with this new understanding, when he left for college, I was better able to let go."

How Much Did You Help?

Go back once more to the last time you helped someone outside your family.

Did you meet a short-term need?

Did you also help develop that person's capacity to meet future needs?

When Gerald Taylor, IAF's lead organizer in the Southeast, approached pastors and lay leaders in white churches to join Shelby County Interfaith, he told them bluntly, "Don't do this if you think you're going to help those poor black folks. They don't want your help."

"The whites were shocked," Gerald remembers. Instead, Gerald encouraged them to examine their *own* interests and ask themselves what they would get out of joining the effort.

When we make ourselves servants, we not only ignore our own needs but often fail to listen to others. We imagine that we already know what their needs are. In Part Three, when we discuss the arts of democracy, we'll explore what happens when we take the opposite approach, listening deeply to grasp the interests of others.

 ### Myth Six: Public Life Is About Pursuing Our Selfish Interests

The Limiting Myth

Selfishness—pursuing one's own immediate gain—is inevitably what brings us into public life. We figure out our own self-interest and fight for it in public life.

The Empowering Insight

Selfishness can defeat our own interests. As individuals, we come to understand and fulfill our self-interests fully only when we interact with others.

Selfishness—if by this we mean an unreflective demand to protect or further ourselves—is what some people *do* bring to public life. That's true. Other people's needs seem less important than our own. But remaining in such a framework can defeat our own ends.

Practically speaking, few of us—even those who appear to have many resources—can accomplish much by ourselves. We need other people's cooperation and support. We may need their insights, their willingness to help. Thus if we are unwilling to listen to others' interests, to incorporate their concerns into our own goals, we may not move very far towards the goals we consider most important.

Confronting Narrow Self-Interest

When was the last time you got angry at someone's selfishness in public life? Imagine you have a chance to speak to that person tomorrow for fifteen minutes. What will you say?

A New Concept: Relational Self-Interest

All across America, people engaged in Living Democracy are learning two critical lessons:

- It's hard even to *define* one's self-interests without interacting with others.

- It's often impossible to *achieve* one's self-interests without considering and incorporating the interests of others.

Becoming effective in public life means developing *relational self-interest*—our own interests as they are linked to those of others. Relational self-interest is easiest to see when we're in a close-knit group such as a family or team. "It's in our self-interest to help your fellow team members," GM worker Joe Caldwell told us. "You're shooting yourself in the foot if you don't."

In other cases, relational self-interest is somewhat harder to see. It evolves as our awareness grows. Diana Steck, a young woman who developed an active public life through the Pennsylvania Environmental Network, described in front of her colleagues how many of them began with a narrow view of their own interests: "Let's face it. When we started, everyone was a NIMBY (Not in My Backyard). Well maybe not everyone—just 99.5 percent of us! People come in [to the Environmental Network] asking what you can do to help *me* with *my* problem. It's self-preservation. But something happens along the way. People *think* they are totally alone. But they discover they are not alone. They see the problem is much bigger than their problem. Their view broadens. It's a definite process."

Others see relational self-interest evolving in response to society-wide change. Monty Bruell, a young African-American man in Chattanooga, a construction contractor and head of a broad citizen alliance called Chattanooga Venture, believes the environmental crisis and rising crime are forcing the lesson of relational self-interest on all of us:

The environmental crisis has changed how people think. It's a hot issue. And people know they can't make enough money to get away from the polluted environment. Or crime. By the time you have the fourth burglary in your neighborhood, you throw altruism out the window. Solving the crime problem is about *your* self-interest. In other words, there may be no purely 'selfish' solutions. All solutions involve us with others. To act in one's best interest in today's world is to get people to act *together.* So now we have white attorneys working with poor blacks because they're realizing that's the way to get what they want in their *own* neighborhoods.

Recall Gerald Taylor's warning to whites in Memphis: don't get involved if it's just to "help" the poor blacks. Many took his advice. Whites and blacks met first in their own churches to figure out what their own interests were, what issues were most important. And the result? Gerald explained, "Whether it was wealthy Memphis or poor Memphis, people told of the *same* concerns, only in a different order of priority. The wealthier people realized that if Memphis was to survive, the working class must have a stake in the future." Once their interests were defined, negotiation on what gets attention first could move forward. "These decisions were then based not on paternalism but on mutual respect," Gerald emphasized.

In truth, all our biggest problems today are the kinds that Monty and Gerald describe. Lasting solutions depend upon meeting the needs of others along with our own needs.

Discovering Relational Self-Interest

List three very important interests you have in public life.

1. _____

2. _____

3. _____

Now list who besides yourself will benefit if each interest is served.

1. _____

2. _____

3. _____

The following chart summarizes this chapter. If we see ourselves as providing service, we can find rewards, but they may be limited. If we enter with selfishness to get what's ours, again the rewards can be real yet limited. Developing relational self-interest requires more time (for interacting and reflecting), but the rewards are unlimited. If you allow yourself some time to read this chart carefully, you'll deepen your understanding of your approach to your own self-interest.

Comparing Three Reasons for Entering Public Life

Service	Selfishness	Relational self-interest
I want to do for others.	I want to look out for myself.	I want to live well and fully in a community that works.
Reactive to others ("What others need")	Reactive to internal needs; unreflective ("What I need")	Pro-active; reflective ("All I care about—family, faith, career, justice . . .")
Defined by oneself	Defined by oneself	Develops from dialogue and interaction
Develops empathy but can foster paternalistic attitudes	Provides short-term material or other gains	Develops reflection, empathy, critical thinking, knowledge, hope
Sometimes offers recognition	Sometimes offers visibility	Offers recognition, visibility, meaningful relationships
Can increase self-respect	No increase in self-respect	Increases self-respect, respect from others
Limited creativity; can relieve immediate suffering but sometimes fails to address its roots	Limited creativity; shapes communities in ways that often have negative consequences	Unlimited creativity; shapes community life in ways benefiting long-term community health

4

Discovering Power
(It's Not a Dirty Word)

IN RECONCEIVING PUBLIC LIFE as potentially a source of enormous satisfaction, many of us stumble as soon as we realize the obvious: public life is all about *power.*

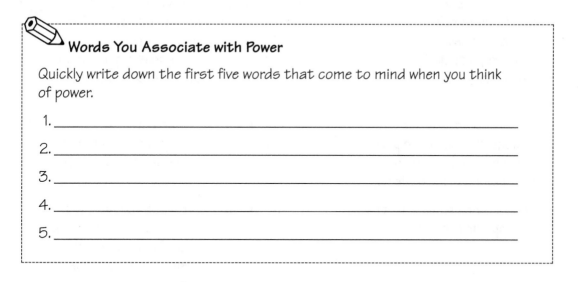

Words You Associate with Power

Quickly write down the first five words that come to mind when you think of power.

1. _____

2. _____

3. _____

4. _____

5. _____

Look over your list of words that came immediately to mind when you thought about the word "power." How many are positive? How many are negative? When teacher Seth Kreisberg asked his tenth graders in Massachusetts to state the first words that came to mind when they heard the word "power," they responded with "money," "parents," "guns," "bullies,"

"Adolf Hitler," and "Mike Tyson."[1] When we ask adults, they often start with "force" and continue on to "police," "law," and "politicians." The notion of power as control or domination permeates our culture.

If we conceive of power as control over others, as the capacity to exert our will over another's will, then it is something to be wary of indeed. It can manipulate, coerce, and destroy. But in developing healthy public lives, many people are rejecting this narrow notion. They are reconceiving power more realistically and thus becoming more effective, more powerful themselves.

Rate Your Feelings About Power

Think about your attitudes toward power. Rate yourself on a scale from one to five for each of the contrasting positions expressed below. Circle the appropriate number in each scale.

I distrust people in positions of power. I assume they must be corrupt to get where they are.	1 2 3 4 5	Everybody has some power, so I trust (or distrust) people not on the basis of their power but based on what they do.
I'm afraid to assume power, either because people will think badly of me or because I can't handle it.	1 2 3 4 5	I value power. We all have some, and many of us need to develop more of it.
I'm uncomfortable with the concept or the use of power.	1 2 3 4 5	I feel comfortable with the concept of power, my use of power, and my desire to always use it well.
In many aspects of my public life I feel fairly powerless and not very effective.	1 2 3 4 5	I feel powerful, competent, and effective in my public life.

In this chapter we ask you to challenge another four myths, these about power. Once again we'll contrast each myth with an empowering insight that successful problem solvers are using to change their lives and their communities.

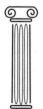 ## Myth Seven: Power Is a Dirty Word

The Limiting Myth

Power is evil. It's always corrupting. It's always used by a few power holders to block change benefiting others. To be good people, we should avoid power.

The Empowering Insight

We cannot realize our values or goals without power. Power is the capacity to act publicly and effectively, to bring about positive change, to build hope.

If we are convinced we have no power, it's easy to see power as bad. And that means keeping it at arm's length. *Mother Jones* magazine once praised some populist heroes, declaring, "We celebrate them because they *challenge* power."[2] The implicit message is that power was something to confront, not to participate in.

The notion of power as something to avoid is changing. In Hammond, Indiana, for example, a far-reaching reform began in the city's public schools in 1985. Decisions that had previously been handed down from the school board became the responsibility of school committees that included teachers and parents. Patrick O'Rourke, head of the city's teachers' union, was used to blaming management when anything went wrong. But now that teachers are sharing in the development of power, he says, "We are moving away from 'us versus them.'" Patrick went on to explain the change: "Solving problems—rather than assigning blame and responsibility to one side or the other—is becoming the operating principle. That is a fundamental shift in attitude."[3]

Building the Capacity to Make Things Happen

"People think, power . . . oh, that's bad. But, *powerlessness*—that's *really* bad," says Margaret Moore of Allied Communities of Tarrant (ACT) in Fort Worth, Texas. ACT is successfully taking on problems that range from economic development to school reform. She, too, is learning to build power, because "Power is necessary to produce the changes I want in my community."

We heard Margaret's realization voiced repeatedly from Albuquerque, New Mexico, to Hartford, Connecticut. Whenever we asked, "What *is* power?" we received thoughtful responses. People defined power as what they know they want, not just what the oppressor holds. "Power," we heard, "is the capacity to make things happen." "It's the ability to change things in your interest for the good of everybody." Throughout our society, we're finding many Americans, like Patrick and Margaret, returning power to its original meaning—from the Latin *posse*, "to be able."

People everywhere are overcoming their fear of contamination in order to participate in power, not just defend themselves against it. They are replacing righteous indignation with the greater satisfaction of real effectiveness in problem solving.

Myth Eight: There's Only So Much Power to Go Around

The Limiting Myth

Since there's only so much of it around, the more power you have, the less there is for me.

The Empowering Insight

Relational power expands possibilities for many people at once. The more you use it, the more there is.

In American culture, what is public life about?

Mainly, it's a fight over whose interest will prevail. In this view, power is something we contend for, not something we develop together.

But emerging in our culture is another concept, one that some call *relational* power. In this new view, power is not a fixed commodity to be fought over. Instead, as we just noted, power is about our capacities to *do* things. And these capacities can only be developed *with* others. Power, in this view, expands for many people simultaneously. And as one person's power grows, it often enhances the power of others. Thus power can be both enabling and creative.

The concept of relational power represents a profound rethinking of the nature of power in American society. With this new perspective, power is no longer a zero-sum concept—the more for you, the less for me.

For most of us, nothing seems to confirm the prevailing zero-sum notion of power more than school life. Teachers often struggle with administrators to determine what goes on in their classrooms, administrators fight with state officials, and the states do battle with the federal bureaucracy. But Patrick O'Rourke described the beginning of a redefinition of power in Hammond, Indiana, that takes us far beyond a zero-sum notion. "We're not talking about taking power away from one group and giving it to another," he said. "We see this new governance structure [decentralized and team-based] rather as broadening the base of decision making in a way that empowers everyone involved because it results in better, more informed, more accepted programs and policies, with everyone on board. Building administrators don't lose out if teachers are more enthusiastic and creative, if schools are better run, and if students learn more. They don't lose, they win. Everyone wins."[4]

For students even more than teachers, the zero-sum experience of power in most schools is still a daily reality. Standardized tests pit kids against each other. One child's A will shift the grading curve, making it harder for others to succeed. But, fortunately, a surprising number of America's schools are discovering another kind of power.

"Before entering Central Park East Secondary School (CPESS), I got in so many fights that I thought fighting was just another course in school," one teenage student told us. Fighting was his means of maintaining power, status, and self-protection. If someone else gained ground, he lost.

But at CPESS he began to experience the possibility of power that expands with others. CPESS is a public school in East Harlem, but it is quite unlike most schools. At CPESS this student's advancement in school-work was not at the expense of his peers; it gave them an advantage, because teamwork on class projects is the norm. And the school's community service program means that he could see another kind of power growing as

One Easy and Two Tough Questions

Think of one serious problem that confronts our society and write it down.

_____

_____

To do something about it, what groups of people need power?_____

_____

_____

What is one important step that they and we can take to develop this power together? _____

_____

_____

well—power in the form of communication skills and practical problem solving.

We Americans also expect our workplaces to be arenas in which we vie for power. We compete for pay, for clients, for the boss's approval, for promotions. Power is our capacity to outsmart and out-position our co-workers as we climb the career ladder. And on that pyramid-shaped ladder, the rungs narrow as we climb. So to reach the top, we have to become ever more powerful in knocking off our competitors.

But today's jobs require that workers become problem solvers—taking the initiative, not just following orders. Sheila Martel, a worker at Polaroid, described such a change in her work this way: "Now we're pushing the decision-making process downward. It means _you_ are accountable. You have the authority, versus your boss or bosses. If you see a quality problem, you have the responsibility to shut down the line. You have the power to do that. Before, you'd have to call a meeting and the line would be running for weeks making mistakes. That's what I mean by empowerment."

Think about your job. Who holds the power?

What kind of power do you have? How do you use it?

The power to make decisions and to create solutions requires that workers share information and decision making. Power, then, is no longer simply divided up; it is continually growing. "I have to believe I am strengthened when I spread power around," says the Tucson, Arizona, school superintendent, Paul Houston. "And the more I hold power to myself, the weaker I get."[5] By this logic, those leaders who know how to spread power downward actually wind up heading more powerful organizations. "You consolidate and build power by empowering others," notes the CEO of one of our country's biggest firms.[6]

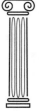

Myth Nine: Power Is a One-Way Force

The Limiting Myth

Power is a one-way force over someone. It means you're in control and can get others to do what you want.

The Empowering Insight

Power always exists in relationships, going both ways. In relationships, the actions of each affect the other, so no one is ever completely powerless.

In American culture, power is considered one-directional. It moves from you to me, or vice versa, not both ways. You either have it or you don't. And unless you hold the commonly understood sources of power—wealth, status, or force—you don't perceive yourself as having any power at all.

Again, as with the notion of zero-sum power that we just discussed, many Americans are discovering that this one-way notion is simply wrong.

"Before we began to think about organizing ourselves, we'd tell officials, '*You* solve it,'" said Dulcie Giadone, who heads Hartford Areas Rallying Together (HART), a broad-based citizen organization in Connecticut. The assumption was that only officials hold the power to solve public problems.

"But they *didn't* solve it," Dulcie told us. Now, Dulcie—a preschool teacher who had never before been involved in public life in her community—has rethought this one-way view of power, where all that is left to the average citizen is voting and praying. "So now we try to be proactive," Dulcie declared. "We try to think ahead. What will happen if we do nothing? What can we offer to make a difference?" From this approach has come a string of successes: passing a bond measure to relieve school overcrowding, shutting down a drug-plagued apartment building, and creating a home-ownership program for low-income residents.

And among the human services as well—our health, employment, welfare, housing, and counseling agencies—power is often experienced as special expertise that someone *else* has, as a thing to be offered. The subtle-yet-powerful message is: "I have power that you, unfortunate client, do not. But, take heart, for I can use my power to help you."

But many professionals and clients are challenging this model of power. Increasingly, they are learning that it doesn't work. After all, can I heal physically or mentally as long as I believe the power to heal is in the hands of someone else, a professional who knows more about me than I know about myself? Or can I ever move out of poverty if all the power rests in a welfare bureaucracy?

Power Exists in Relationships

What Dulcie and many others are realizing is that power is never simply one-way. It is not only what public officials or other so-called experts have. Power always exists in relationships among people. Someone has the power to create, to block, to enable, to oppress only insofar as other people accept, respond to, or honor that power.

Once we come to see power as never being completely one-way, it's possible to acknowledge our own responsibility—the first step in perceiving the sources of power open to us. "We're the ones who let them roll over us," said Pauline Thompson, in York, Kentucky, as she acknowledged her part in enabling coal companies and toxic waste disposers to defile much of the Bluegrass State.

Once we see our responsibility, we can appreciate and cultivate the sources of power we *do* have, instead of seeing all the power as being on the other side. We can even plan the reactions we seek. And we can consciously create relationships with those we think hold more power, knowing that in relationships the flow of influence is never entirely one-directional.

Understanding power as a relationship need not obscure the very real power imbalances, based on wealth, status, prejudice, and long-existing "connections," that define our society. Understanding power as a relationship is a tool which those with less power can use to establish relationships that are at least partially "on their own terms." Here's an example of an organization that insisted on a relationship of mutual respect.

The Reverend Terry Boggs told us how the citizens' organization Allied Communities of Tarrant (ACT) made itself a key decision maker in a choice that could have been the death knell for a poor Fort Worth neighborhood. When Texas Wesleyan College announced it was moving to a more upscale part of town, the college was reacting to the neighborhood's decay, a result of "white flight," absent landlords, and poverty.

But if the college pulled out, ACT feared, the neighborhood had virtually no chance of recovery. The campus provided the last point of stability on which to rebuild the neighborhood. So ACT leaders and members—mostly moderate- and low-income blacks, whites, and Hispanics—contacted the board of trustees and the college's president. "To prepare, we conducted a two-and-a-half-hour role play," Terry recalled. "We went over every eventuality. We were ready! At the appointed hour, all of us—fifteen lay people and pastors—arrived at a parlor off the president's office. There we saw chairs lined up in two rows, all facing a table where the president was to sit. Immediately, we started rearranging the furniture, so that we could sit in a circle."

ACT organizer Perry Perkins explained what happened next: "At that point, the president's assistant walked in. 'What are you doing?' he asked. We said, 'We want a *meeting*. We don't want a lecture!' We were polite, but our actions communicated that we were an organization with *power*. We deliberately created a certain tension. Our action produced some discomfort that the president and his assistant had to deal with. We created a 'public moment' which focused people's attention. They had to deal with it."

The meeting worked, and the college eventually re-committed itself to the community.

ACT is clear about its philosophy of public life. Members know effectiveness in public relationships sometimes requires not nastiness but *polarization*—creating enough tension to make those with more power aware that they have to take seriously the voices of those they've perceived as powerless. "Sometimes we have to polarize in order to depolarize," is how Perry Perkins puts it.

Confrontation: Sometimes a Step to Relationships? Now, don't misunderstand us here; just because these diverse Americans are learning to develop power and self-interest relationally doesn't mean they still don't have to deal with folks who operate by a zero-sum notion of power. Veteran citizen organizer Mike Miller of San Francisco's Organize Training Center describes his experience with just such folks—landlords, for example: "Often landlords want nothing to do with a tenants' union. They don't want to negotiate. They simply resist *any* relationship. But when the tenants' union stands firm and succeeds in establishing its power, concrete improvements occur. Vandalism goes down, vacancy rates go down, the building stabilizes. Then, the landlord becomes a convert to bargaining relationships. He can see his interest in it."

Mike Miller's experience has taught him that at the initial point of conflict, one's adversary may well see power as a one-way force. Citizens have to establish themselves as players to be dealt with seriously—as, say, ACT did in its confrontation with Texas Wesleyan College—in order to be in a position even to demonstrate the possibility of relational power and self-interest.

Discovering New Sources of Power

Once citizens learn to let go of the old zero-sum, one-way notions of power, once they begin to understand power as a *relationship* among people, many new sources of power become possible.

Power, as it is being lived and learned, is neither fixed nor one-way. It is fluid. Based on relationships, it is dynamic. It changes as the attitudes and behavior of any party change. This understanding of power offers enormous possibilities: it suggests that by conscious attention to the importance of one's own actions, one can change others—even those who, under the old view of power, appeared immovable. All this allows us to discover new sources of power within our reach.

Your First Thoughts on Sources of Power

How good are you at identifying the sources of power you have? If you want to find out, please complete one (or both) of the following exercises.

Think back to a recent problem or confrontation in your public life. At that time, what power did you think you had? Now, with the advantages of hindsight, reflection, and creativity, what power could you have developed and used? Write it here. _____

_____

_____

Now let's use our imaginations. Your neighborhood is being threatened. City hall has informed you and your neighbors, one month after the legal notification deadline, that an incinerator is going to be built not far from your daughter's elementary school. The residents are up in arms over the aesthetic, traffic, and toxic problems that will result. You're part of a four-year-old neighborhood group. You've joined other members at a neighbor's house just three weeks before the city council will vote final approval.

Quickly list the sources of power you and your neighbors have:

_____

_____

_____

Typically, Americans think of power in the form of money, the law, force, and status. But if power is perceived relationally, it can be found in knowledge, numbers of people, creativity, moral persuasion, perseverance, organization, and even humor. The bonds among people may be the most important source of power.

The behemoths of our modern world—the GEs and Citicorps, the mass media, big-city governments, the White House—all maintain their wealth, size, status, and other trappings of power. But even their power can be limited. Yes, they have the power to produce commodities, to expand, to accumulate, to manipulate, to block, and even to move armies. But do they have the power to solve problems, to create solutions?

What Do You Think?

Here are some common perceptions of power sources:

FORCE   MONEY   LAW

ASSUMED STATUS   RACE/PRIVILEGE

EXPERTISE   AUTHORITY   OFFICIAL POSITION

FAME   "CONNECTIONS"

But can't many of these sources of power be

COUNTERED AND MODIFIED?   WORKED WITH?

CHANGED, PERSUADED, CONVERTED?

SUCCESSFULLY OPPOSED?   DEVELOPED FOR OURSELVES?

Everyday citizens are successfully developing new sources of power in order to address the usual sources of power from positions of power.

Today's problems—homelessness, poverty, joblessness, environmental devastation, drugs, crime, faltering health care, failing schools, AIDS, racism, and discrimination—defy top-down answers. These problems are complex and interrelated. They touch us all. They cannot be solved simply by material changes, such as new technologies or new goods. They cannot be solved by giving orders. Solutions require that we *all* change our way of thinking and our behavior.

Effective solutions to our country's biggest problems, therefore, demand:

- Ingenuity and insight of those most directly affected

- Creativity that emerges only when diverse perspectives meet

- Commitment to actually "making it happen," which arises when citizens know they've helped arrive at answers and understand how they themselves will benefit.

After all, discovering our role in public life means much more than simply resisting the power of others. It means developing our own. Here are six ways successful people are learning to do just that.

One: Building Relationships Becomes a Source of Power. "Organizing is a fancy word for building relationships," is how Ernie Cortes, the Southwest leader for the Industrial Areas Foundation (IAF), likes to put it.[7]

When we talk of relationships, we mean those within an organization or with friends, interested supporters, and allies as well as those with key decision makers in the larger public world. Ken Galdston of the Merrimack Valley Project in Massachusetts describes his organization's primary process for reaching out to others in the community: members simply sit in the homes of their neighbors. And they listen.

What a simple concept—so fundamental, so uncontrived. "We don't have an end goal, like 'join our organization and give us dollars,'" says Ken. "We try to go to a deeper level. We don't go in and say, 'We're canvassing your neighborhood to find out what you don't like.' Instead, we approach

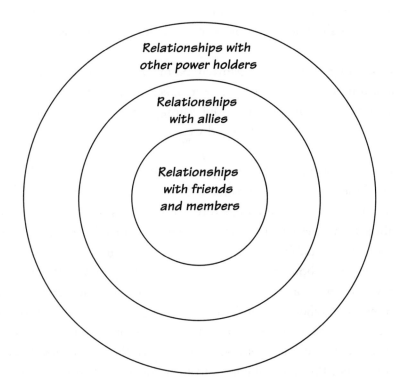

Relationships with other power holders

Relationships with allies

Relationships with friends and members

people with questions like, 'How long have you lived here? What forces and people shaped your life? Where do you work? What's happening in your company? What do you think about TV? About advertising?'"

These straightforward questions establish a relationship of trust. And this is where effective citizen action begins, long before any decision is made on which issues to address. This approach is a far cry from asking people simply to sign on to *your* campaign.

After the initial relationship has begun, the most effective citizen organizations attend to rituals and celebrations. They strengthen the bonds among members. Skits, potluck dinners, work parties, demonstrations with a humorous edge, victory celebrations, annual meetings with banners and noisemakers to add festivity—all these elements sustain the bonds of friendship and common purpose that begin with listening.

Relationship building creates power, because it transforms people's sense of their own potential. "My organization saw qualities in me that I didn't see in myself," said Elena Hanggi, a homemaker and part-time hospital aide when the Association of Community Organizations for Reform Now (ACORN), a national citizens' organization, came to her door and asked about her concerns. She never viewed herself as a public problem solver, yet in a few years she rose to become an effective leader of ACORN.

Two: Building Power in Organized Numbers. "Organized people and organized money"—that's what power is, according to the grandfather of community organizing, the late Saul Alinsky. And since most of us don't have much money, Alinsky believed we must find our power in organized people.

Today, several national and regional organizations are developing the power of their members, not as mere donors but as the very core of their effectiveness. When these groups turn out hundreds or even thousands of members to a meeting or an action (that's shorthand for a public confrontation with a public official or institution), decision makers listen.

Turning out a thousand or more people is no longer unusual in the most effective citizen organizations. "We got thirteen thousand people out for our meeting on school reform," said the leading organizer in California for the IAF, which Saul Alinsky founded. "That's what established our credibility on the issue of failing schools." It's not just the head count that matters, of course. People's willingness to turn out is visible evidence of their commitment to act. It's pretty basic, but that's what establishes citizens as a force to be taken seriously.

But the term *organized people* can mislead if it conjures up the notion of people *being* organized, of a leader lining up people behind a pre-set agenda. Lasting power lies in a very different process. The source of power comes less from people being organized than from their having become *connected*. Developing bonds with each other through their common work is the key. And in these bonds there is strength and hope—power.

Three: Demystifying Expertise and Discovering the Power of Knowledge. In the process of discovering power within themselves, people who have never before been involved in public life often make another important discovery: those to whom we have so often deferred—the so-called

experts—are frequently *less* knowledgeable and competent than we have assumed. At the same time, we can make ourselves *more* knowledgeable and thus increase our power relative to these same so-called experts.

"How do you gain confidence?" we asked Eddie Anaya, a leader with Valley Interfaith, an IAF organization working in the Hispanic community around Harlingen, Texas. He did not hesitate to respond: "By learning the issues. This organization is our university. It's a big fallacy that the legislators know a lot more than we do. In some cases we know more than the politicians. We've educated *them*. Now they know they have to be accountable to the people. After we got funding for water to the *colonias* [poor Hispanic communities unserved by public utilities], we had to teach the water development board how to manage the public funds!"

ACORN, a well-grounded national organization with five hundred chapters and one hundred thousand members, mostly in low-income communities, develops this power of information and knowledge in dramatic ways. One of ACORN's primary concerns has been the lack of affordable housing for people of color, in part because of what it suspected were the discriminatory practices of banks. How did ACORN counter the power of the banking industry while building its own power? By doing its own study of twenty banks in ten cities, discovering that the rate at which whites got mortgages was much higher than that of equally qualified blacks. That research itself—published in a number of major newspapers—had national impact. "Just the threat of disclosure of the data has prompted many banks to launch efforts to reach minority borrowers," observed the *Washington Post*.[8]

We had the privilege to sit for several hours with ACORN members in their modest offices perched over a storefront on Flatbush Avenue in the heart of Brooklyn, New York. Some were white, some African-American. None had more than a high school education, yet they taught us about banking reform. Steve Kest, an ACORN staffer, stressed how much ACORN members have learned about banking practices. "A professor of finance who attended an ACORN meeting told us, 'These folks know more about banking than the finance professors I know.'"

In San Antonio we heard about how an IAF group called COPS (Communities Organized for Public Service) made themselves into the city's leading experts on job training. "To develop our job training plan," one leader told us, "we interviewed hundreds of people frustrated with the current job training system. We set up meetings with corporate executives. We

Two Ways of Thinking About Power in Public Life

Power is:

Zero-sum. It strengthens some at the expense of others. It divides what already exists.

A one-way force; either you have it or you don't. It's the powerful versus the powerless.

Limiting, intimidating, scary.

Controlling.

Rigid, static.

Derived mostly from laws, status, force, and wealth.

All about what I can do— or get—now.

Power can be:

Mutually expanding. It builds capacities of all involved. It's creative, offering new sources, new possibilities.

A give-and-take, two-way relationship. No one is ever completely powerless, because each person's action affects others.

Freeing.

Collaborative.

Dynamic, always changing.

Derived from many sources: relationships, knowledge, experience, numbers, organization, creativity, vision, perseverance, discipline, humor.

Concerned with how decisions get made—and how power is built— over time.

asked them what they needed. We studied job training programs in Europe to figure out why they work so much better."

Out of this process, COPS came up with an innovative plan passed unanimously by the San Antonio City Council. Ordinary people developed their knowledge, and used the power that the knowledge gave them, to change their lives. And now the COPS plan is being studied as a model by other cities around the country.

Four: Having Fun with Power. Drama, surprise, and humor tend to "shake things up." They help people to see old issues in a new light. That's part of their power.

Daymon Morgan told us a story about power that had all of these elements. Daymon, who's in his sixties, appears the classic farmer figure, with overalls and hat. He's also chairman of Kentuckians for the Commonwealth, the group you heard about here through Jean True and Pauline Thompson. With a broad grin, Daymon told us how KFTC's members focused attention on the dumping of out-of-state waste: "We conducted a funeral at the capitol. We buried the state of Kentucky. We made it just like a real funeral. We had funeral music, a real hearse, and everything. People were crying. We asked the governor to sign either a moratorium on out-of-state waste or a death certificate for the state. This was all a member's idea. We sure got people's attention."

Daymon also told us about a creative skit KFTC staged at the capitol in Frankfort when KFTC members carried a bed into a legislative hearing room. In it were Daymon and others wearing stocking caps. Some were dressed in costume to represent the state's biggest coal and waste companies; others represented the legislators. And under the covers they passed large wads of fake cash. The message of who was in bed with whom was quite clear: corporations control the legislators' votes. The media loved it, conveying a message to Kentucky's citizens and helping KFTC consolidate its support for limiting corporate influence on the state's politicians.

Five: Power in Discipline. The Youth Action Program (YAP) in New York involves poor teenagers in a self-governing training program in the construction trades. These young people taught us a great deal about the power of discipline. "When we were organizing to appear at the city council, calling for jobs for young people, we practiced every Wednesday night for three months," says a YAP organizer. "We practiced walking in an organized way, in single file, filling up every successive seat in a row rather than flowing in to the council in an undisciplined way. We practiced standing in unison and clapping together at the close of every speech of one of our supporters. Nobody wore hats or chewed gum. We knew that this degree of self-discipline, implying no threat but demonstrating internal unity, would have an impact. It did."

Reflecting on Discipline

Let's explore your feelings about self-discipline. Try listing below the advantages (and disadvantages) of self-discipline, or think of one part of your public life where you could develop more of that power.

Advantages: _____

_____

Disadvantages: _____

_____

I could develop more self-discipline in this part of my public life: _____

_____

_____

Or use the following hypothetical case to start thinking about how important self-discipline is to your public life.

For the next three minutes, imagine you are vice president of a parents' group. At the last school board meeting, your members created quite a ruckus. Upset over proposed budget cuts, one of your members shouted down the school board president. Another member of your group stomped out. Not one school board member, even your two former allies, appeared sympathetic to your cause.

But the media loved the meeting. For the first time your parents' group made the six and eleven o'clock news. While the confrontation caused several of the members of the parents' group to drop out, newfound visibility had your phone ringing off the hook with people offering support and encouragement.

You're now sitting in a major strategy session with your group's most active members. You've got only about ten minutes to make a case for the power of self-discipline in public action. You don't want to be viewed as weak or intimidated by the school board. But you also know you need a long-term collaborative relationship with the school board to solve a number of complex issues. Most importantly, you want the board to agree to become accountable to the parents.

What do you say to your fellow parents' group members?

"We knew that the more respectful the group, given how scared the white society is of black and Latin young people, the greater the power of the group, because they would inspire respect, trigger surprise, and in fact generate gratitude, because people with the right to be mad are reaching for alliances instead of attacking."9

These young people succeeded. They won millions in city funds for job-training programs that have benefited hundreds of youth.

Discipline, of course, involves more than self-control. It suggests the capacity for perseverance. ACORN's James Shearin, a low-income African American, told us of the power of simple stamina. The Community Reinvestment Act—which requires banks to invest in local communities—resulted in large measure directly from citizens' organizing efforts, especially by National People's Action. Under pressure from the banking industry, a congressional committee held hearings in 1991 to consider changes that would have effectively gutted the law. James told us of the final hours of ACORN's effort to defend the reinvestment act: "ACORN members stayed in line all night long to get seats in the hearing room. When the paid representatives from the banking industry got there in the middle of the night, the ACORN people were already ahead of them. They were amazed."

The commitment and discipline of the low-income ACORN people undercut the ability of the wealthy banking industry to hire "seat-takers" in order to reserve places at these crucial hearings. Eventually, the banking lobby was defeated.

Six: Power in Vision; Power in Tapping Human Compassion. YAP members used the surprise (and relief) created by their discipline to break through to city officials in New York. But Ken Galdston of the Merrimack Valley Project (MVP) in Massachusetts illustrated for us another key source of relational power. MVP has saved many jobs and successfully created worker-owned businesses out of failing companies. They have not achieved these goals simply by threat or organized demand, Ken explained. "By employing a democratic economic strategy with community action, our vision *catches*. Some of *our* vision starts to become part of *their* vision— our antagonists' vision. Given the imbalance in our practical power, we have to make our vision part of our strength."

Examples of Underdeveloped Sources of Relational Power

Power Source	Example
Relationship building	One-on-one organizing strategies, allowing ordinary people to discover their own capacities because someone—finally—is listening.
Ability to analyze power and self-interest	Communities Organized for Public Service (COPS) in San Antonio analyzes corporate interests in job training reform before bringing corporations into dialogue on reform.
Knowledge	National People's Action's documentation of redlining contributes to passing the federal Community Reinvestment Act. Workers at Weirton Steel buy the company and apply knowledge from their direct experience to make the company profitable.
Numbers	Ten thousand Texans with the IAF gather on state capitol steps, commanding attention of lawmakers.
Discipline	Young people in the Youth Action Program handle themselves with such decorum that New York's city council is moved to act.
Vision	In the Merrimack Valley Project in Massachusetts, some businesses "catch" the citizens' vision of industry responsive to community values.
Diversity	Memphis's Shelby County Interfaith links distinct black and white interests on school reform.
Creativity	Citizens in St. Paul devise their own neighborhood network to help the elderly stay out of nursing homes.
Persistence	ACORN members stay in line all night to squeeze out paid banking lobbyists for seats in the congressional hearing room.
Humor	Kentuckians for the Commonwealth stage a skit at the state capitol. In bed are KFTC members portraying legislators and their farmer chairperson as a coal company lobbyist. They pass big wads of fake cash under the covers.
Chutzpah/ nerve	Sixth graders in Amesville, Ohio, don't trust the EPA after a toxic spill in the local creek, so they make themselves into the town's water quality control team.
Mastering the arts of democracy	Groups regularly evaluate and reflect after each public action or event, asking, What did we learn? How did we grow? How can we do better?
Organization	Several citizen organizations, now with two or more decades of experience, are successfully institutionalizing the development in their members of all these many sources of power.

In a similar vein, citizens are learning how to tap the innate compassion of their neighbors. A good example comes from Orange County, California. There, the group called Orange County Congregation Community Organizations (OCCCO) has tackled the community's drug problem. It identifies its power in numbers; it turned out twenty-five hundred members for its meeting with the county commissioners. But it uses an additional source of power: when its members testify before public bodies, they're encouraged to be brief, relate the facts as they know them, and express any emotion they genuinely feel. Rabbi R'Moshe ben Asher, now of the Organize Training Center in San Francisco, described the impact of this approach: "We compel officials to listen to the real pain of these problems. When one member gave testimony in the meeting with the mayors of Anaheim and Santa Ana, she talked about her drug-addicted brother who died in a county jail. Probably more than half the people in that auditorium had tears in their eyes, and the two mayors were obviously moved. We have learned that the most cynical, indifferent, hard-bitten officials respond to human pain when it's communicated *without subjecting them to personal attack.*"[10]

We added the emphasis in Rabbi ben Asher's account because it's so critical. Only when we can express our own pain without causing others to feel personally accused do we allow them to experience their innate capacity for compassion.

These underappreciated, and therefore often underdeveloped, sources of power—from numbers of people and knowledge, to humor and the tapping of others' compassion—aren't sources that we as individuals acquire, as one might acquire traditional power. After all, one can, individually, gain the power of wealth simply through inheritance, or a lucrative investment, or the power of position by individually holding a post with top-down authority.

Not so the types of power we've seen flourishing in the lives of those who appear in this book. These types of power are realized differently. They are developed from within ourselves. And they grow as we deliberately begin to make them part of our daily interaction in the schools, businesses, and other institutions that shape us and that we, in turn, shape by our actions. The exceptional organizations cited here suggest the possibility of creating institutions in which people build power through cultivating their internal strengths and relationships of mutual accountability.

Myth Ten: Power Is About Today's Victories

The Limiting Myth

Power is measured by the victories you achieve now.

The Empowering Insight

Power is more than today's visible results. You can reach your short-term goals and still have *lost* power. Wielding power relationally builds *future power.*

More than twenty years ago, one of us—Paul—was the executive director of the FIGHT (Freedom, Independence, God, Honor, Today) organization in Rochester, New York, the largest African-American organization in the entire state. I remember it was a heady time. Black power was big. FIGHT was big. We managed to intimidate the city fathers into all sorts of concessions for people of color. Two decades later, looking back on FIGHT, I had to reconsider. On balance, Rochester's African Americans are in worse shape. Although we won some important battles, we lost the war. No fundamental alteration of the political culture that excluded us has taken place. Minorities in Rochester are still shut out from all too many centers of power. This reflection led to my recognition that organizations such as FIGHT have been able to wield power but not *create* power, at least not 'future power'—power that alters not just today's decisions but the way decisions get made from now on.

Future power is a continuing process of relationship building. It's not a single action, no matter how victorious that single action may appear.

Creating future power—a changed public culture in which today's victories establish an ongoing place for citizens in public life—depends on many developments in which we each can take part. They include:

- Citizen-controlled organizations with staying power
- Reshaping official public procedures so they are open and accountable to citizens—and stay that way, and
- Wielding power relationally—carefully assessing the impact of one's actions on others as well as grasping and incorporating their interests.

Looking Back on Future Power

Think of a social cause—civil rights, abortion, women's rights, fair taxation, ecology, or another—with which you most agree. Are you satisfied with its progress? If not, what could those concerned have done to build more future power?

Building Relationships for Future Power

Shifting the goal from winning a single issue to changing the very nature of public life—what does this mean in action? How can we actually create future power?

The Texas Industrial Areas Foundation groups discovered that an inordinate portion of school funding is eaten up by administration. But instead of moving forward with IAF's own reform agenda, the organizations in the IAF network began to build what they called "a constituency for change." It set out to build relationships among teachers, community leaders, and state and local officials.

The IAF statewide citizen network conducted thousands of face-to-face discussions with parents and teachers about what specific reforms *they* wanted for their children. Out of these discussions came a provocative vision statement that took pains *not* to point the finger of blame. The Texas IAF is building power—future power—by drawing all stakeholders into the reform process. In just a few years this process generated reform in fifty-five schools. Most important, it has created a foundation for ongoing change.

In short, Americans from all walks of life are letting go of purely negative definitions of power in order to see power as a tool "to make things happen," "to achieve what we believe in," "to do something important." Similarly, they are discovering that self-interest, when it is developed through interacting with others, need not be simply destructive selfishness.

Consequently, they are discovering many sources of power that involve more creativity than those traditionally honored in our culture. The complexity and depth of today's problems require just such creativity.

What Happened to You While You Read This Chapter?

- Can you identify sources of power in your life you didn't previously realize you had? Write them down.

  _____

  _____

- Return to your responses at the beginning of this chapter when you were asked to rate your feelings about power. Which attitudes would you most like to change?

  _____

  _____

  _____

- List three ideas about power that can be useful to you.

  _____
  _____
  _____

  How might you apply each idea in your life?

  _____
  _____
  _____

What is the first step you are willing to take to improve your understanding and practice of power?

  _____

  _____

PART TWO

—

America Coming Alive: The Invisible Revolution

WELCOME TO PART TWO OF OUR JOURNEY. Here you'll find the seeds of Living Democracy. You'll read about people in every walk of life who are tackling America's biggest challenges, discovering lessons they've generously shared with us.

Important breakthroughs are being made in every dimension of American society. In Part Two we highlight just five.

Chapter Five takes you to work. Beneath the bad news of layoffs and working-harder-for-less, we pinpoint other trends—and some dramatic stories—that demonstrate Living Democracy's potential to address our society's most profound economic ills.

Chapter Six explores radio, TV, newspapers, and more—that portion of public life that leaves so many Americans feeling frustrated and powerless. Here you'll find stories of Americans who are learning that they don't have to remain passive and frustrated.

Chapter Seven takes you into the offices and agencies of what's loosely called human services, that realm—from health care to anti-poverty programs—which touches all of our lives. We explore the quiet revolution that may well influence your own treatment the next time you need services.

In Chapter Eight you'll find more surprising revelations. Regular citizens are discovering ingenious ways to make government accountable. And some local governments are learning that only citizen engagement can make cities work.

This part of the book ends with Chapter Nine. It cuts through the seemingly endless debate about how to help our failing schools. We look at what's really working. We explore the actual changes underway in classrooms and schools that are succeeding in preparing young people to be effective adults.

If you have a special interest in one aspect of public life—education, say, or workplaces, or the media—you may wish to turn to that chapter first. Skip a chapter and come back to it later if you wish. Always use this book as it meets your needs, and remember that delving into interests you don't usually explore may give you a richer appreciation of the many ways you can realize the potential of Living Democracy.

So in Part Two you'll meet people *applying* the useful concepts we explored in Part One. From a workplace in Pittsburgh to senior housing in New York, from health clinics in Oregon to a youth organization in California, from barrios in Texas to a newspaper in Kansas, from a classroom in Florida to city hall in Seattle—all across America an invisible revolution is taking shape. There is one unmistakable common thread among the lessons of Part Two: it's dawning on more and more of us that *the best decision making is shared.* In virtually all settings, authoritarian decision making may appear more efficient, but it isn't. True, it can be quicker, but we pay for that speed later when decisions are not as useful and their implementation is weaker. Across many arenas of American life, citizens are discovering that human beings grow into the most effective problem solvers when we ourselves "own" the challenge—when we participate in defining the problem and devising the solutions.

You can decide whether the Americans you meet on this journey are finding ways to solve the problems you care most about, and whether they offer you practical lessons and ideas you can apply in your own life.

We'll begin with a sensitive subject these days—workplaces and the economy.

5

Our Jobs, Our Economy, and Our Lives

FIVE YEARS AGO, Florinda DeLeon was on welfare, a single parent bringing up three children by herself. Today Florinda makes $6.50 an hour as a home health care worker. She loves her job. And with her company's revenues growing by 20 percent a year, Florinda boasts that "I don't ever have to think about being back on a welfare line."

Almost everywhere else, home health care workers suffer a precarious existence: no benefits, irregular hours, and tough working conditions. But Florinda DeLeon's life is different. Not only is she earning higher-than-average wages for her industry, she receives health benefits and a paid vacation as well. She gets top-notch training, and she's treated with respect by her company's owners.

Why? Because she—along with 170 of her co-workers—*are* the owners. Florinda works for Cooperative Home Care Associates (CHCA), founded in the Bronx in 1985. Florinda also recently completed a two-year term on the company's board of directors. "Being worker-owned means we decide what's best for us," she says proudly.

Irma Johnson is a member of ACORN, a national organization of low- and moderate-income people. In the late 1980s, ACORN concluded that too many banks were refusing to grant mortgages to low-income people who had very good credit. And some federal rules also unreasonably stood in the way of first-time home buyers. Irma and other ACORN members took action. First, they did their research. Then fifteen ACORN members from eleven cities met with senior staff members of the Federal National Mortgage Agency, widely known as Fannie Mae. During long hours of tough debate, these self-taught negotiators convinced this government agency to make key policies more favorable to low-income home buyers.

Florinda and Irma are shaping economic decisions that most Americans feel are beyond our reach. Most of us grow up believing the economy runs not by *our* having a say but by fixed rules that operate almost automatically to protect our well-being. After all, in a market economy, don't we all have the freedom to choose our jobs and select among countless consumer goods? Shouldn't we leave the large economic decisions—from corporate investment to banking policy—in the hands of big-business owners, Congress, and the Federal Reserve?

In the 1980s, some deeply disturbing economic trends forced many Americans to doubt these easy assumptions. Even many who were working felt their jobs threatened. Housing costs skyrocketed, helping to create the most widespread homelessness since the Great Depression. And more and more of us were working longer hours for less pay—still without being able to afford health care.

While millions of Americans were hurting badly, it became obvious that others were doing better than ever: during the 1980s, the wealthiest one percent captured more than half of the rise in the nation's wealth.[1]

For growing numbers of Americans, the old notion that our economy operates almost automatically to satisfy our needs no longer holds water. How then do we Americans reconceive economic life? What does economic life mean in a Living Democracy?

In a Living Democracy the economy is no longer understood as a set of fixed rules operating almost automatically, aided by the occasional tinkering of a handful of corporate and public guardians. Instead, the economy is a *web of human relationships* in which we each play critical decision-making roles.

Questions About the Economy

Thinking about the economy as a web of human relationships encourages each of us to ask:

• Who really makes the decisions in my economic relationships? Do I have an important voice?

• Who is accountable? Whom can I hold responsible for making wise decisions?

• What economic results do I want?

TOWARD AN ECONOMY BASED ON HUMAN RELATION- SHIPS
___

Each of us participates in, or could participate in, six types of economic relationships. Some we experience every day. We may think of these simply as roles we play individually, but each actually represents a complex set of links to other people. They tie us to each other. And they play a major role in determining not only our own well-being but the health of the environment and how our society uses its resources.

In three of these roles—consumer, voter, and investor—many Americans are discovering we do have some power, some control over economic decision making. Their impact is not yet large enough to offset the way many of America's largest corporations do business. But through such efforts as selective shopping, consumer boycotts, and socially aware investing, millions of Americans are already learning that in these roles we can each have a voice in creating a Living Democracy.[2]

In this book we've chosen not to focus on the roles of consumer, voter, and investor but instead to focus on the other three economic roles that form the heart of economic life: worker, employer (owner of economic resources), and direct shaper of economic policy. Most Americans remain unaware of the power they could have in these roles, the power that some citizens are building for themselves.

The first part of this chapter highlights our roles as workers and how relational self-interest applies to the workplace. We then discuss Americans as employers—workers who are also owners and who thereby gain considerable control over their economic destinies. The last part of this chapter

Economic Relationships in a Living Democracy

Six economic relationships	Who participates now?	Who has a voice and is accountable now?	Who has a voice and is accountable in a Living Democracy?
1. Consumer.	All of us.	All of us, but in proportion to how much money we spend and how deliberately we spend it.	As income is more fairly distributed, more people have a voice. As consumers make more deliberate choices, we gain a voice.
2. Worker/earner.	Most of us.	Owners/employers/managers.	As worker participation, worker ownership, democratic unions, and self-employment spread, workers have a greater voice.
3. Voter influencing economic policy via elected representatives.	Regrettably, only half of us exercise our right to vote. The potential remains for virtually all of us to participate.	Those with the biggest campaign contributions.	All voters equally, as candidates gain more equal access to voters and voters gain more equal access to candidates and officials.
4. Investor/saver.	Those with surplus income.	Disproportionately those with the most money to invest.	As wealth is more evenly spread, more of us will have a voice. Those who direct savings in keeping with their values will have a say, too.
5. Direct shaper of economic policies for government and/or corporations.	Very few of us.	Those with the most dollars for lobbying, and the Federal Reserve and other government agencies.	More and more citizens with vision, shared public values, and skills in using the arts of democracy to shape policy.
6. Owner/employer.	Few of us.	10 percent who own 86 percent of financial wealth, plus corporate management and directors.	More and more of us as worker ownership expands and as wealth becomes more evenly spread.

tells the stories of regular people who are developing their power to become *economic innovators and policymakers.*

But first, the setting: just what is happening in our economy that is prompting change?

What's to Come

- Some key reasons our economy is failing

- Rethinking workers' roles

- Other forces pressing for change

- How relational self-interest produces better companies

- Three attributes modern businesses need in their workers

- What workers want most

- Five lessons successful businesses are learning

- Worker-owners and economic innovators—everyday Americans, who are changing the way our economy works

Old Strategies Fail

In today's economy there's good news for the few who are prospering quite well. But most of us can only see the bad news, and the bad news is *really* bad.

For two decades now, the American economy has been on the skids, with the real earnings of most workers falling since the early '70s. Shortly after World War II, the U.S. economy was King of the Mountain internationally. But by the time America's baby boomers were reaching young adulthood, that boom had ended. Europe and Japan had recovered from the war's devastation, and the economies of several so-called third-world countries had begun to take off.

U.S. corporations, unconstrained by legal or moral obligations to *America's* need for good jobs and productive investments, made what they thought were shrewd analyses of their self-interest. "If you want to compete in the world economy," they asked, "what do you do?" Their answers were as follows:

Go Where Your Costs Are Lower. By the mid-1980s, our corporations were exporting more from their foreign affiliates back to the United States and to other markets than they were from their plants here at home.[3] With the factories went American jobs paying middle-class incomes. Two million American manufacturing jobs were lost in the 1980s. General Motors alone laid off tens of thousands of workers over the last decade, while opening huge plants in Mexico.[4]

Get Tough with Workers. To reduce costs at home, some companies began to systematically defeat striking workers by simply replacing them with those who were more desperate. Companies reduced wages and benefits, sped up production, and used more temps and part-time workers who get low wages and no benefits.[5] American workers' lives moved closer to what we associate with third-world working conditions. "There is a narrowing gap between the average American's income and that of the Mexicans," said the president of Caterpillar when he pushed for wage cuts in 1991. "I think what is going on is positive."[6]

Narrowing the gap between his salary and his workers' pay was never a consideration, however. Trimming CEO salaries just hasn't been a part of corporate cost cutting. In 1980, a top CEO earned about forty-two times more than the average factory worker. But by 1990, a mere decade later, the executive was making 157 times more than the worker![7]

Why hasn't this two-pronged strategy—move out or reduce labor costs—worked? Why is our economy weaker than at any time in our memory? Why is homelessness spreading, and why do we have an increasingly frightened middle class?

Some would say no society can improve by impoverishing its work force. But the decline of the American economy may have deeper roots; it may result from our *culture*—from self-defeating assumptions still governing our economy.

Measure Your Sense of the Economy

Circle yes or no:

1. I feel less sure of my job security
today than I did five years ago.   Yes   No

2. Generally, I think other Americans
are also less sure of their jobs.   Yes   No

3. My children are likely to have a harder
time establishing a good career than I did.   Yes   No

4. Many minorities are having a harder
time in today's economy than in previous years.   Yes   No

5. I think it's harder for most people to
make ends meet than it used to be.   Yes   No

6. Overall, it seems most members of my
family are working harder than they used to.   Yes   No

7. I don't see a clear way out of this economic
morass. I don't yet hear our elected representatives
proposing a way out either.   Yes   No

8. I resent the Savings and Loan bailout. It
seems like a huge amount of money, and I'm
not sure it's necessary or that the right people
are getting the right portions of it.   Yes   No

9. My neighbors' children are having a tougher
time finding a summer job than in years past.   Yes   No

10. I've even imagined the possibility of
homelessness if I lose my job.   Yes   No

Fortune magazine aptly described American corporations as "hierarchical systems designed to control workers and break down production into its smallest component tasks."[8] In these systems:

- Executives issue orders.

- Workers take orders.

- Workers are responsible for "doing a job." The rest is the boss's headache.

- Owners and workers are two distinct categories, with different motives.

- All this activity has one goal: the highest return to shareholders.

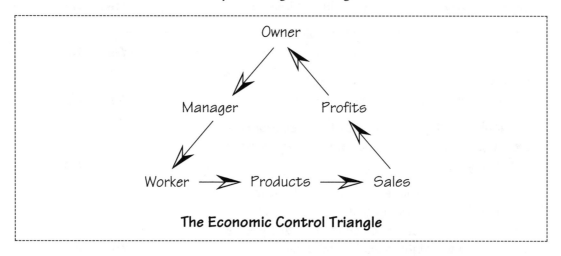

The Economic Control Triangle

But this approach has backfired. It erodes the very productivity so essential to the corporation's profits. Robert Levering, coauthor of *The 100 Best Companies to Work for in America,*[9] offered one explanation for our continuing slide in productivity: "When employees feel the bottom line matters more than anything else, their productivity suffers and they see little reason to care about the company."[10]

Another Way to Be Successful

Our continuing economic failures push the less dramatic news off the front pages. But an invisible revolution is under way in American corporate life. The best companies, and some of the biggest, are finding another way to be successful.

The extent of this invisible revolution first hit us as we sat in the cramped San Francisco offices of Robert Levering and his research team. He told us, "Ten years ago, we had a helluva time finding a hundred companies" that seemed worth praising for how they treat employees. Now, it's much easier.

"We've seen a sea change in the last decade. It seems like companies are realizing that all the rhetoric about 'people being their most important asset' is really true. In order to tap that asset, they have to treat people as something other than machines.

"Today's fad is 'quality,'" Robert went on. "But now it's more and more broadly understood that worker participation is part of quality. More people feel they are able to be themselves at work—really be more than they thought they could be."

Others call it *self-management*. Henry P. Sims, a professor at the University of Maryland, claims, "When I first started teaching self-management in 1980, no one had ever heard of it. There was slow growth until 1987, and then it started to accelerate. Now it's turning out to be a resounding success."

The Spread of Teamwork: What Do You Think?

By the early 1990s, almost half of Fortune 1000 companies had begun using self-managed teams. And more than half said they planned to expand teamwork.[a]

Has this trend reached your workplace? Should it?

"Empowerment of employees is happening," says Professor James Koch at Santa Clara University's business school, "not because of human relations considerations—not because it's the 'right' thing to do—but because of the need to adapt in order to survive in a much more complex world."

Fred Eintracht, a manager at Texas Instruments, was quite blunt in his agreement with this point: "When we were in a growth market and the competition was not quite as keen, our old ways were okay. But now we're competing in a global market," he noted. "We need to empower people to get that extra crucial competitive edge in performance."

Having more women in the work force is also bringing about changes. Women tend to have a different decision-making style, one that challenges the notion of one-way, hierarchical power. Management professor Judy Rosener says that women managers typically "encourage participation by making people feel part of the organization."[11]

Forces Driving Corporate Change

- Global competition

- The need for more productive employees

- The need for better-trained employees, continuing learners

- More women in positions of authority

- Fewer middle managers to oversee workers

Additionally, the cost cutting that corporations imposed in the 1980s itself has changed the way work gets done. "Cost cutting meant getting rid of middle management in the 1980s," says company-watcher Robert Levering. With fewer supervisors to oversee things, top executives had to rethink what workers could do *on their own.*

But how does that happen? What change of attitude has to occur for companies to fully make use of all that their workers have to offer?

"Basically, they have to realize that the key to corporate success is to link the success of the individual and the success of the organization," says Professor Koch. "And democratization is the key to both."

Dr. Koch's point summarizes what hundreds of researchers and thousands of managers are finding: Living Democracy *works*, because the closer workers feel to the company, the more their front-line experience informs the core decision making that creates business success. When workers have an important voice in a company, they have a crucial incentive to invest both their brains and their hearts in their work.

DISCOVERING
RELATIONAL
SELF-
INTEREST
IN THE
WORKPLACE
———

Professor Koch's observations recall the concept of self-interest explored in Chapter Three. Relational self-interest—self-interest defined in relation to others' interests—emerges at the workplace when owners, managers, and employees begin to see their interests linked.

How then can businesses succeed by uniting the worker's and the company's interests?

What Do Employers Need?

As business rethinks its self-interest, many business leaders, *for their own reasons*, are concluding that treating workers as one-dimensional cogs in the corporate machine doesn't work. Instead of needing the "yes, boss" faithful worker, today's executives are realizing that to increase productivity and improve quality—maybe even to survive—they need instead:

Lifelong Learners. In today's fast-paced economy, no one can afford to work from yesterday's knowledge. "Learning, striving people are good workers and happy people," says Ralph Stayer, who revolutionized decision making in his own Wisconsin sausage factory, Johnsonville Foods. "They have initiative and imagination . . . So we replaced our personnel department with a 'learning and personal development team.'"[12]

Planners and Problem Solvers. "In the past, the planning function was separate from those who do the work," explains Professor Koch. "Now planning is an ongoing process of learning and reflecting on experience." But these more efficient planning systems depend on the full participation of the workers, he notes.

Team Players. Better solutions derive from team problem solving. A decision reached by several minds, including those who work close to the problem, is almost always better than one arrived at by a single executive.

What Do Workers Want?

Top money is *not* the American worker's highest concern or biggest reward. More important is a secure job and a sense of accomplishment. And today, some 40 percent of our work force believes (at least in part) that work should be personally satisfying.[13]

Sandra Woolsey worked at Texas Instruments for twenty years. "I never used to brag about my work," she says. "The only thing I ever used to brag about was that I managed to hold on to my job all those years." But in the late 1980s, Texas Instruments introduced self-managing teams, breaking down their rigid hierarchy. "It has changed everything," Sandra reports. "Now I brag to my family all the time. I regularly tell them what I've accomplished."[14]

Workers say they want more involvement at work. This includes a sense of dignity—a need to make meaningful, recognized contributions. It also includes a need for growth—not just decent pay. Fred Eintracht, a manager at Texas Instruments, put it this way: "It can't be the old way anymore, where you check your brains at the door. Now people have a vision of the total process. They want to know *why* they're doing what they're doing."

Businesses' need for lifelong learners and problem-solving team players certainly dovetails with these interests of workers.

What Do You Want Most?

Job security   Learning   Respect

Accomplishment   Financial rewards   Benefits

Managers and other experts as resources

Sense of responsibility   Enhanced relationships

Intellectual growth   Creative outlets

Participation in shaping the future of
companies and communities

Circle the three or four items that mean the most to you.
Then underline the ones you actually enjoy at your job.

Throughout corporate America, successful employers and employees are not talking about a simple change in workplace rules. They're talking about a *change in the culture of work life*—new assumptions about what works, about how people treat each other, and about what skills and attitudes must be valued. Put another way, they're talking about the fact that democracy actually works.

Five Principles for Putting Relational Self-Interest to Work

Five key principles are advancing businesses beyond an authoritarian culture—beyond what one auto worker at GM's Saturn plant calls the "old world"—toward a Living Democracy based on collaborative human relationships.

Principle One: Workers Gain a Real Voice in Decision Making. At one of America's smartest companies, Polaroid, a new practical conclusion has been reached: "To have more brainpower at work, employees must take part in decision making." Consequently, at Polaroid there's a worker's representative on the board of directors and a peer review process for grievances. Plus, workers can vote their 20 percent of Polaroid's stocks. There's also a new emphasis on shared day-to-day decisions.

And when we talked with Joe Caldwell at that Saturn plant in Spring Hill, Tennessee, he told us emphatically, "Employees here are self-hiring. The final decision is ours. You think that's not crucial to how we think about personnel?"

Joe explained how it works: "Each team of twelve to sixteen people is set up as a business, with our own purchasing, budgeting, and maintenance. The team leader is elected, not as a boss but as a resource to give direction." Joe Caldwell's plant remained profitable in the early nineties, even when GM was suffering record losses and layoffs at plants all across the country.

At the Xerox Corporation as well, employee teams have gained real decision-making power. At Xerox, a fifteen-to-twenty-member team assembles the cases for copiers, for example. They take responsibility for scheduling themselves for virtually everything—days off, hours of work, and so on. "They never used to ask us anything," workers at Xerox told author Robert Levering. "Now they listen." One worker summed it all up: "That makes all the difference in the world in how we think about this company and what we'll do for it."

You Are About to Start a Company . . .

You've lined up the concepts, plans, financing, and sales outlets you'll need for the next two years. Everything is in place, except for hiring the twenty to twenty-four people you'll need in your new organization.

What will you do? Think about these options:

1. Hire workers and make sure they know I'm the boss—because I developed the concepts, the goals, and the organization, and I know best how all these elements should fit together.

2. Hire a few workers and give them the authority to hire others. Have as many of them as possible involved immediately in planning and decision making, sharing authority with everyone.

3. Hire workers and invest heavily in training so they'll eventually be prepared to assume more and more authority for making important decisions.

4. Share ownership (and profits) with employees who work with the company for more than two years.

5. Try to involve workers in important decision making and use their experience, but hold on to the power to make the final decisions.

6. Keep a wary eye on my competitors and emulate the personnel practices of the more successful among them.

7. Develop a team of top-level, competent people. Make them executives, rely on them, and reward them well. Let *them* be concerned about the other workers beneath them.

8. Another strategy:

_____

_____

_____

_____

_____

_____

_____

_____

_____

_____

_____

_____

Principle Two: Information Becomes a Tool, Shared Democratically. At Tandem Computers in Silicon Valley, California, top management holds a teleconference with ten thousand workers four times a year. Employees ask any questions they wish.[15] At Connor Formed Metal Products in San Francisco, employees now have access to computers on the shop floor with detailed information about the company, including such sensitive data as pricing and profit margins.[16] Companies are discovering that the best decision making grows out of the best information. And the highest employee commitment to a company is based on a full understanding of the company's business.

Principle Three: Every Employee Is Rewarded for Learning and Innovating. At Chaparral Steel, Charles Clifton, Director of Continuing Education (notice his title), told us that all 950 employees go through "The Chaparral Process." "That's an overview of the whole plant," he said, "from sales and marketing to processing and shipping, so everyone gets a bird's-eye view of what is going on in the entire plant."

"Cross-training here is the norm," declared crane operator Jim Stamey. "Everyone learns everyone else's job. That's one of the beautiful things about Chaparral."[17]

Charles Clifton told us what gives him special satisfaction: "Our workers probably put in two hundred hours a year in formal coursework. Some of them have been out of school for a long time, and this wakes them up, and they discover qualities they'd forgotten. They come alive. We've had a lot of men with reading difficulties, but they became so inspired to learn that we gave them manuals for their wives to read to them. Some started at third-grade level, and now they're at high school level. First they have to break out of the fear. They begin to start up the ladder at the plant, and they perform better while they're learning more. They become quite different people. You can see it in their faces."

The Chaparral Process is hardly typical. While U.S. corporations spend nearly $30 billion educating and training their employees, only one in twelve American workers receives any kind of training at all.[18] Where does all that money go? Most training dollars get spent on managers and other professionals, according to studies by the AFL-CIO.[19]

Charles Clifton described how learning gets rewarded at Chaparral Steel: "People are trained to do several jobs, and they rotate. They're tested and if they pass they move up the pay scale. In three-and-a-half years an employee can move all the way up. We've provided a way for everyone to reach the top of the pay scale."

Profits have increased steadily at Chaparral Steel despite an industrywide slump.

Back at GM's Saturn plant, union leader Mike Bennett told us how much time workers are expected to spend in training. "In three years, you'll get 20 percent of your income for training. That," Mike stressed, "speaks to the company's commitment." While reward systems for training are relatively new for U.S. auto makers, their success has been proven. Honda plants in this country offer their employees a wide array of free classes in everything from problem solving to the technical details of a job. "All you have to do is go over and say, 'I'm interested,' and they'll let you study anything," says worker Sandy Johnson of the Japanese car giant. That learning is rewarded as well: line workers have become supervisors and even senior managers through Honda's training program.[20]

Principle Four: Employees Are Trained for Teamwork. Because human beings are not born as skilled team players, training has to include special training for teamwork. When Ann Donnellon at Harvard's School of Business Administration studied four major firms using team management, she found that in three, the teams were failing miserably. Workers were confused and suspicious. In the fourth, teams were working beautifully. Why the difference? The fourth company trained for teamwork. "Training is critical," she says. "Training can reduce . . . the aversion to conflict . . . that our culture breeds." In fact, she adds, "It can teach team members the process of negotiating differences. . . ."[21]

Teamwork gets directly rewarded in companies that are moving toward a more democratic work culture. For example, when CEO Ralph Stayer set out to revamp Johnsonville Foods, he made sure the visible rewards were given less for technical expertise than for "demonstrated abilities as a teacher, coach, facilitator." Johnsonville stresses group as well as individual accountability. So in its personnel evaluations, this company makes teamwork as important as other types of performance.[22]

Principle Five: Innovative Changes Foster a Culture of Mutual Respect. Joe Caldwell described the culture at GM's Saturn plant: "Everybody here is an adult. No time clocks. No guards at the door. You are a grownup. It makes you feel a whole lot better. It's the way everybody wants to be treated."

This heightened respect flows not just from boss to worker. It emerges among workers as well—through teamwork. "I think being on a team changes the old attitude of prejudice," said Joe. "In the old world [the plants he worked in before], you didn't know the guys that well. Here I've met the families and the kids. Some of my best friends at Saturn are black, even though I come from a very prejudiced Southern state."

Changing Old Habits: It's Tough, But It's Hard to Go Back

America's forward-looking corporations are learning a few more lessons about Living Democracy. For example, the transition to self-management requires considerable patience. "Employees are likely to test the system, do something management doesn't like, to see whether management is sincere

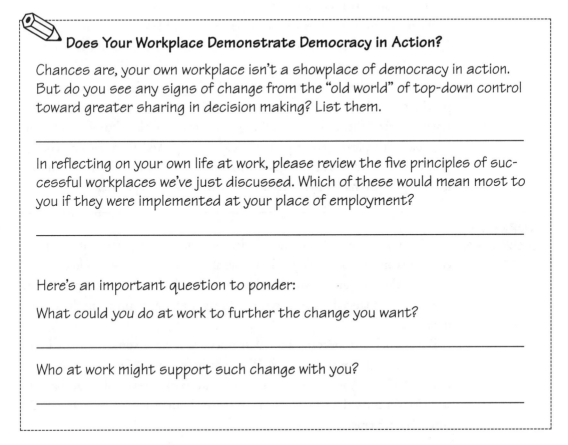

Does Your Workplace Demonstrate Democracy in Action?

Chances are, your own workplace isn't a showplace of democracy in action. But do you see any signs of change from the "old world" of top-down control toward greater sharing in decision making? List them.

_____

In reflecting on your own life at work, please review the five principles of successful workplaces we've just discussed. Which of these would mean most to you if they were implemented at your place of employment?

_____

Here's an important question to ponder:

What could you do at work to further the change you want?

_____

Who at work might support such change with you?

_____

or will retreat on self-management and clamp down at the first excuse," says Professor Sims from the University of Maryland.

And because the transition to self-management is so difficult, it often requires leadership. "There has to be an executive driver—a bit of a paradox, of course," says Sims, "so that decision making is pushed down in the organization." "Without support from top management," adds Robert Levering, "people get good ideas and can't go anywhere with them. They get very disappointed."

Let's not get carried away; the millennium has not yet arrived. We've drawn these lessons of Living Democracy from only a small minority of American firms. The top-down model of control still dominates corporate America. But in talking with the people whose job it is to study trends in American business, we found a consensus: despite the difficulty of changing, *American companies have little choice.* Teamwork and genuine employee participation are taking hold. That's because *they work.* There is no other way to meet the competitive challenges of the nineties.

Professor Sims told us that Procter and Gamble increased productivity 60 percent using self-managed teams. GM, he says, finds a self-managed plant 30 to 40 percent more productive than a traditionally structured one. Impressive studies now back up these findings. Studies now confirm the productivity benefits of self-management.[23] Business analyst Edward Lawler writes, "It is hard to kill a good thing. People who become comfortable with participative practices can be expected to resist any change [back to the 'old world']."[24] As Ford's former CEO, Donald Petersen, put it: "People who have tasted freedom just won't let you go back."[25]

WORKERS AS OWNERS
—

Ownership is the buzzword among advocates of worker participation. Typically, this means psychological, not legal, ownership or—as some prefer, stakeholding. In other words, when workers feel it's *their* company, they develop an enhanced sense of responsibility for what happens in their organization.

But if ours is to become a truly democratic society, some ask, why legally separate workers and owners? Why not have workers as owners *in fact* as well as feeling? And indeed, experiments in worker ownership go back to the last century. The most recent historical surge ended with the 1929 stock market crash.

What's to Come

- How employee stock ownership plans help workers become owners

- Whether unskilled, undereducated workers can run a company successfully

- Why worker-owners make better investors than old-fashioned investors

- Dramatic stories of regular people everywhere who are reshaping our entire economy

---

Today, the advocates of worker ownership span the ideological spectrum, from Jesse Helms to Jesse Jackson.[26] And it's a fast-growing phenomenon. By the start of this decade more than eleven thousand companies were owned in whole or in part by their twelve million employees. These workers had accumulated $60 billion in stock.[27]

That's only about 3 percent of the value of all stock, but in four important industries, workers own the majority of stock in companies that rank among the top ten. Those industries are private hospital management, shipbuilding, construction, and steel manufacturing.[28] In just the last few years, the steelworkers' union has arranged sixteen major employee buyouts.[29] And what's more, fifteen employee-owned companies now rank among America's largest four hundred private firms—and they're growing faster than non-employee-owned companies.[30] Most significantly, during the first quarter of 1993, employee ownership stocks outperformed all market averages.[31]

Advocates maintain that workers are more committed than outside investors to long-term profitability. What's more, they argue, the reason worker ownership has not spread faster is quite simple: top managers and investors—*not* the workers—take home the profits needed for business development.

This giant stumbling block—the fact that workers often lack access to capital—has been partly overcome by a financial mechanism devised by an investment banker named Louis Kelso. It's called an ESOP, an acronym for Employee Stock Ownership Plan. It's a benefit program for employees, funded by the company, that invests in the company's stock.

To entice employers to help their workers become owners, the ESOP plan became a federal law in 1974 and provides significant tax benefits to participating companies. And ESOPs have grown steadily ever since. By the 1990s, through their ESOPs, employees owned at least 25 percent of many companies that are household names, including J.C. Penney, Kroger's, Avis, and Coldwell Banker.[32]

It helps to view worker ownership across a wide spectrum. At one end are companies whose workers own a minority of the firm's stock through an ESOP. Typically, daily work life is unaffected. (Although at Polaroid, where employees own 20 percent of the company, even partial ownership seems to be creating a culture of ownership. When employee Sheila Martel told us about workers' efforts to reduce costs by taking vacation time during the slow sales periods, she concluded, "It's *our* money we're saving.")

At the other end are worker cooperatives. Here workers are full owners and often very much in charge of daily work life. They even elect the board of directors. There are roughly one thousand worker cooperatives in the United States, although most have only a few workers.[33]

Some people are dedicated to employee ownership because they think it's fairer and more democratic. But worker ownership has other merits. For one, it can increase productivity when combined with real participation. Corey Rosen and Karen Young, founders of the National Center for Employee Ownership, argue that neither participation nor ownership *alone* has much effect on the bottom line. It takes both.[34]

To illustrate, we'll look at a sampling of today's many worker-owned, or partially-owned, firms. How are the "stakeholders" of these worker-owned companies making the transition to Living Democracy in the workplace?

Former Welfare Recipients Help Raise Industry Standards

Cooperative Home Care Associates (CHCA) in the Bronx, New York, is a worker-owned cooperative. Co-ops differ from other businesses—including those with ESOPs—that operate by a one-share, one-vote rule. Decision making at CHCA is strictly one-*person*, one-vote.

At CHCA, workers become owners by investing a thousand dollars through small weekly deductions over five years. So far, 170 of its 270 workers have become owners. Eighty percent of CHCA workers—roughly half of all employees are African-American and half Latina—were welfare recipients who had never before worked in formal jobs.

Rick Surpin, one of the prime movers behind CHCA, says, "Owners shouldn't be just the first people to walk in the door. They have to *earn* their membership by proving they are good workers."[36] CHCA works hard to develop professional managers, people who know their jobs and their clients and are willing to fire employees who can't meet the company's high standards. It's entry-level training program has earned the New York City Department of Employment's highest evaluation.

CHCA has now achieved the status of "yardstick" company—one setting higher standards for the entire New York home health care industry. CHCA boasts one of the lowest client complaint records in the New York area. Rick and other worker-owners believe that the company's better client care comes from its culture of ownership—and the better working conditions that result. After all, aren't workers who enjoy above-average pay, job security, benefits, and the dignity that goes with ownership more likely to have the peace of mind needed to provide responsible care?

CHCA is also seeding its organizational model elsewhere. "When people, even from other countries, visit us to see how we've done it, the sense of pride is tremendous for all the worker-owners," Rick beamed. Two groups—one in California and one in Connecticut—have been inspired to replicate the CHCA model. And CHCA and its Training Institute are themselves starting two other home health care cooperatives in Philadelphia and Boston.

Steelworkers Sacrifice Because They're Owners

Weirton Steel in West Virginia is one of the country's top ten steel makers. And it's also the country's second largest majority-worker-owned manufacturer.

Weirton's experience challenges a common fear about worker ownership: that worker-owners will take their profits home rather than invest in their company's growth. During the last four years of the 1980s, Weirton was the only U.S. steel company to show a profit every quarter. For over five years, employees each took home an average of over twenty thousand dollars in profit sharing. Then, in 1989, the employee-owners decided to decrease profit sharing for several years and do what the former parent company, National Steel, refused to do: invest in new equipment.

"Back then, we made a lot of money for them [National Steel], but they didn't reinvest in us," Walter Bish, co-manager of worker participation, told us. So workers voted to undertake a $500 million, five-year plant modernization program. And they are enduring the consequences. With big craters in the factory floor and major engineering projects under way, keeping up production "is like trying to change a flat tire on a car going down the highway at sixty-five miles an hour," Walter said. But the worker-owners are willing to endure the nuisance and postpone their profit-sharing bonuses because they know they will be the long-term beneficiaries of the modernized plant.

Weirton is also taking steps toward greater worker participation, translating the workers' legal ownership into a real say in important decisions. When three hundred worker-owners applied for three new positions as trainer-facilitators, a joint management-labor committee chose two mill workers and a non-management employee from accounting.

Today, twelve trainers—all but a couple of whom were previously mill workers—conduct three-day training sessions for workers. In addition to teaching problem solving and communication, the classes end with a decision-making activity that "brings home to the workers that 'participation is easy to say but hard to do.'" About 40 percent of the workers have completed the training so far. Weirton claims these employees have created major innovations, saving the company millions of dollars.[35]

EVERYDAY CITIZENS AS ECONOMIC INNOVATORS

At the beginning of this chapter, we charted six of the roles Americans play in economic life. Consumer, voter, and investor were the first three. But we chose to focus on three others: worker, employer (particularly worker-owner), and direct shaper of economic policies. It's to this third role that we now turn.

Growing up in America, we learn that *policymakers* are "experts" and politicians. So it's been hard to imagine ourselves in that role. Yet more and more of today's citizens feel poorly served by these so-called leaders. Here is just a bit of what we've seen in the last few years:

- Scandal and fraud throughout America's savings and loan industry, burdening taxpayers for years to come with bailout costs that some estimate could go as high as $1.2 trillion (yes, that's trillion with a "t").[37]

What's to Come

Citizens actively taking charge in order to:

• Monitor and save companies in trouble

• Influence banking—get money to regular people

• Make our biggest expense—homes—affordable

• Put it all together—implement a range of innovations

• Change the big picture, too—even national policies

• A $2 trillion military buildup, with no tax increase to pay for it, that helped quadruple the national debt, with interest payments that now take a big bite of every tax dollar.[38]

• A one-third decline in the incomes of young families with children in the last two decades. This has directly contributed to an unprecedented increase in child poverty.[39]

• A burst of mergers and leveraged buyouts in the 1980s, creating companies so shackled with debt that bankruptcies reached near record highs and layoffs became common even in blue-chip companies.[40]

Yet there's good news here, too. As these failures by our elected officials and corporate leaders become more and more obvious, citizens are becoming emboldened. Terms like capital flight, deindustrialization, and redlining are no longer considered esoteric. Millions of regular citizens are demystifying economics and becoming innovators themselves. Let's look at a few citizens who have become public problem solvers and created new economic tools to deal with our economic problems.

Workers Learn How to Save Jobs Themselves

In Pennsylvania, citizens concerned about the disappearance of good jobs have decided they're *not* voiceless and powerless in economic decision making. Imagine this: It's late December, 1989, it's snowing in Pittsburgh, and the storm is heavy. Trucks bringing in the city's bread supply can't

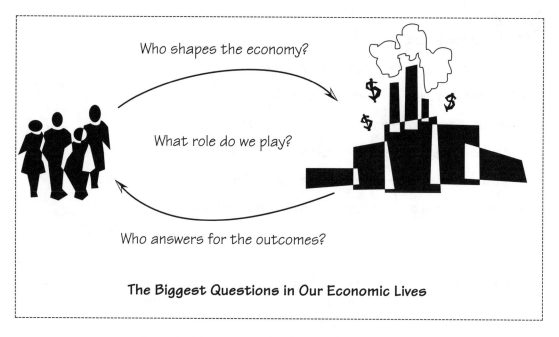

Who shapes the economy?

What role do we play?

Who answers for the outcomes?

The Biggest Questions in Our Economic Lives

get through. For two weeks during the holiday season no one can buy bread.

"I remember looking at the empty shelves and thinking 'this is amazing,'" said Tom Croft. "There was no bread, period."[41] Tom heads the Steel Valley Authority in Pittsburgh. For him, the dearth of bread at holiday time came as a welcomed gift. It proved what he and others had been arguing for some time: that a recent multinational corporate takeover—which closed Pittsburgh's only bakery and cost hundreds of jobs—left the city vulnerable.

At the time, Tom's job at Steel Valley Authority was to help the unemployed workers, their local union, and other concerned citizens find a solution. Three-and-a-half years later—with forty of the laid-off bakery workers as team leaders—a new bakery with the apt name of City Pride opened in Pittsburgh.

To make City Pride happen, banks, the union, churches, local government, and a local community development corporation all joined forces as investors. Tom attributes much of the project's success to what he describes as "the workers' undying patience, wisdom to self-govern, and capacity to rally against overwhelming odds.".

But why is Tom, someone from the Steel Valley Authority, involved in helping to open a new community-owned bakery? In the 1980s, hundreds of corporations pulled out of Pennsylvania. Dislocated workers, religious leaders, and community activists decided that protests weren't enough. They succeeded in creating a new type of public authority—perhaps even new in America. The Steel Valley Authority, chartered by the state, has a clear mission statement: "to provide a 'voice at the table' for the working people who suffer the hardest-hit industrial relocation in the nation."

The Authority even has the power to hold on to corporate property when selling it would destroy jobs. And it acts as a broker for the purchase and sale of plants that might otherwise close. "In Pittsburgh it's clear we can't be passive and wait for things to happen," the Authority's Robert Erickson told us.

Workers in the Midwest are also learning new roles in economic decision making. "In Chicago, three thousand out of seven thousand manufacturing companies disappeared in the 1980s, and the 1990s don't look any better," Dan Swinney told us, "and many of those companies that closed didn't need to." Dan heads the Midwest Center for Labor Research in Chicago, supported by a broad base of union, religious, and community groups.

In their search for practical solutions, the Midwest Center focuses on what workers *themselves* can do. "We're offering training classes and workshops for non-management people to learn to think of themselves as fully involved in the company," Dan told us. "We're helping them recognize the indicators of when a company is in trouble: when the machines aren't getting repaired, when there's no research and development of new products, when there's an aging owner and no successor."[42]

This training has created the Center's Early Warning Network to help workers monitor their companies for signs of trouble so that they can turn things around before it's too late. The network is expanding at the rate of thirty plants a month. The Center also helps workers buy out a failing company or find an appropriate successor if, say, an owner is about to retire.

And there's a larger vision taking hold as well. Both the Midwest Center and the Steel Valley Authority take part in a national network of thirty-two local and regional groups: the Federation for Industrial Retention and Renewal. Launched in Chicago in 1988, it spreads innovative solutions discovered by everyday citizens who want to save and enhance their jobs.

Ultimately, however, whether it's starting a new bakery in reaction to corporate desertion in Pittsburgh or helping a failing company to save jobs in Chicago, one question is paramount: how do we create economic institutions accountable to communities?

Ways for Citizens to Become Problem Solvers

- Employee stock ownership plans

- Worker cooperatives

- Worker buyouts

- Early warning monitoring, training, and networking to prevent job losses

- Public agencies to save and create jobs

New Community-Based Economics

One way to create community-based economics is through citizen innovations that address our most basic needs for housing and jobs.

Banking on Communities. In 1980, Bonnie Wright and her husband, Martin Eakes, roamed North Carolina, counseling unemployed workers on ways to deal with plant closings. They worked out of their car. When their car caught fire ("There went our office!") the two set up a "real" office. It became the Center for Community Self-Help.[43] In just one decade, the Center has become a national model, showing how a financial institution—not a charity—can help citizens gain an economic stake in their community.

Bonnie Wright and Martin Eakes realized that among the biggest reasons people stay impoverished is lack of capital, plain and simple. So they set out to create a financial institution that would be financially sound and at the same time provide capital to those who usually can't get it. With seventy-seven dollars in profits from a bake sale, they launched the Self-Help Credit Union and the Self-Help Ventures Fund in 1984. Now with $35 million in assets, they've made more than $18 million in loans.[44]

They loan to minorities and low-income people, including 120 former public housing residents. In addition to home ownership loans, Self-Help has assisted scores of employee-owned businesses, from a minority-owned sewing company to a recreation services company.

Far away from North Carolina, in the heart of Chicago, is the country's first development bank—Southshore Corporation. It was launched in 1973 in a deteriorating African-American neighborhood where a third of the area's apartment buildings were tax delinquent and in danger of being abandoned by their landlords. Southshore began with home ownership loans to stabilize the neighborhood but soon began supporting local entrepreneurs willing to reclaim run-down apartment buildings. By the 1990s, close to a third of the housing stock in the vicinity had been rehabbed with Southshore loans. Now other Chicago banks are competing to make loans there.

It's Southshore's combination of profit making and social purpose that its founders hoped others would be eager to copy. But no. After twenty years, only two other similar ventures have taken hold. In 1992, however, the social unrest in Los Angeles shook up a lot of people. Community-based solutions gained appeal. And citizen groups across the country began working to ensure that the Clinton administration lives up to its promise to promote one hundred new community development banks, à la Southshore, all across the country.

Few people feel they have less of an economic voice than the rural poor in a state like North Carolina or inner-city residents in a place like Chicago. But community-controlled financial institutions, including Self-Help and Southshore, are working to change that in cities all across America. They are establishing relationships of mutual accountability between citizens and financial institutions. Such relationships lie at the heart of a Living Democracy.

And there's another innovation that's making it possible for economically disenfranchised citizens to gain some measure of "voice" in our economy. It's a means to self-employment, something that most of us assume is open only to the better-off. And it's true: most of the eleven million Americans who work for themselves (compared to only half that number twenty years ago) are at least middle-class.

One citizen who has been intrigued by the potential that self-employment holds for poor people is Susan Matteucci. A graduate of the Massachusetts Institute of Technology's urban planning school, Susan visited Bangladesh in 1988, immersing herself in the experience of the Grameen

Bank. It's a lending network operating in eighteen thousand villages, through which more than a million landless, mostly desperately poor women in Bangladesh are receiving small loans to invest in money-making projects.

Susan came back to Chicago's inner city and started the Full Circle Fund at the Women's Self-Employment Project, one of about a dozen successful lending programs throughout the United States inspired by Grameen.

She is adapting the lessons she learned in Bangladesh to poor women in Chicago. The key lesson to success, she's learned, is about the *power of relationships* and the feelings of mutual accountability they make possible. "There's a wide perception that no one will trust each other in the inner city. Wrong!" says Susan. The Full Circle Fund made fifty-five loans in its first three years. The repayment rate was a complete 100 percent.

Citizens Figure Out How to Keep Houses Affordable. The people at Community Self-Help, Southshore, and the Full Circle Fund are right: creating community-based economic programs is key to expanding economic participation by citizens who are now shut out. Without access to capital—credit—we can't become owners, whether of our own homes or businesses.

A Lending System That Works

Here's how a Grameen-inspired lending system builds on the power of relationships:

• A group of four to seven people (often women) are jointly responsible for an individual member's loan; they are, in effect, cosigners.

• The group helps each member develop a business plan and offers support in seeing that it's carried out.

• Each member of the group is dependent upon the other because no new loan will be issued to any member if one of them defaults on a loan.

• If any member defaults, all are responsible for making good on the loan.

But access to credit is meaningless if what we need—a home, for instance—remains so expensive that it's still unaffordable, despite the credit. And by the early 1990s, only 9 percent of the nation's renters could afford to buy a median-priced home in their region.[45] As the housing crisis worsened, so did the concerns of many ordinary citizens. People began asking such core questions as:

- How do we create *permanently* affordable housing?

- How do we promote home ownership and eliminate absentee owners who drain money from our community?

- How can home ownership become possible for all those people who don't have large down payments, people whose incomes will always be modest?

One answer, citizens have discovered, is to separate ownership of the house from ownership of the land it's on. Here's how that concept works in actual practice: Rob and Mary live in Burlington, Vermont. He's a social worker, she's a day-care worker. With three kids, they were bursting out of their small apartment. After beginning to search for a house, they sat down and figured out a budget. Only then did the impossibility of their dream hit them. "What are we going to live on after mortgage payments?" These people—good credit risks—simply couldn't afford monthly payments on a house the size their family needed.

Then they learned about the Burlington Community Land Trust. Through the Trust, they were able to afford a $54,000, four-bedroom home. The Trust paid $12,000 for the land. The couple only had to take on a mortgage of $42,000, bringing their monthly payments within reach of their income.

Rob and Mary own their own home. But if they sell, the Trust has the first option to buy. After compensating the couple for the improvements they've made, the Trust keeps 75 percent of any appreciation in value.[46]

The beauty of this scheme is that the Land Trust uses its share of the increased value to subsidize the price for the *next* purchaser. The house itself remains affordable for others and becomes more affordable over time. Instead of ongoing government subsidies to cover a mortgage that is larger than Mary and Rob can afford, all that's needed is a one-time subsidy that will eventually be replaced.

Community land trusts are now springing up in 23 states and 120 communities, from New York City and Chicago to Wichita, Kansas, and Menomonie, Wisconsin. The idea came not from real estate professionals or financial wizards but from average Americans who decided to go beyond despair or protest to become public problem solvers.

After the successful land trust in Burlington, Vermonters who rarely sit in the same room, much less see eye-to-eye—*forty* environmental, farm, and community development groups—collaborated to take the land trust idea to the state. In unprecedented unity, they convinced the governor and legislature to create an ongoing revenue stream from property taxes to support permanently affordable housing, as well as to preserve important farm land. "We've never seen anything like this coalition," said one supportive state senator.[47]

What's going on here? Land trusts for permanently affordable housing, banks focused on community development, training programs to help workers avoid plant closings, public support for worker-owned start-ups—these are among the economic tools citizens are devising across our nation. They are expanding the number of citizens who have an economic voice. They are creating relationships of mutual accountability. They are moving us toward a Living Democracy.

Putting It All Together. In Connecticut's Naugatuck Valley and Massachusetts' Merrimack Valley, tough times have challenged citizens to develop most of these tools for public problem solving—and more.[48]

Once the center of the nation's thriving brass industry, Naugatuck Valley by the 1970s was losing dozens of factories and plants. And those remaining behind were increasingly owned by large conglomerates based around the world. Many once-thriving communities were dying.

So in the early 1980s, Naugatuck Valley residents started meeting to ask the key question that led them to action: *what can we do?*

Ken Galdston, a veteran citizen organizer and management school graduate, helped pull together diverse community, religious, and union leaders. At age thirty-five, Ken felt frustrated that other citizen groups he'd worked with had focused on "neighborhood issues but ignored people's life at work." In the Naugatuck Valley, however, work issues couldn't be ignored. People were in too much economic distress.

From those early meetings was born the Naugatuck Valley Project (NVP), whose members now include sixty-eight religious, union, community, and business organizations. Their goal (and that of NVP's sister project, the Merrimack Valley Project in eastern Massachusetts, which Ken also helped to found) is ambitious: "to create new democratic institutions as models of how we can restructure our society."

NVP models many of the lessons about power we stressed in Chapter Four. Most important, its strength comes from its members—now thirty-thousand families. It's these families, not an organizer's agenda, that guide the progress. "What we are all about is developing leaders who take control of their lives," says director Susan Wefald. By leaders Susan means regular people who are encouraged to discover their power.

Since NVP is member-driven, it can't be a single-issue organization. It must respond to members' concerns as they evolve, member Theresa Francis told us. "Recently the main things that come up for people are affordable housing and care for our senior citizens," she noted. From these concerns has grown the worker-owned Valley Care Cooperative Home Care company modeled after New York's successful Cooperative Home Health Care. And a land trust that's already generated one hundred units of permanently affordable housing is also under way. Additionally, NVP defeated a city plan to replace a park with an incinerator.

"The people in these projects are making things happen," Theresa declared proudly. "They don't just talk about housing, saving jobs, and all the other things folks like to talk about. They *do* it!"

These local and regional citizen efforts benefit from parallel efforts that are creating new roles for citizens in shaping *national* economic policy.

Citizens' Action on the National Level

It's January 1991. We sit down with several hundred members of National People's Action (NPA) in a large, crowded basement office in a working-class Chicago neighborhood. At least half are African Americans; several are Hispanic. Most would call themselves low-income. They are gathered to protect their recent gains and raise their sights. Those sights are focused on enforcement and expansion of the federal Community Reinvestment

Act (CRA), which requires a bank to make loans in every neighborhood in its service area; otherwise federal approval for expansion or other requests will be denied. The act took effect in 1979, and the NPA estimates it has kept up to $8 *billion* in communities across America that banks would have sent elsewhere. Some of the people meeting with us played a key role in the passage of this historic legislation.

We listen to NPA's chairperson, Gale Cincotta, a large, forceful woman who raised six children in a working-class Chicago neighborhood. Years ago she became outraged that banks were redlining—discriminating against minorities, even though she herself is white. She became angry that real estate agents were fostering white flight out of inner-city neighborhoods. Gale decided to fight. Her efforts led to the founding of the NPA, among the most important forces behind the passage not only of the Community Reinvestment Act but also of the Home Mortgage Disclosure Act, the federal law requiring banks to reveal exactly where they've made loans.

"You do *not* have to be a banking expert to negotiate with a bank," is the message from the NPA and its National Training and Information Center. "All you need to do is prove they discriminate (this is easy) and know what you want from them." With that, NPA has helped to create federal law and policy. They've demonstrated citizens' ability to make change affecting the entire nation.

ACORN stands for Association of Community Organizations for Reform Now. Founded in Arkansas in 1970, it is one of the country's largest low-income membership organizations, with one-hundred thousand members living in twenty-six states. Unlike the Industrial Areas Foundation (IAF) organizations or the Naugatuck Valley Project—whose members come from already existing community institutions like churches and unions—ACORN organizes *new* neighborhood groups that become chapters of the national ACORN network.

ACORN jumped into the housing crisis in the late 1970s, when members in Philadelphia started "squatting" in abandoned, city-owned houses. "We got the properties, but we needed the money for rehab," Deepak Bhargava explained. Then their members ran into the same bank redlining that had propelled Gale Cincotta into action in Chicago.

ACORN used the Community Reinvestment Act to press banks not just for loans but for lower interest rates and more flexible lending practices.

The organization and its allies also succeeded in creating one seat on the Federal Housing Finance Board and two seats on each of the twelve district Federal Home Loan Bank Boards for directors representing community interests. Then in 1991, ACORN got its former president, Elena Hanggi, appointed to fill a seat on one of the Federal Home Loan Bank Boards. Soon she became chairperson. Elena told us that her first goal was simply to change the way work gets done on the board. It operated as a "rubber stamp" for the banks, without serious attention to the community consequences of its decisions, she explained. She wanted to change that, so banks would serve the *entire* community.

Elena, who began as a homemaker in Little Rock, and ACORN members like George and LaVerne Butts, who have worked for years on ACORN projects, would argue with Americans who see the system as, in LaVerne's words, "untouchable." "Local people are getting involved in the biggest issues," George points out, "so it is the locals that affect the national picture. We went to Congress and told them what we wanted in the S & L legislation. The heart of it all came from us."

George's satisfaction comes from more than changing specific policies: "LaVerne and I have been doing this long enough to see that the debate has shifted. It's now about *including* us rather than excluding us." ACORN members know that in many ways they are changing the rules that banks have to follow. "Because of us," adds LaVerne, "they know that it *does* matter what they do." Indeed, it matters plenty.

THE PUBLIC FACE OF PRIVATE ENTERPRISE

Perhaps the biggest handicap in solving today's social problems by moving toward Living Democracy is our inherited notion that public life excludes our work lives and economic decision making. We usually assume that we go to work to make money—a private pursuit. We try to earn enough to meet our private needs and indulge our private tastes. It's *private* enterprise, after all.

By taking this view, we miss the public nature of today's economy. Sure, corporations are owned by investors and not by the public at large. But it is crucial to appreciate the enormous public consequences of their choices.

Those choices—where to invest, what to produce, how to produce it, how to reward employees and executives, where to pay taxes, how to influence government—determine where people live; what schools, roads, and hospitals are required; whether the environment will be destroyed or protected; and whether people will be able to meet their basic human needs.

In fact, some analysts argue that decisions made by corporations and their leaders, whom we do *not* elect and seldom see, determine our well-being more directly than those made by the governments whose leaders we *do* elect.

It's within this context that we hope the stories we've described in this chapter have meaning and import. They suggest that millions of Americans—both employers and employees—are awakening to the need for *shared accountability in our economic lives.*

Corporations are learning they can no longer succeed without sharing decision making with their workers. And in the process, workers are becoming more accountable in their workplaces. All the while, citizens and workers are creating new economic tools—from community-based banks to lending circles—to give more citizens a greater voice in our economy. And they are learning how to hold even the largest corporations and government agencies accountable for the public consequences of their actions. They are developing their power to change the way decisions get made in America.

 Taking the First Step

Is there one innovation you've just read about that you'd like to see spread?

Should you tell someone about it?

Does it prompt you to write a letter to the editor of your local newspaper suggesting some Living Democracy ideas that could be implemented in your town?

Should you discuss it with any group you're a part of?

Should you contact one of the organizations mentioned here to find out how to organize a similar effort in your community?

What one step do you resolve to take during the coming week? Write it down.

_____

6

Making the Media Our Voice

THE POWER OF TALK RADIO is the empowerment of the public," says Mike Siegel, radio talk show host on KVI in Seattle. "The mainstream media think they have all their own answers, and they pontificate about them," he said. "But they seem to have no idea what the people are feeling—no clue. Talk radio is a facilitator, a change agent, a catalyst."

Mike cited an example: "Shortly after the Exxon oil spill in Prince Edward Sound, a columnist in the Seattle Times suggested people contact me to talk about a boycott of Exxon. The station got inundated with phone calls. And in the end we helped pass a national law requiring all tankers to have double-hulls [safeguarding against spills]."

In El Paso, Texas, small-business owner Jule Zimet and others helped launch a series of discussion groups on pressing concerns, from schools to abortion. Soon they decided that TV would allow them to include many more people. So now, three times a year, representatives of face-to-face discussion groups appear on a prime-time televised forum with viewer call-ins. "Ballots" register citizens' opinions before and after the program. And these views are then sent to El Paso.

Both Mike and Jule are eager to prove that citizens can *use existing media* to make themselves heard. Other folks you'll meet in this chapter already work in the media, control media, and are discovering the value of *moving the media closer to ordinary citizens*. And still other Americans are *creating new media*—controlled in part by everyday citizens—to increase the opportunities for people to voice their views.

How do Mike and Jule's stories, and those of all the new pioneers in democratic media, differ from Americans' typical experience of the media?

The content of their programs affects the lives of listeners directly. The medium is interactive, and it's not just a vehicle for selling. It's also a means for *action*.

But most of us experience the media very differently. They're one-way. They come *at us* with almost hypnotic power. The media—those floods of images affecting our moods and opinions and spending—loom as a distant

---

Your Personal News Media Audit

How many hours each week are you involved with the news media? Write down your estimates.

Medium	Numbers of Hours Per Week
National newspapers (USA Today, Wall Street Journal, New York Times, etc.)	_____
Local newspapers	_____
Network TV news (including news magazine programs such as "60 Minutes")	_____
Local TV news	_____
National radio news (including programs such as NPR's "Morning Edition" or "All Things Considered")	_____
Local radio news	_____
Magazines and newsletters	_____
Computer bulletin boards	_____
Other: _____	_____

Now circle those you would like to use more.

Next, strike a line through those you would like to use less.

force, beyond the control of ordinary mortals. As viewers and listeners, we remain passive.

It doesn't surprise the two of us that when we speak publicly about the possibilities for Living Democracy, someone from our audience invariably presents the challenge, "But what about the power of the *media*? How can we have the democracy we truly want when the media are controlled by a handful of corporate giants?"

Indeed, just twenty-three corporate conglomerates now own most media outlets in the United States, from newspapers to TV to motion pictures.[1] And in 1992, the Federal Communications Commission more than doubled the number of radio and TV stations it will allow one individual, company, or religious group to own.[2] Big media conglomerates like this arrangement, but most Americans are not pleased with what this highly concentrated, narrowly controlled industry offers us. Roughly two-thirds of us believe the media don't deal fairly with all sides, are influenced by powerful people, and focus too heavily on the bad news.[3]

Yet not all Americans are throwing up their hands in defeat. A strikingly diverse number of citizens are turning media into true mass communication: *mass* suggests that we *all* can participate. And *communication* is by definition more than one-way. In so doing, they are making themselves heard—and showing what a democratic future might hold for the rest of us.

The people you'll meet in this chapter see genuine public talk as essential to democracy. By *public talk* we mean people expressing their views, hearing different views, weighing the differences—we mean all that goes into forming public judgment. Public judgment is not just public opinion—the undigested, knee-jerk reactions to the questions of pollsters. Instead, public judgment requires that we ourselves help shape the questions and frame the issues. It means we have the opportunity to reflect, to weigh alternative solutions, perhaps even create some ourselves.

Let your imagination roam as you read this chapter. Imagine mass media becoming true mass communication—a vehicle for public dialogue, discussion, and debate, helping Americans form public judgment. Many folks you'll meet in this chapter are beginning to tap just such a resource.

What's to Come

Some news about the media that may be news to many Americans:

Newspapers . . .

- Discover citizens want more than sound bites
- Help the disenfranchised gain voice
- Find new ways to create communities

Radio . . .

- Becomes the new town meeting
- Can be owned and operated by regularcitizens

Television . . .

- Becomes a forum for citizen dialogue
- Can be produced by lay people
- Opens up politics to regular Americans and revitalizes grassroots democracy

Computers . . .

- Increasingly link citizens to each other
- Link citizens to their local governments

REDIS-COVERING THE POWER OF PRINT

Despite the spell cast by electronic media, over a third of Americans cite newspapers as their major source of information about the world. Each day, sixty-three million Americans read a total of sixteen hundred newspapers, but their numbers are rapidly dwindling, a disturbing trend for our democracy.[4] While America has five times as many cities as it did at the end of World War II, the number of daily papers has shrunk by more than one quarter.[5] Only thirty-seven U.S. cities still have competing, separately owned daily papers.[6] In fact, ours is the only industrial society in which most large cities no longer have competing dailies.

Enriching Your Use of the Media

Put a check mark next to the ways you would like to enrich your link to the larger world through the media.

I would like to:

____ Become more selective in what I watch and read

____ Become more critically aware of the messages I receive

____ Find new sources of information about the things I care about most

____ Participate more through letters to newspaper editors, call-in talk shows, and electronic bulletin boards

____ Create my own news medium through a regular column in a local news-paper, a newsletter, or a public access cable television program

---

Citizens Want More than Sound Bites

The debate over the media's function in a democracy often gets stuck on this unhappy note: people get what they ask for. The reason that media coverage has become so superficial, so this argument goes, is that citizens just don't *want* anything else. Our attention spans, we're told, have been permanently stunted by the fast pace of TV, where we spend, on average, one quarter of our waking hours.

How, then, can we explain the following story?

During October 1991, two reporters at the *Philadelphia Inquirer*, Donald L. Barlett and James B. Steele, ran nine fact-filled, lengthy articles that analyzed what's behind the crisis of our economy—who's getting rich and why the rest of us are suffering. Immediately, circulation rose by ten thousand copies.

When the paper issued a reprint of the series, citizens mobbed the doors for copies. The *Inquirer* had to call in extra security to handle the crowds. Four hundred thousand copies later (plus twenty thousand calls and letters), reporters Barlett and Steele believe they've proven a point. Citizens *do* want to know.

Then the journalists turned their series of articles into a book.[7] In their public appearances since its release in 1992, they've described the sentiments expressed in many letters from readers: "You're doing what newspapers are supposed to do—telling us what's going on in our lives as part of a larger picture." Another reader put it this way: "You've given me the hard facts about what's happening. You articulated what I felt but didn't have the facts to back up."

Did the *Inquirer* tap into a public sentiment that other papers have ignored? Let's look at another newspaper that has refused to accept the notion that "lite" news—personality profiles and human interest stories—are all we Americans can handle.

A Big Newspaper Discovers Its Relational Self-Interest

Beginning in 1990, in Wichita, Kansas, editors at the *Wichita Eagle* began an experiment that changed the way their newspaper sees the public. In so doing, they discovered the relational self-interest we discussed in Chapter Three. Managing editor Steve Smith put it this way: "People who feel connected to their communities are more likely to read newspapers. In the newspaper business, your self-interest tells you that if you can find ways to connect people to the community, it will loop back to benefit you. They will become newspaper readers down the road." So the *Eagle* staff developed a multi-edged strategy to "make it easier for people to connect to the community."

It didn't require genius to figure out where they could begin to more closely meet the needs of readers. Starting with the 1990 gubernatorial race, the *Eagle* vowed never to let political candidates off the hook. "We ask questions relentlessly, insisting that their positions be made clear and understandable," editor Davis (Buzz) Merritt, Jr., told his readers.

In the newspaper world, running an article more than once is considered bad form. But the *Wichita Eagle*'s commitment to voter education proved stronger than newspaper custom. On seven consecutive Sundays, a "Where They Stand" section ran summaries of twelve key issues along with candidates' views on each. "You have to give information over and over again, so people will have it when they need to use it," Steve Smith explained.

The new issues section had an immediate impact on candidates. Just a few days before "Where They Stand" appeared, the front-running candidate, who had refused to take a clear stand on anything, suddenly came up with positions on all twelve issues.

For each subject, the *Eagle* published in-depth articles. An "Ad Watch" feature analyzed the candidates' TV and radio commercials for accuracy.

("As we reported on them, the spots became cleaner, more accurate," Steve observed.) And a twenty-four page "Voter's Guide" ran the Sunday before the election. In addition to this extraordinary coverage, the paper sponsored public service TV spots encouraging people to register and vote.

And the response?

The three-week campaign to increase the number of voters generated 50 percent more requests for voter registration material than had been made in the previous nine months. Research showed that the print coverage did help increase voter turnout in the *Eagle*'s circulation area. Pre- and post-election surveys showed that people's understanding of the issues also increased substantially.

Steve and other *Eagle* staff members see themselves doing more than in-depth reporting of elections. They're also making a fundamental shift: "We're adopting the *community*'s agenda. We're not pulling the issues out of a top hat," Steve stressed. "We're not making these issues up. We're going to both readers and the larger community. We're asking *them* to tell us what is most important to them."

Managing editor Steve Smith is convinced any newspaper with some guts could be doing the same thing, and a number of others are following their lead.

Special Newspapers Build Communities

Large daily newspapers such as the *Philadelphia Inquirer* and the *Wichita Eagle* are discovering that their self-interest lies in moving closer to their communities—learning to become especially responsive to the needs of their readers. Other newspapers, usually smaller and more specialized, are springing *from* their communities' need for a voice and a link to others. They help build ties and understanding within such communities as Native Americans, the homeless, or the citizens of a specific neighborhood. And they help these groups voice their concerns to the larger public. Along the way, they encourage other Americans to develop voices in print that might otherwise never be heard.

A Fearless Newspaper Stirs Useful Controversy. Take an important part of the Native American community, for example. In 1981, Tim Giago, a member of the Oglala Sioux tribe in South Dakota, asked himself: How can a community make decisions without information? How can we

Anytown Times

VOLUME XII   NUMBER 75   Monday, January 1st

The Power of Print:
How Some Newspapers Are Connecting Citizens and Their Communities

Put a check mark next to any of these innovations your local paper is making:

_____ Conducting surveys or town meetings to learn citizens' concerns

_____ Publishing in-depth articles connecting social issues to people's everyday lives

_____ Pressing candidates aggressively for clear, full explanations of positions

_____ Publishing special voter guides

_____ Repeating issue summaries and analyses several times during electoral campaigns

_____ Sponsoring public-service TV spots to encourage voting

_____ Connecting people to citizens' groups working on particular issues

_____ Furnishing a meeting place for citizens to discuss key issues

_____ Forming task forces to sponsor discussions of key problems

Monday, Jan. 1st   •   Living Democracy Section   •   page 1 make up for the lack of positive role models of Native Americans in the newspapers?[8]

Tim's questions led to *Indian Country Today,* the largest independently owned Native American newspaper in the United States. Since each issue is passed among several readers, changing hands an average of five times, its weekly readership approaches numbers reached by the largest South Dakota dailies.

Indian Country Today isn't afraid of conflict. Some whites complained bitterly about its series on bigotry in Rapid City. Then when the paper criticized management on the reservations, tribal authorities were furious. *Indian Country Today* has been willing to investigate fake medicine men and women, while celebrating authentic Native American life. And it has regularly pub-

Improving Your Local Newspaper

If your local newspaper received very few check marks on the list of innovations in the *Anytown Times* on page 114, what can you *do*?

Why not suggest that your class, civic group, or other organization meet with the editors of your paper? Explore the newspaper's self-interest in expanding readership. In addition to the innovations already suggested, you might recommend:

- Transforming the "letters to the editor" section into a real dialogue, organized by key topics

- Starting an expanded community bulletin board that provides information about events

- Launching a "citizen of the week" profile highlighting community problem solvers

- Initiating a regular column written by students and/or teachers about reforms needed or under way in the local schools

- Providing any other ideas you think up

Remember, it's in the relational self-interest of your local paper to reconnect with your community.

lished unvarnished accounts of alcoholism, domestic violence, and vandalism in Indian society.

The paper has also served as a conciliator. South Dakota is still divided over a 1975 gun battle killing two federal agents and one Native American. So the publisher invited Governor George Mickelson to make 1990 a year of reconciliation. The Republican governor accepted, joining the leaders of nine Sioux tribes in a peace-pipe ceremony at the state capitol in Pierre. Prompted by the newspaper, the state changed the name of "Pioneer Day," always celebrated on Columbus Day, to "Native American Day."[9]

Publisher Tim Giago believes his paper is helping to open communication well beyond its own pages. "We've got a long way to go, but I see whites who are trying. Two years ago you didn't see Indians working in stores in Rapid City. Now they recruit and employ Indians. In the public schools they're now teaching children about the Fort Laramie treaty of 1868, the treaty the government made with the Sioux people. I can't tell you how important that is."[10]

A Newspaper Gives Voice to the Voiceless. In San Francisco and several other major cities, homeless people have started their own twelve-page tabloid, called *Street Sheet*. Half the publishing staff, the Coalition on Homelessness, are homeless or formerly homeless people who are paid to work on the paper.

Street Sheet gets the word out about meetings and demonstrations that call for solutions to the housing crisis. It analyzes government policies that touch poor people's lives. But *Street Sheet* is also a vehicle for homeless people to earn money. Thirty thousand are printed monthly. They are sold for a dollar apiece by homeless people who can keep the money. "It's a way for people to get by, an alternative to panhandling," editor Lydia Ely explained. "But it's not a job, since we publish only once a month."

Still, "the vendors get the cash they need to start rebuilding their lives," Lydia added. Being on the street selling the paper encourages "interaction that homeless people don't often have. And that sometimes leads to job offers, too."

While newspapers have been the focus here, magazines can also be critically important in spreading news of citizen-led developments—stories that don't often make the evening news. For your convenience, we've included in the Resources section a list of magazines we find most helpful.

Does Your Neighborhood Need a Newspaper?

Creating one can be easier than you think, now that desktop publishing on home computers has become so readily available.

Think about the role a newspaper could play in improving life in your neighborhood. Consider involving children and teenagers in gathering information and writing copy.

Answer yes or no:

Do you think you might like to publish a newspaper? _____

Do you know others who might want to? _____

If you answered yes to either question, what is the next step you should take? Write your idea here.

_____

_____

_____

Since TV dominates most debates about the media, it's easy to forget the humble radio. Yet surveys show the average American listens to the radio for about three hours a day. During prime time, two out of every three Americans listen to their radios.[11]

RADIO BECOMES THE CITIZENS' TOOL

Talk Radio: Manipulation or Dialogue?

Radio has become the first widely used interactive medium. Nationwide, there are as many as nine hundred stations that present talk radio in some form or another. In Los Angeles alone there are seventy-nine talk shows; in Washington, D.C., forty-nine.

At the beginning of this chapter, talk show host Mike Siegel used the Exxon oil spill to demonstrate the impact of talk radio. In another case, in 1989, the public interest group Congress Watch used talk shows in a successful campaign to halt a congressional pay raise. About fifty talk show hosts prompted thousands of angry letters and calls to congressional

Radio Talk Shows: Tips on How to Be Heard

When you call a talk show radio program:

- Be patient. Don't expect to be instantly connected.

- Don't sound angry. Since the screeners seek a variety of views, stress that you have an additional perspective to contribute.

- Be prepared. Remember you're likely to have only thirty to sixty seconds. So make some notes in order to be concise.

- While you're waiting your turn, keep listening. You'll want to know what others are saying and adjust your comments, if necessary.

- Support your views with hard facts wherever you can.

- Pause after your first point so that the host can comment. Work for a dialogue.

- Pretend you're talking to a friend. This helps reduce nervousness.

Source: Adapted from the Center for Media and Values, "Rethinking Democracy: Citizenship in the Media Age," *Media and Values*, no. 58, Spring 1992, 21.

offices.[12] Talk radio helped to kill a congressional bill that most congress-people wanted.

Talk radio has proved its power when people want to voice their outrage. But what about when they want to calmly exchange views on serious problems? Isn't talk radio just a lot of gab prompted by superficial, fast-talking hosts who are mainly interested in attracting large audiences and advertising dollars?

Just as the *Philadelphia Inquirer* showed the newspaper industry that citizens really do want more substance in their news reports, some radio stations are creating stimulating talk shows that depend entirely on thoughtful analysis from everyday citizens. From San Francisco to Boston, stations are providing a forum to hash out community issues, make government more accountable, and dialogue seriously with experts and their fellow citizens. The largest of these efforts came in 1992, when National Public Radio launched a midday, nationwide call-in show, "Talk of the Nation," hosted by John Hockenberry. John has since moved to network television, but he and his colleagues at NPR intentionally created a climate distinctly different on "Talk of the Nation" from that of many commercial talk radio shows. On "Talk of the Nation," people from across the country discuss topics ranging from multilingual education to the impact of legislation protecting the interests of citizens with disabilities.

"A lot of talk radio is wild, pressure-valve style. There's a lot of primitivist anger being expressed in the guise of democracy," asserts John. "There are so many cues in American culture to connect with anger, money, image. But we stumbled on an intellectual formula and discovered that people are dying to connect with intellect, with brains. People haven't had their brains work in a while. We tapped into more than just eggheads; we quickly heard from smart, ordinary people."

John also worries that talk radio sometimes talks down to people. But, he said, "We found out that if we behave in a certain way, if we create a responsible show, we don't get jerks. We get responsible people."

Can Low-Income People Run Their Own Radio Station?

"Talk of the Nation" proves that people will make good use of opportunities for serious public talk. Amazingly, there are now entire *stations* dedicated to public talk by everyday people. We visited one in Dallas, Texas.

We had a hard time even *finding* KNON. As we drove up and down some depressed residential streets in Dallas, nothing looked like a radio station. Finally, we decided, "This must be it. What else could those huge cables be, hanging out of the windows?"

Everything about KNON seemed makeshift. Paint cans littered the lobby, and furniture had obviously come from a salvage store. We kept open minds: something different was going on here. But was it also important?

At the top of the rickety stairs, the haphazard appearance dissolved. In front of us, a serious live broadcast was under way. A skilled interviewer, African-American and middle-aged, was asking probing questions of two women, one a black female physician who was explaining in careful, easy-to-follow detail just how women should do breast self-examinations regularly to detect cancer. We were impressed as we realized that *this* station was covering an important subject that can't be found on a typical American radio station.

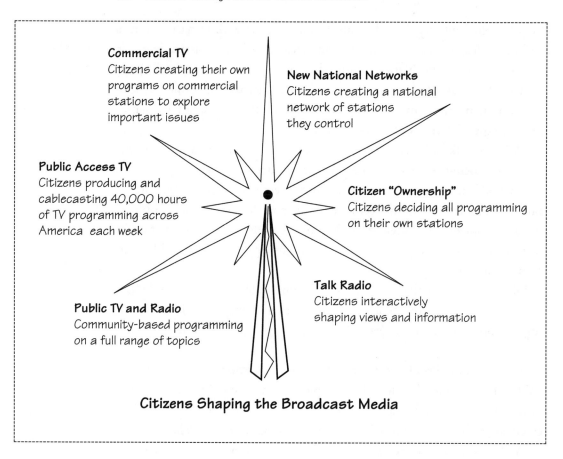

Commercial TV
Citizens creating their own programs on commercial stations to explore important issues

New National Networks
Citizens creating a national network of stations they control

Public Access TV
Citizens producing and cablecasting 40,000 hours of TV programming across America each week

Citizen "Ownership"
Citizens deciding all programming on their own stations

Public TV and Radio
Community-based programming on a full range of topics

Talk Radio
Citizens interactively shaping views and information

Citizens Shaping the Broadcast Media

Launched in 1983, KNON is owned and controlled exclusively by low- and moderate-income people. It now attracts 100,000 listeners. And one of its goals, says station manager Mark McNeil, is "to provide a voice to those usually disenfranchised from the media."

In Chapter Five you met ACORN, a national organization of low- and moderate-income people who are having a powerful influence on the nation's banking and housing laws. KNON is just one outcome of ACORN's decision fourteen years ago to set up a national association of community organizations, labor unions, church-based organizations, and broadcast facilities. They're all dedicated to one goal: using radio and television to organize their communities. They call the association the Affiliated Media Foundation Movement (AM/FM).

AM/FM's strategy is ambitious, aimed at forming a national network of radio and television stations owned and controlled by low-income communities. AM/FM has assembled the technical expertise to assist community groups who wish to apply for Federal Communications Commission (FCC) licenses. So far, in addition to KNON in Dallas, they've put two other FM radio stations on the air—one in Tampa, Florida, and one in Little Rock, Arkansas. In Watsonville, California, AM/FM has launched a television station owned and operated by low- and moderate-income people. Station manager Richard Helmka described it to us as a "training ground and forum for the cultural diversity of the community." And pending before the FCC are AM/FM applications for stations in half a dozen more states.

AM/FM's achievement is all the more striking when we realize that, although less than 2 percent of the entire broadcast industry is owned by people of color, AM/FM boards and broadcasters are almost *entirely* people of color. Every day they demonstrate what many Americans feel is impossible: even in the face of media conglomerates that are trying to gobble up as many stations as possible, ordinary Americans *can* control some of the airwaves.

Let's switch channels now from radio to TV to explore citizen innovations in that medium.

CITIZENS CREATE THEIR OWN TELEVISION

Talk radio, drawing on the views of everyday citizens, is all the rage. But what about television? Is talk TV, created by local citizens who want to focus on serious topics, even *feasible?*

El Paso is a city in west Texas with problems. Poor people, mostly Mexican-Americans, live wedged between a river and a mountain range, isolated from wealthier neighborhoods and a military community.

"We're not one community but many different communities, with a lot of reasons to be divided and not a lot that helps us realize the shared nature of what we face," said Jule Zimet. So Jule, manager of a family-owned moving and storage business, decided to help bring the National Issues Forum (NIF) to El Paso.[13] She felt that these citizen discussion groups, guided by outlines of diverse views on important issues, would draw El Paso's citizens into the public dialogue.

Jule and her friends decided to produce something more than just discussion groups, however. They wanted their discussions of community problems televised as well. And they wanted that televised public talk to come not from so-called experts but from everyday citizens.[14]

Now, three times a year during prime time, El Paso's citizens can participate in a televised issue forum called "Paso del Norte." On the Sunday before the forum, the local paper carries an article on the upcoming television show topic, along with a "ballot" soliciting citizen opinion.

Ismael Legarreta, a local engineer, has been part of the issue forums for five years. He explained how the citizen discussion groups are linked to the televised programs: "We always have at least five sites where people gather to talk before the TV program. At each site there's a trained moderator and a trained recorder. We show a film clip on the topic and then we talk. The recorder notes conversation that spurs others or which stops a conversation, plus any consensus the group arrives at. And there's a pre-forum ballot and a post-forum ballot on which people can state their views."

Organizers also make background information on the topic available at the local library ahead of time.

Then each discussion group sends representatives to the televised forum. On the air, everyone uses first names, "taking away authority so everyone feels comfortable speaking," Jule told us.

Telephone lines are always busy during a program. While only about fifteen callers get through, all callers' comments are recorded. Responses through all the formats—TV, newspaper, and public forums—are tabulated and sent to public officials.

Jule Zimet has observed people change and grow, too, when the forums expose them to another's point of view. She remembers a forum on health care when advocates for the elderly came face-to-face with groups who had *no health care at all*—poor people and their children. Activists for the elderly ended up saying their needs were not the most pressing.

"Discussion also sets the stage for action," Jule told us. "It gives people the confidence to come together when they need to come together to do something. The station manager has told us that he'd like to do one of our forums once a month because it's the most important programming they're doing." It appears that participation in TV by everyday people is not only feasible, it's a powerful tool for citizen learning and action.

Public Access Television Strengthens Community Life

Today in the United States, two thousand public access TV channels carry a total of forty thousand hours of programming each week. (Roughly one-half of U.S. households are now wired for cable, which is where these public access channels appear.) Typically, public access refers to an arrangement in which a commercial cable company agrees to provide free production facilities and channel time as a condition of obtaining their license. Through public access, regular citizens and community groups can create their own shows and have them sent out to all the customers in the cable system. Let's get a sense of its possibilities.

In the mid-seventies, a breakthrough in the use of television occurred in Reading, Pennsylvania. Here's how a key player, Red Burns, described it at the time: "Senior citizens are programming, operating, and financing their own two-way TV system. . . . For two hours each weekday, local people can turn to Channel Three and participate in the only TV system of its kind in the world. Senior citizens are not only responsible for operating the system, they are pioneering the exploration of a medium which is radically different from [traditional] broadcast television."[15]

Red Burns is the director of New York University's Alternate Media Center. With support from the National Science Foundation, she helped initiate this experiment, which had lasting results for community-based television.

Three existing centers where seniors gathered were given television cameras and video recording equipment. Special equipment installed in the homes of about 125 seniors allowed them to receive the cable programming over their TV sets and to respond by telephone. Everyone on the system could see and hear each other. "We used the metaphor of a telephone to suggest conversation rather than one-way television," explained Red.[16] The experiment caught on.

The project became Berks Community Television (BCTV), now operating as a nonprofit community access channel on the local cable system. Ann Sheehan, who works at BCTV, told us that a lot has changed in the last sixteen years, but not the basic idea, "because it works." Seniors are still involved, but so are many others. BCTV functions as a community organization that gives citizens access to TV.

BCTV televises city council meetings, as well as city budget and community development hearings. Citizens can also phone in their views to public hearings, knowing their views will count just as much as those participating in person.

As Red Burns looks back to BCTV's beginning, she underscores the points so many effective citizens have stressed to us: "First and foremost, an atmosphere of trust between the implementers, researchers, and users had to be created. *A great deal of time was spent listening to people.*" The entire original staff was recruited from Reading and none had previously been trained in video. The project drew out the innate capacities of local people, rather than simply adding outside experts.[17]

Community TV Opens Up Politics to Citizens

Max Nofziger lives in Austin, Texas. The musician and former flower salesman never imagined himself running for office. But his concern about energy and the environment motivated Max to run for city council. And Max is convinced his victory is partly due to Austin Community Television (ACTV).

In Austin, every citizen—including candidates for political office—gets access to ACTV on a first-come, first-served basis. In campaigns for the last city council elections, candidates produced or appeared on twenty public access programs. "Many candidates can't afford to buy broadcast time," says Melissa Hield, president of ACTV's board. "This is an opportunity

Accessing Public Access

Does your community have public access cable?

Do you watch? Do you wish the quality of the programming were better?

Do you belong to a religious or civic organization that might use public access to share its program with the community?

Would you or the organization to which you belong like to learn new media skills?

Why not call the cable station and find out more about how your local public access cable channel works in your community?

For assistance in figuring out how to make public access a positive tool in your community, you might contact the National Federation of Local Cable Programmers. Their address can be found in the Resources section at the end of this book.

for the public to see more candidates." "Free time for candidates is fantastic," says Bill Turpin, a retired air force officer who produces and hosts a conservative public affairs series, "Freedom and Peace." Turpin produces programs with candidates running for U.S. Congress in his congressional district. Other shows on ACTV allow viewers to engage in dialogue with officials and candidates.

The Growth of Public Access TV

In its capacity to expand communication beyond the elite to regular people, public access television has been likened to the invention of the printing press. Conceived during the 1960s, it was given a huge boost in 1972 by a Federal Communications Commission requirement that the emerging cable companies had to provide public access.

Cities were soon awash with proposals to establish channels to serve the public interest. One of us—Paul—worked in Rochester, New York, at the time. I remember that proposals came from citizens for a channel that would be devoted entirely to health issues. Another would be dedicated to residents of one low-income area, another for Hispanics, another for African Americans, another for persons of Italian heritage. Still more community leaders called for separate channels devoted to personal finance, house repairs, and other "modern living skills." Some of the people I worked with wanted one for use only by community organizations. Ideas for useful channels seemed endless.

Advocates for public access pressed their case directly before city and state agencies that had been empowered to grant franchises (long-term contracts) to cable companies. And often they succeeded. In many cities those with authority *required* cable companies to include public access channels and equipment as a condition for obtaining a franchise. "To make television—which is the most dominant form of media—accessible to everyday citizens by federal law is pretty revolutionary," declares Paula Manley, the station manager of Tualatin Valley Community Access (TVCA).

Paula sees access to the electronic media as a logical extension of our First Amendment rights as citizens: "People need to become literate with the tools of media in order to communicate . . . in order to come together to solve problems. *This is not a luxury; it's a necessity for a working democracy* [italics added]."

Public access hasn't come close to the potential foreseen by its early enthusiasts. Only about one-tenth of all cable systems have access channels.[18] And unfortunately, the poor quality of too many public access programs prompts viewers not to become engaged, but to reach for the remote control.

Still, public access's growth is steady. From Portland, Maine, to San Diego, California, citizens tune into their own communities and watch their neighbors discussing day care, cheering the hog races at the county fair, or protesting CIA recruitment at a local college. In Seattle, citizens can see live training under way in five high schools to assist citizen organizations in applying for city funds for community improvements. The potential for community involvement through public access TV is seemingly boundless.

COMPUTERS BECOME CHANNELS FOR PUBLIC TALK

While breakthroughs in consumer electronics are triggering fears of information control and invasion of privacy, they are also opening a new world of direct citizen-to-citizen communication, as well as creating a more direct link between citizens and their government.

Computer Networks Expand Conversation

Electronic systems now link millions of Americans. More than eleven million of us have computers and modems. And approximately thirty-five thousand computer bulletin boards now connect people who have common concerns.

Among the commercial on-line services, you'll find CompuServe, Prodigy, America Online, Genie, and the WELL. While all involve users in ad hoc discussions of issues, the process of involving users in more formal conversations is still being developed.

The Institute for Global Communications (IGC) in San Francisco provides the organizational umbrella for three interrelated computer networks or bulletin board systems. The oldest of these is PeaceNet, which has spawned networks in ten countries that together make up the Association for Progressive Communications (APC). Over fifteen thousand APC members in Australia, Brazil, Canada, England, Germany, Nicaragua, Russia, Sweden, Uruguay, and the United States share information about world crises and workable solutions for everything from disposable diapers to human rights violations and nuclear waste. They chat quietly with friends or argue politics with adversaries. They plan demonstrations and write proposals. And they reach eighty news and information services, making the Association for Progressive Communications a giant clearinghouse for alternative views and information. In the United States, over seven thousand subscribers pay ten dollars per month for one hour of computer time dedicated to peace issues, environmental sustainability, and human rights.

If you'd like to explore computer bulletin boards—perhaps helping to use them to expand genuine dialogue—the book *Ecolinking* by Don Rittner can get you started.[19]

Computer Bulletin Boards Encourage Debate

In Colorado Springs, sixty-five diverse computer bulletin boards connect citizens with common interests. Since 1981, Dave Hughes—with his Stetson hat, Justin boots, and laptop computer—has provided inspiration and instruction. Here's how Dave describes the genesis of his work: "From day one I saw that these things [computer bulletin boards] are communities, in a sense, if you define community as a group of people that relates to each other personally, socially, economically, educationally, politically, culturally. A bulletin board is like a neighborhood or small town."[20]

What motivates Dave to develop computer networks is his concern about what's missing in our democracy. Democracy needs three elements to work, argues Dave. The first two are information and the right to vote. These we have, he says. "But the thing that had been warped and distorted for a lot of reasons is the third—debate and discussion. The news anchors arguing with each other have become the substitute for debate, except in your own tiny circle."

So Dave set up electronic bulletin boards with names like Old Town Bank and Little Red Electronic Schoolhouse. Dave explained, "The bulletin board is a place where people can come at their own convenience. And they use the written word. . . . People can discuss public issues and have a chance to be heard.

In a one- or two-hour city council meeting, with a hundred people in the room, only a few people can talk. But on-line, everybody has their say because there's a differential in speed. We can read 600 to 800 words a minute, whereas speaking you can only talk 120 words a minute."

Dave's system first became known in Colorado Springs with the Home Occupation Ordinance battle in 1983. The city planned to revise a law that governs what work you can do out of your home. But, Dave told us, "I was the only person to show up at the planning commission meeting."

Dave considered the ordinance discriminatory toward people trying to bring in extra income during a recession. At the planning commission meeting his objections led to a thirty-day tabling of the ordinance. And, according to Dave, here's what happened next: "I carried the three-page ordinance back and typed it into my bulletin board and put it on-line. I wrote a letter to the editor saying I don't like this ordinance, and if you (reader) have a modem, dial 632-3991. See for yourself. Hundreds of people who didn't know me, the bulletin board, or the issue, dialed in—plus regular callers. It took off like a shot. At the next meeting, 175 people showed up at the planning commission. From longhairs to libertarians. It was 'just people.' And no activist organization."

The planners hammered out another version. And regular citizens went at it again. They "downloaded" the ordinance, rewrote it, and "uploaded" onto the network again. Dave continued: "You don't get that in front of normal planning bodies. When it finally went to city council, it was passed *because* a lot of people had expressed their opinions and revised it. It was now an acceptable ordinance. The process worked."

Dave believes that computer linkups diminish "force of personality" as a factor in communication. "TV politics emphasizes the emotional, the images, and appearance. The on-line computer world is a corrective. It's more substance- and issue-oriented, even though personalities are in there," says Dave. He's convinced this type of electronic advocacy also powerfully reinforces democracy by providing time for reflection.

Government Links Citizens Electronically

Santa Monica, California, began an ambitious public access computer network in 1989, sponsored by the city's information department. The response has surpassed all expectations.

The Public Electronic Network (PEN) is free to all residents. PEN boasts thirty public modems in libraries, schools, and other convenient locations around the city, and the system can be accessed by citizens with modems from their homes. PEN's nine thousand registered users grow by

What's to Come

More ways citizens are shaping media today:

• Educating reporters through tours and meetings

• Creating attention-grabbing public service announcements

• Producing high-impact videos to bring home important points

• Using media to watchdog media

• Gaining control through media literacy

about a hundred per month, and the system now has ten thousand log-ons per month.

PEN helps bring city hall closer to citizens. It provides information about city services and allows residents to communicate with city hall and with each other. Users can get a library card, access the library's catalogue, file police reports or job applications, submit consumer complaint forms, sign up for recreation classes—all without having to go to city hall.

PEN also offers 250 menus of information, including recycling tips, city jobs, how to obtain city services, the agendas and minutes of city meetings, and a social services directory. Its "Public Square" feature allows PEN users to join in computer conferences—community-wide discussions on pollution, the homeless, development, traffic, and any other concerns citizens wish to bring to it.

Citizens' organizations are discovering they do not have to sit back and wait for the media to cover their issues. They are creatively influencing and using a variety of media to further their goals.

CITIZEN GROUPS CAN USE AND INFLUENCE THE MEDIA

Citizens Educate the Media

Louis Head of the Southwest Organizing Project (SWOP) in Albuquerque explains that at SWOP they don't just rely on the media to get their news out. "We educate them," he says, adding, "We spent 1985 researching environmental degradation in communities of color and came up with a day-

Tips for Building Relationships with the Media

- Get to know the reporters as people. Take them to lunch. Give them background materials on your issues.

- Sponsor a tour so that the media can see first-hand the problem you're talking about.

- Hold press conferences whenever appropriate. Meet the needs of the media for hard facts *and* dramatic images.

- Meet with the editorial board to provide background on the issues that concern you and listen actively to understand the paper's views.

- Telephone reporters when you think they've done a good job and write letters of appreciation for effective coverage. Remember that members of the newspaper staff will read your letter, even if it's not printed.

long tour for the media. It had about twelve stops. We take media people on buses into neighborhoods—to the dump, to industries, and through communities that are having big problems. People on the tours get a chance to talk with people from other organizations The mixing—that's a big piece of it. We've developed a lot of relationships this way. We call it a 'Community Environmental Tour.' It's a model we still use today."

Tours typically last an hour and a half to two hours, followed by a stop at a community center or a volunteer fire station. After watching a video to further illuminate the issues, participants reflect together on their experiences.

"Anytime we do a tour we get good TV coverage," Louis told us. "But there's a bigger context in terms of how we work the media. We're very deliberate about developing media contacts and strategies." Here Louis underscores a key insight of Living Democracy: being effective in public life requires attention to building relationships.

"We make sure that certain reporters have a jump on the story," Louis explained. "But we're not afraid to hold the media accountable. We do 'accountability sessions' when there's been any misrepresentation of us."

Using the Media to Attract Attention

Some citizens are especially creative in using the media to attract support. With just a half-dozen people sitting in her living room, Dorothy Green started an organization in 1985 to protest the impending death of the Santa Monica Bay caused mostly by the dumping of raw sewage in the Pacific Ocean just west of Los Angeles. Heal the Bay now has nine staff members and a half-million-dollar budget.[21] The organization was instrumental in the passage of ordinances promoting conservation and linking growth to sewage treatment capacity. They also got a commitment from the Los Angeles City Council for $3.4 billion to expand the inadequate existing system.

Heal the Bay produced public service announcements to appear in movie theaters before the main feature. "We scrounged around for old home movies of people playing at the beach, fooling around, learning how to surf, doing stunts in the sand. We strung these together with a voice-over saying, 'You know, we've always had so many good times together, but you haven't been treating me very nice lately, and we want these good times to continue. If you love the beach, call Heal the Bay, 1-800-HEAL BAY.' People just loved it!"

The success of this approach spurred the organization to try more ads at theaters and on late-night TV. Dorothy is convinced her group's work— including their successful use of the media—is having an impact. "The ocean is getting cleaner!" she exclaimed. "People are coming to us now and saying, 'I see dolphins playing in the bay. We haven't seen dolphins here for years and years and years.'" Dorothy told us she can see the difference in front of her own home: "There's a tide pool there, and we're seeing starfish for the first time in years. And the pelicans are back, stinking up Marina Del Rey. That's what makes us feel the best!"

Citizens Make Videos to Make Waves

Citizen groups are using video to document public concerns and to let others in the community know what they're doing about it. The Interfaith Organizing Project (IOP) of greater Chicago set out to block the building of a major new professional football stadium that threatened the West Side. They videotaped news reports on the issue and their own meetings and demonstrations. "We used these tapes to show what was going on

Around the country there are now about 125 media arts centers—nonprofit groups available to assist in the use of video. Look for the National Alliance for Media Arts and Culture in the Resources section.

around the stadium issue and inside our organization. The tapes also provided a good visual history of our organization," says IOP director Ed Shurna.

IOP blocked a stadium for the Chicago Bears, in part because the developers refused to negotiate with the IOP about including neighborhood improvements in the development plan. Later, other developers, proposing a new stadium for the champion Bulls basketball team, *would* negotiate. And IOP used its clout—built in part through skillful use of video—to win $20 million in new affordable housing, a new park, and street improvements.[22]

Citizens as Media Watchdogs

Is Americans' stance toward the media like the old joke about the weather: everybody complains about it, but nobody *does* anything about it?

The stories we've recounted suggest that many Americans *are* doing something—stepping over the line from passive reader, listener, or viewer to become *shapers* of what they watch or listen to. But citizens are also discovering we can influence the way mass media functions, and we can change its negative impact on us.

Fairness and Accuracy in Reporting (FAIR) provides one example of citizens talking back to the corporate-controlled media. FAIR is a New York-based nonprofit organization that aims, according to founder Jeff Cohen, "to eliminate bias and censorship in the media." With a small staff and equally small budget, FAIR has been able to exert significant influence, mainly by using the power of hard facts and hard work. "We are known for doing our research before we criticize," Jeff stressed with evident pride.

In 1990, for example, FAIR released its six-month study of the "MacNeil/Lehrer News Hour," analyzing who made up the guest lists. It reported that 90 percent of the guests were white, and 87 percent male. Only 6 percent of the guests were from labor groups, public interest

How Representative Are the Broadcast Media?

Do your own research to see how fair and accurate the media are. Make it a family game:

- Put a big sheet of paper next to the TV with columns marked to indicate white, minority, male, and female.

- During selected broadcasts, ask family members to make a mark in the appropriate column for each lead actor, commentator, or "talking head" they see giving a view of current events or of that day's news.

- At the end of the week, add up the totals. Or better yet, let your kids do it.

Roughly speaking, do the results reflect the proportion of each group in your city? (This "game" might lead into a valuable family discussion.)

---

groups, or racial or ethnic minorities. "Reports of our study appeared in several hundred daily papers," Jeff said.

"And they ['MacNeil/Lehrer'] are now somewhat less biased. A couple of people within 'MacNeil/Lehrer' told us that it was our efforts that made the difference."

Jeff Cohen is convinced that FAIR has accomplished more than opening up the guest lists on a few programs. "We have helped change the way media bias is understood. In 1986, Ted Koppel worried that the media were too hard on government. Three years later he admitted that the media are a "discouragingly timid lot."[23]

Jeff believes a healthy skepticism is growing as more and more people talk about who "owns the media and who sponsors the show. The fact that GE owns NBC is still not widely known," he notes, "but we are raising consciousness among a broader audience. Our critique of the media gets on talk shows in Tulsa and San Antonio, places where our views were never heard before."

A New Literacy: Helping Citizens Gain Control

A whole new kind of literacy is required in the modern world. Being able to read and write will no longer suffice. Today's powerful media evoke feelings without our conscious awareness. They bring distant reality into our living rooms without our knowing what to make of it. So how can we learn to interpret the messages that bombard us daily?

In some schools, television is now being taught directly as a college-credit subject—not producing it, but *watching it*. It's called "Media Literacy," "Visual Literacy," or "Critical Viewing." From Oakland, California, to Norman, Oklahoma, and Bethesda, Maryland, students are learning to analyze television and the other media. They're taught the differences between news reports, editorials, and commercials. They study how color, focus, and camera angle influence the appeal of television messages, and how the length of a presentation and the type of information can distort a viewer's understanding of an event. They learn the concept of *target audiences* and various ways advertisers skew programming to meet their commercial needs.

Jay Davis of the Center for Media and Values in Los Angeles, California, believes that consumers of the media can gain the power to change the mass media themselves *by changing the way they respond to it and interact with it*.[24] In Bedford, New York, parents at a local school decided to change the way they responded to the media. About twenty-five parents asked for training in media literacy.[25] Bruce Campbell, at the local Episcopal Church, offered to lead a workshop, with a guidebook developed by Jay's center. "The parents were feeling beleaguered by the media in their homes," Bruce told us.

The most powerful exercise the first night was viewing a clip from the popular TV show "Beverly Hills, 90210," after which participants were asked to guess which commercials would follow. "They were surprised at how far off the mark they were. About half the commercials were for movies, even R-rated movies. This was a lesson in how the media reinforces its own usage," Bruce noted.

The parents also became aware that the commercials were produced in the style of the program, Bruce explained. "You could visually see a linkage in the production style of "90210"—clothes, editing, etc.—and the commercials. The programs and the commercials are a package."

Just preaching at people—young or old—to beware of TV's seduction doesn't help much. So these parents are gaining some ideas for helping their youngsters become critical viewers. Children, fortunately, have a healthy desire not to be fooled or "taken in," a desire that can be reinforced through media training.

What is Freedom to Speak in a Living Democracy?

Let's pause to ask two questions about the future of our society: *Why* the trend toward fewer and fewer decision makers in the media? (Recall that just twenty-three corporations now control most media outlets.) *Why* do more and more of us feel like passive observers of the media, rather than becoming more like the active participants we've described in this chapter?

A common answer is that only the large corporations can *afford* to gain access to the media. But for us, the explanation begins one step earlier, with the widespread acceptance of the media as a commodity. As long as the media are a mere commodity, responsibility for their use rests with the shareholders of media conglomerates. The shareholders' goal, understandably, is the highest return on their investment. (Today, only one hundred corporations sponsor 85 percent of TV programming.) One TV executive recently summarized the significance of seeing media this way: "The networks," he said, "define their business as delivering audience to advertisers."

But as the media become communication tools in a Living Democracy, they no longer are simply a commodity. They also become a *community good*. By this we mean something on which we all depend and, therefore, in which we can all have a say. In fact, all citizens hold an interest in mass communication, for at stake is the health of our communities and our nation.

Right now, however, it's not just the money or sheer power of corporations that block our participation in the public world of media. A big obstacle lies in the world of ideas—how we *think* about freedom of speech. Supreme Court rulings suggest that almost any limits on the right to buy airtime infringe on freedom of speech and therefore are unconstitutional. The Court defends the right to spend money in order to enter our living rooms via the media.

But this narrow focus ignores a much broader right in a Living Democracy: *the citizens' right to speak.* If the right of free speech means anything in today's high-tech world, it must mean more than the right to stand on a soapbox and preach to crowds on a sidewalk. To be meaningful, the right to speak freely must involve the right to be heard by our fellow citizens.

Can Citizens Mediate the Media?

Shifting our society's definition of the media from mere commodity, a medium for selling, to a "community good," raises questions about its governance:

- If we Americans reject government-run media because of the danger of top-down control, what are the possibilities for citizens to have a direct voice in corporate-controlled media programming?

- Might we imagine elected citizens who sit on the boards of media-owning corporations?

- Might we imagine vigorous antitrust enforcement to ensure much greater competition among media outlets?

- Could we require media-owning corporations to involve citizens in planning community-enhancing programming?

And having access to the mass media is virtually the only way to be heard widely in today's world.

The narrow focus on the "right to spend" ignores another key value in a Living Democracy: the right we all have to hear alternative views. We need vigorous, diverse speech that is not dependent on wealth or the popularity of the speaker's views.

So as we work to bring democracy to life throughout our media, we must probe certain questions deeply: What does freedom of speech mean in the modern world? How important are our freedoms to be heard and to hear diverse views? These aren't easy questions. But they lie at the heart of the Living Democracy practiced by all those in this chapter who insist that those freedoms are indeed vital.

7

From Client to Citizen

CHRISTOPHER HATCHER lives in one of the toughest neighborhoods in New York City. He's nineteen, African American, and has two kids. He told us he'd been in trouble with the law more than once. Now Christopher is part of the Youth Action Program (YAP).[1] Its goal is not to "treat" him. In YAP, he participates in a team of young adults who work part of the week learning construction by restoring abandoned buildings to create homes for homeless youth. The rest of the week the team is in class, studying toward a high school equivalency degree. YAP helps young people make smart decisions and learn new, marketable skills. It is governed by a policy committee whose members are mostly drawn from the young adults themselves. Committee members get extensive training on everything from drawing up agendas to how to handle anger.

Lionel Kupersmith has fought manic depression for twenty-six years; his wife, Susan, has struggled with an anxiety disorder for a decade. "Now we're both almost totally healed," Lionel told us. Their cure, he is convinced, was not handed to them by professionals. "Today, I represent a picture of health. . . . This is something I created *by myself*."

Central to Lionel's healing has been his work with On Our Own in Montgomery County in Maryland, run by people Lionel calls "mental health consumers"—those who have suffered mental disease. On Our Own is a drop-in center with *peer* counseling for support and guidance. It also offers classes in everything from auto mechanics and organic gardening to computers. There are now several dozen On Our Own-type groups across the country.

A SHAKE-UP IN HUMAN SERVICES

Everywhere in America, the field of human services is experiencing a profound shake-up. From cancer patients to those suffering mental illness, from youth "at risk" to public housing tenants and the elderly, people are rejecting approaches that define them by their so-called problems or deficiencies. In this chapter, you'll meet many such people. They are defying the notion that solutions come solely from the outside. You'll discover that lasting solutions depend instead on pragmatic partnerships—the kind that in many ways define what we mean by Living Democracy.

But before we tell their stories, let's look at the big picture. Just what is this revolution of expectations all about, and what are its roots?

Our society's dominant notion of social services grew out of two distinct historical strains. One is our long Judeo-Christian tradition, which obligates believers to "care for the less fortunate." It furthered the emergence of two social categories: the caring and the cared for.

Then, during the early twentieth century, this tradition converged with a second strain: the newly emerging social sciences. Psychology, for example, helped establish the role of the professional therapist who diagnoses an individual's illness and guides the cure. And sociologists began to describe pathologies and prescribe solutions at the level of society.

Slowly the dominant view of social aid moved from the care giver offering charity—which often left the recipients dependent and powerless—to the care giver as agent of change—as the problem solver who finds solutions and acts on the client's behalf.

But by mid-century, what happened? Our nation discovered "the other America," those vast numbers of citizens who had been poorly served by our dominant notions of social aid. At the same time, many Americans began to question certain givens in America, and one of them was the notion that charity alone—simple care giving—could alleviate the terrible problems associated with poverty.

By the 1960s, President Lyndon Johnson's War on Poverty, with its dictum of "maximum feasible participation of the poor," opened the door to a whole new way of perceiving the role of client. Neighborhood councils—part of the federal government's Model Cities program—thrust the poor into positions of decision-making power. The civil rights and other so-called liberation movements began to proclaim the value of self-determination.

Further challenging the social science paradigm was the growing perception that our old assumptions simply weren't working. Throwing more professional services at people didn't seem to make their problems go away. In fact, some conservatives began to attack what they called the poverty industry—that is, the professionals paid to deal with poverty—for siphoning off resources while contributing little. Today these critics point out that in New York City and Chicago over 60 percent of all public funds for low-income people are allocated to professionals rather than to the poor.[2]

At the same time, several revolutions were taking place within the field of psychology. Cognitive therapy and humanistic psychology taught that the self could improve the self. We aren't simply at the mercy of external forces; we are learning organisms, capable of great strides in personal growth. One trailblazer in cognitive therapy defined the fundamental new insight this way: *the individual could choose to act on himself.* For example, curing mental illness no longer rested solely in the hands of therapists, social workers, and asylums. It now passed in part into the hands of the sufferers."[3]

Your Reflections

We've just summarized dramatic changes in how we as a society understand the best way to solve social, and even individual, problems. During your own lifetime, how has your perception changed?

Out of your own experience, have you come to appreciate the capacity of the non-expert, or the "client," to contribute to solving problems?

Have you ever found yourself questioning the effectiveness of top-down, or expert-driven, decision-making?

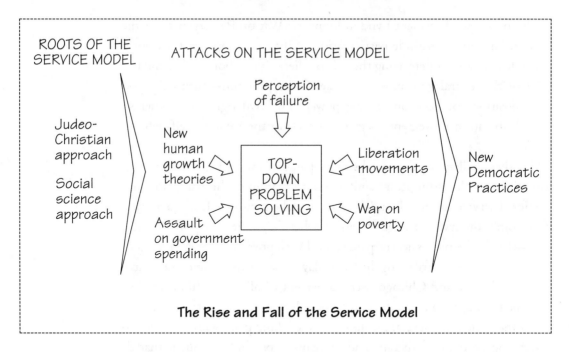

The Rise and Fall of the Service Model

The 1980s delivered yet another blow to the dominant social service model of professionals delivering care to clients. The public purse seemed to have been emptied. Ronald Reagan's anti-government campaign convinced many Americans that government itself was the problem. And taxpayers responded by tightly capping taxes at the state level. Washington slashed social spending that had benefited the poor, while pursuing an unprecedented peacetime military buildup and handing billions in tax breaks to the better-off. The federal deficit ballooned out of control. Add to this the cost of the savings and loan fiasco and burgeoning government-covered health care costs. By the 1990s many Americans had concluded that, like it or not, our problems can't be solved solely by professionally run programs—if for no other reason than we don't have enough money to pay for them.

All these forces, both positive and negative, have created an opening into which Americans are walking with new ideas and new energy. Core themes of Living Democracy are fast emerging within the human services. In fields long dominated by top-down, expert-driven approaches, we see a growing appreciation of the power within ordinary people to become problem solvers. And there's increasing awareness of the creative power of collaborative human relationships.

What's to Come

This chapter moves from clients who solve their own problems—and who actually teach the experts—to professionals who build problem-solving partnerships with their clients. It highlights people who are turning self-help into public problem solving.

Here are the ten exciting developments you'll find in this chapter:

- Ten million "victims" become helpers.

- Neighborhood support networks build power for low-income people.

- Self-governing tenants use government to bolster their self-reliance.

- Cancer patients join together for mutual support and new influence.

- Four thousand young people successfully fight crime—their way.

- Psychologists become respectful partners with the poor.

- Social workers function as coaches to help families.

- Disabled people learn to enable themselves—and change public policies.

- Moving beyond bootstraps to mutual healing and problem solving.

Self-help was born, many would say, in 1935 in Akron, Ohio, when the two founders of Alcoholics Anonymous hit upon a powerful mix of ideas:

- The healing power of being understood, which we often feel only from others who have "walked in our shoes"

- Heightened self-esteem that derives from being helpful to others

- Increased determination when one feels part of a group effort

They developed a twelve-step approach that at least two hundred types of organizations have adapted to their own needs—from Debtors Anonymous to Workaholics Anonymous.

SELF-HELP: NEEDS BECOME ASSETS

Test Your Own Beliefs

Here are eleven common beliefs about the social problems in our midst. How do you react to each of them? Put check marks in the appropriate boxes.

	Strongly agree	Agree	No opinion	Disagree	Strongly disagree
We should care for the less fortunate. I'm partly responsible for what happens to my fellow human beings.	☐	☐	☐	☐	☐
People are largely responsible for their own misfortunes. It's not my responsibility to care for others beyond my immediate family.	☐	☐	☐	☐	☐
America needs more government programs directed towards the poor.	☐	☐	☐	☐	☐
Mostly, people have to learn to solve their own problems. Ultimately, no one can do it for them.	☐	☐	☐	☐	☐
We know how to cure poverty. It's only the will to do it that is lacking.	☐	☐	☐	☐	☐
Part of the problem of the poor is what's been called the "welfare mentality," the notion that "if I just sit back, someone will have to take care of me."	☐	☐	☐	☐	☐

	Strongly agree	Agree	No opinion	Disagree	Strongly disagree
It all begins with education. If people were well trained at an early age, they'd have the personal skills to deal with whatever life throws their way.	☐	☐	☐	☐	☐
If we dismantled the poverty industry and redirected the money we now pay for social workers and bureaucrats towards the poor themselves, everyone would be better off and we'd probably save money.	☐	☐	☐	☐	☐
We live in a racist, greedy, dog-eat-dog society. Lots of people can't survive in such a society. This me-first culture fails people in trouble.	☐	☐	☐	☐	☐
People can choose to act on themselves. That's the heart of the problem: people need to learn to change themselves.	☐	☐	☐	☐	☐
More Americans should have a real say in how we use our resources. Then we'd use them more wisely to make sure more people have the opportunities they need.	☐	☐	☐	☐	☐

What do you actually believe about the large issues raised in these questions? What are the causes of human misfortune and deprivation? Whose responsibility is it to deal with those causes? Who should help those in trouble? And what is your role?

The twelve-step approach is only one part of a much larger phenomenon, loosely called the self-help movement. It now embraces over half a million groups involving fifteen million participants across the country, according to Dr. Frank Riessman, Director of the National Self-Help Clearinghouse in New York. Adding all those who are interested but not now active in a self-help group, that number climbs to twenty-five million supporters. That's 10 percent of the American people.

Frank has seen the power of self-help in his own life. Coping with Parkinson's disease, Frank said that when he first found a support group, "it was a blinding experience of identification." Discovering other people who understood his experiences, he says, "was one of the pinnacle experiences of my life."[4]

But to Frank, self-help groups are part of a much larger social transition. He sees them as "an extension of the worldwide democracy movement." To Frank, self-help extends Living Democracy, what he calls "participatory involvement," to the field of human services.[5]

Similarly, Jerry Goodman, co-director of California Self-Help Center, thinks of self-help groups as "miniature mental health democracies where power resides in the membership." In such support groups, he experiences "equal rights . . . and free expression of thought. . . ."[6]

But critics hardly see self-help groups as miniature mental health democracies. For some, self-help is a know-nothing dead end where folks who don't understand much about their own illness attempt to treat people who know even less. It's the blind following the blind. Other skeptics imagine self-helpers simply identifying with their condition, rather than helping each other go beyond the condition. Still others can't fathom self-help

Meeting Your Needs

Have you ever joined with others in what might be called a self-help group?

How about your family members: have any of them ever taken a problem to a group of people who share the same problem?

Are you satisfied with the results?

What might have made the experience better, more effective?

support groups going beneath members' immediate pain to address the underlying social conditions that help cause the condition in the first place.

But when self-help allows people to discover their own resources—and join a common problem-solving effort—it contributes to the emergence of the Living Democracy we're finding in other areas of society. For us, the irony is that the organizations we highlight in other chapters of this book, from Kentuckians for the Commonwealth to worker-owned businesses, are not typically seen as part of the self-help movement. Yet all these efforts have people discovering their own power, developing that power in relationships, and solving real problems together.

What typically gets tagged as self-help are support groups dealing with health and other personal problems. But the line between personal self-help and self-help with a strong public dimension is a blurry one indeed. Personal support groups bring people out of their homes into situations in which they learn to solve their problems. Moreover, these groups often evolve into vehicles for their members' expression beyond the group, sometimes bringing about significant changes within the larger community, as you'll see below. They become what might be called *public self-help*.

The power of self-help is that it turns problems into solutions. Needs become resources, says Frank Riessman. From the self-help perspective, Frank notes, one sees not ten million alcoholics but ten million potential helpers in overcoming alcoholism. Self-help, he argues, "expands the help-giving resources . . . by converting helpees into helpers." And there's qualitative improvement as well, because "self-helpers possess an inside understanding of the problem."[7]

Hard evidence supports Frank's view of the inherent advantages of self-help over the pure medical model in which physicians are responsible for the cure. In one study, for example, people with emphysema who joined mutual support groups were only one-third as likely to be hospitalized as those not in such groups.[8]

So with millions of people involved in reaching out to strangers both *for* help and *to* help, the self-help movement re-weaves our social fabric, establishing connectedness based on mutual responsibility and mutual respect. Healthy public life depends on this connectedness.

One way to understand this transformation within human services is to listen to someone who might be typically viewed as a client by many social workers but who rejects the label and the attitudes it suggests.

Beyond Client to Problem Solver

Julia Dinsmore is a so-called welfare mother. She and her three children live in a diverse inner-city neighborhood of Minneapolis. Julia is also a musician who can be found on a summer's evening sitting on her front porch singing and playing the guitar for herself and anyone within earshot. As we talked with Julia in her home on a quiet Sunday morning, the phone rang more than once. Other single mothers were calling for advice.

Julia believes in power. Even the power of those who have, as she says, "internalized their oppression"—that is, those who have accepted society's disparaging view of them. That belief led to the Mothers' Union. Julia describes it not as an organization but as a loose mutual support network for families who have been "multi-generationally poor."

The Mothers' Union is appropriately named. Its focus: good parenting and creating stable families. Poor people have to move frequently, because of shifting rents and changing welfare payments, says Julia. This destroys the basis of stable families supported by healthy communities.

The Mothers' Union approach is not to plead before social service agencies. "We go around educating and building mutual partnerships with middle-class people who can help funnel resources and support to our leaders so that we can secure our lives," says Julia. She criticizes the paternalism of the social services model that doesn't listen to the people it was designed

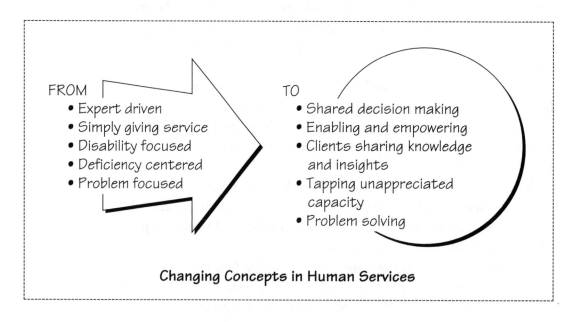

FROM
- Expert driven
- Simply giving service
- Disability focused
- Deficiency centered
- Problem focused

TO
- Shared decision making
- Enabling and empowering
- Clients sharing knowledge and insights
- Tapping unappreciated capacity
- Problem solving

Changing Concepts in Human Services

to serve. "They keep trying to save us from ourselves," she told us. "They keep designing stuff that benefits somebody else in our names. I say no—we need to be in full partnership with people who have the resources."

One example of what partnership means to the Mothers' Union was a joint fundraiser with prominent Minneapolis women, including the mayor's wife. It resulted in a down payment on a house for a family of seven. The group's goal is two houses a year.

Julia Dinsmore is creating new power. She and her friends are breaking free of the narrow assumptions about the limited capacities of welfare mothers.

Creating Your Own Partnerships

You've just seen how the Mothers' Union joined with others to redirect resources and create new power. What resources might be available in your community to share in partnership?

Is there anything you might do to develop the necessary partnerships?

Kids Claim Their Power

If welfare recipients are determined to throw off society's limiting notions about their capacities, many young people feel the same way. One is Linda Warsaw of San Bernadino, California.[9] Ten years ago, when Linda was ten, her family's house was burglarized. "That was really scary," she says. "Someone went through my private things, and I didn't even know who that person was."

For two years, Linda and her mother volunteered at the Victim Witness Assistance Program, exposing Linda to a whole spectrum of crimes against people her own age.

One case made a particularly deep impression. An eight-year-old girl insisted that the neighbor who had molested her be brought to trial. Linda told us the impact the girl's stance had on her: "This little girl decided on her own that she wanted this person put away so no other children would have to go through the pain she'd gone through. It was hard for her, but she went through with the trial. After seeing her courage and conviction, I real-

---

Some Programs of Kids Against Crime

- A peer support hotline where young people address concerns and questions about drugs, crime, and personal problems

- Preventive education programs on topics such as child abuse, suicide, teen pregnancy, and AIDS—includes skits and workshops presented at schools, shopping malls, and other places kids gather

- Graffiti cleanup and neighborhood improvement campaigns

- Project Identification, which has fingerprinted over twenty thousand young people

---

ized kids can make a difference. That's when I went home and drew up the proposal that started Kids Against Crime."

Linda was only twelve at the time. Since then, Kids Against Crime has become an organization of over four thousand young people in forty-five states who create and run crime prevention programs directed to others their own age.

All of these activities are organized by kids, for kids. "Little kids say, 'Oh, I'm not eighteen. I can't vote. What difference can I make?'" says Linda. "But we know they can do a lot, that they do have a leadership role. They can really say no to an adult and avoid becoming victims themselves. We teach them that they have power."

The public life skills these young people are gaining through Kids Against Crime range from public speaking to planning, from active listening to deal-

---

 Your Kids and Others Nearby

Think for a moment about the needs of the young people in your community.

What programs and services are available to kids where you live? Is your community helping them, supporting their development, in the way you could? Are you drawing them into real partnerships as you support them?

Is there any way you might enhance the lives of the children in your community?

ing with the media. "The work here is fun—we like to do this work," Ryan Pena declared. "We're not just talk, we actually go out there and we do it." In Kids Against Crime, young people have moved beyond the position of client or victim. They are, in fact, reshaping their world by their action. Theirs is an approach to self-help that goes far beyond individual change.

Clients Move Toward Self-Governance

To many Americans, the residents of a low-income housing project would be among the last people thought capable of shouldering responsibility for community problem solving. Haven't most housing projects, they believe, become hellholes of grime and crime? And isn't this in large part because residents, trapped in poverty, have absorbed society's message telling them they are incapable of being anything other than wards of the state?

Beginning in the early 1980s, a number of housing project tenants—first in isolation from one another, but increasingly in a network of mutual support—challenged those assumptions of hopelessness.

One hero of this awakening is Kimi Gray.

In the mid-sixties, when Kimi first got her apartment in the Kenilworth-Parkside housing project in Washington, D.C., she fit some of the leading stereotypes of a welfare mother: twenty-one, divorced, African-American, with five children. (In fact, most welfare recipients are white with an average of only two children, so Kimi may have fit the stereotypes, but not the reality.)

Kenilworth-Parkside had gotten so bad that by 1980 Kimi and her neighbors faced what one observer described as "an open-air drug market. And violence was so common that the management company put a bullet-proof barrier around its office. Residents went without heat or hot water for months at a time. . . . Rubbish was picked up so infrequently that rats infested the buildings."[10]

But by 1982, Kimi and her fellow tenants had convinced the mayor that they could manage their housing better than the government. When he finally gave in, the tenants created their own constitution, bylaws, and policies. The Kenilworth-Parkside Resident Management Corporation hired and trained fellow tenants to do what outsiders had previously been brought in to do.

They succeeded in cleaning up the project and getting rid of drugs, in part by involving residents as "building and court captains" to enforce the rules. And they went much further. They set up after-school programs for kids, courses to help adults get their high school diplomas, and an employment office.

Residents also created their own businesses, partly financed with start-up loans from the residents' council. One goal was to keep in their own community the little money they did have. So they created a cooperative store, a snack bar, two laundromats, a beauty salon, a catering service, a moving company, and more. These jobs grew to employ 120 residents.[11]

During the first four years of tenant management, rent collections increased 77 percent. Crime rates reached an all-time low. The proportion of project residents on welfare sank below 5 percent, down from a peak of 85 percent.[12]

In 1990, the residents actually purchased Kenilworth. "The community of 3,000, once characterized largely by single-parent families on welfare is now a community of homeowners, the majority of whom work."[13]

Kenilworth is an exceptionally dramatic story. But the drive and vision behind it are not unique. Today, across America, a score of tenant organizations have signed contracts for self-management. But "there are many hundreds more you could call burgeoning groups," according to Ronica Houston of the National Association of Resident Management Associations. Through NARMA, residents themselves are now pushing for policy changes that favor self-management.

Residents at Kenilworth have become heroes to thousands of public housing residents elsewhere. The world of Kimi Gray and her colleagues could point the way toward a national strategy for creating safe, attractive, permanently affordable housing. Sadly, however, Kenilworth's admirers in Washington during much of the 1980s and 1990s missed its key lesson for government.

The Kenilworth lesson? That government's role should be less to house the poor than to work *in partnership* with low-income people, ensuring that they themselves can assume responsibility for housing.

What would that mean? Greatly increasing assistance for low-income people to buy homes, requiring banks to make loans in low-income neighborhoods, and encouraging land-trust strategies to remove the speculative pressure that pushes housing prices out of the reach of the poor. It would also involve job creation and higher minimum wages. In a Living Democracy, citizen-driven solutions use government to bolster self-reliance.

Kenilworth, by contrast, has been exploited by anti-government dogmatists. It's touted as proof that simply selling off public housing will help end poverty. (Conveniently overlooked by these true believers is that the government put in, on average, over $130,000 in subsidies per unit at Kenilworth to make it salable—a strategy that obviously can't be repeated widely.[14]) In fact, if we continue to lack any national strategy to create *more* affordable housing, selling public housing will shrink the pool of housing available to the low-income people.

Many tenants in public housing grasp this complexity. They have spearheaded a nationwide initiative called the National Low-Income Housing Coalition. In meetings with the federal Department of Housing and Urban Development, these tenants argue that there is no sell-to-the-poor panacea. If Washington is serious about "tenant empowerment," they say, then tenants in each individual project must define what can work for them. The government "wants the poor [who buy their housing projects] to be able to sell the homes for a profit down the road," says Juandamarie Brown, who lives in Boston's Castle Square. "But what we need is [a] permanent . . . guarantee there will always be affordable housing for those who need it." She and others in her tenants' organization have taught themselves the intricacies of housing finance. "*We* should be the consultants," says Juandamarie.[15]

Kimi Gray and Juandamarie Brown demonstrate the potential of even those disenfranchised in part by class and color barriers to move from client to citizen.

Identify Your Housing Issues

You drive around in your community often. You know where the nearest housing problems are. Why do these problems exist?

What do you think are the major housing issues that confront your community?

If you could speak with all those involved—those who live in the housing, those who own them, government officials, taxpayers and all those who care about the housing crisis—what would you encourage them to do?

While not all of us have experienced the disempowerment these two women confronted, almost all of us have felt a loss of control at some point in our lives, regardless of class or color. When we're stricken by disease, that loss of control can feel overwhelming.

Beyond Cancer to Answers

It was 1977. The telephone was ringing in Mimi Kaplan's living room in suburban Chicago. Having just played a vigorous game of racquetball, she recalled thinking to herself, "I feel great."

But the news from her doctor wasn't great. Mimi had breast cancer.

Once the shock of the mastectomy wore off and she learned that she faced two years of treatment, Mimi was seized by terror. How, she wondered, was she going to cope with being a wife, mother, and university professor while undergoing the rigors of chemotherapy? And she had no one to ask.

Through a mutual friend, Mimi met another cancer patient, Ann Marcou. Both felt that while family and friends often mean well, they either

---

✎ What Are Your Needs?

You have just been diagnosed with a serious illness.

Which of the following do you want most? Put a check mark next to the needs that are of greatest importance to you.

- ☐ High-quality medical attention
- ☐ Clear information about your illness, its causes, and treatment
- ☐ A realistic sense of hope
- ☐ Knowledge about the experiences of others who have had your illness
- ☐ Confidence that you, personally, can do something to aid the recovery process
- ☐ Emotional support for the struggle with the illness

Most people find it hard to choose just one of these needs. Most want them all. How can you get these needs met?

skirt the issue or offer false assurances. The women discovered that beyond cancer, their biggest problem was finding people with whom to share their fears and answer their many questions: What relieves the nausea caused by chemotherapy? Which specialists can be recommended? Can I wear a bathing suit? Which prosthesis is best?

From such questions Y-ME was born in 1978. Today, one thousand women a month call Y-ME for help. There are thirteen support groups in Chicago alone, and Y-ME chapters have opened in eleven states. Nation-wide, more than two hundred volunteers—women who've lived with can-cer—share their experiences with women who've just been diagnosed.

"In the early days it was hard, very hard," Y-ME's executive director, Sharon Green, told us. "Doctors didn't want empowered women asking questions. . . . Doctors didn't like us, but now we've proven that we're not interfering with medical care. We're *enhancing* treatment. Informed patients are better patients. Now we're full partners with doctors."

Y-ME's type of support groups can even claim to lengthen women's lives.

How Have You Been Treated?

Recall the most recent serious illness you, or others you know, have had and the treatment received.

- Did the experts treat you (or your family or friends) as a helpless victim?

- Did you (or they) feel as though the experts were condescending?

- Did you (or they) receive enough clearly presented information about the illness?

- Did you (or they) feel isolated from family and friends?

- Did the doctors put you (or them) in touch with others who've had similar experiences?

The women in Y-ME have much to teach all those doctors who are dedicated to their patients' well-being. What might you teach the doctors and other health care professionals who have entered your life? What would improve their care of you?

A recent Stanford University study confirmed that women with breast cancer already spreading throughout their bodies who participate in a weekly ninety-minute support group survive one and a half years longer than comparable women who get medical treatment alone.[16]

Y-ME does more than reeducate doctors one-by-one. "We give workshops for professionals on the psychosocial needs of patients," Sharon told us. "Here, cancer patients are helping the professionals."

PROFES-SIONALS IN PART-NERSHIP WITH CLIENTS

The Living Democracy revolution that is under way in human services stems not just from client initiatives. Professionals, too, are breaking old molds. They're shifting their self-definition from provider of services to coach. They're rethinking their role—no longer simply giving advice but encouraging new ways of thinking among those they formerly served.

The Kenilworth-Parkside housing project, for example, is a stunning victory for self-help. But what about communities in which no Kimi Grays emerge spontaneously? Do professional social workers have any role to play in uncovering such leadership and helping to develop it?

Professionals Help Others Take the Initiative

In 1987, psychologist Dr. Roger Mills took on a project in the Modello and Homestead Gardens public housing projects in Miami, Florida. Funding came from the Department of Justice. "Sixty-five percent of the families were involved with drugs, mostly crack. . . . There were parents prostituting their children for drugs. It was a terrible situation, probably the worst I've ever seen," he said.

Roger Mills believed that change could come directly as Modello and Homestead Gardens residents realized their own potential. Sounds good, but is it possible?

"I was in an abusive relationship, very abusive," project resident Virene McCreary remembered. "I didn't have any self-esteem. I was just at home, having babies. The outside world just didn't matter." Every day, residents like Virene faced the proof that somehow they'd failed. Almost the entire litany of America's social problems afflicted them. And worst of all, society had forgotten them. Under such conditions, would not most of us have difficulty finding realistic grounds for hope?

But Roger and his colleagues believe that hopeful feelings are not just a product of circumstances. They believe that people can tap into innate feelings of self-worth, regardless of how depressed their environment. And once they do, they are able to exercise initiative and gain control over their lives.

So Roger Mills and his team didn't begin by instructing people about what they should do to reform their hostile, drug-ridden housing project. They talked *with* residents in their apartments. Informally, face-to-face, they introduced a startling notion—that people do have personal power and can realize the self-esteem within themselves. And such power can change their community for the better.

Not surprisingly, much skepticism greeted their initial efforts. One resident said, "I went to the first class he [Roger] held, and here he was saying that regardless of what was happening in your unit, if your self-esteem is high then it don't matter. And right away I said, well, he ain't too bright and I ain't got time for what he's talking about."[17]

But something began to change. "If I don't feel good about myself, then nothing is going to go right," is how Virene McCreary put it. "For me, it was just like a light going on—everything seemed to fall into place."

And the change wasn't just in the expectations of the residents about what they could accomplish. The professional team also worked with the schools attended by the children of Modello and Homestead Gardens. And they worked with agencies, including the police, who deal with the project's residents. Each was encouraged to see how their negative expectations created problems, how their tendency to blame only made situations worse. The goal was to introduce the notion of working collaboratively with the residents to solve problems, rather than viewing the residents themselves as the problem.

When hope began to take hold among the residents, here's what happened, according to Roger and his team:

> [The resident-organized PTA] scheduled a dinner at the school to get to know their principal and their children's teachers. They invited the state attorney, the Metro-Dade Police, youth services agencies, and child protective services representatives in to help with the problems of drug trafficking, with problems of family violence and truancy.
>
> ... The PTA then began to more assertively go after programs they felt would help their community. They brought in job training and

placement programs, G.E.D. classes, and wrote grants for after-school programs for youth. They formed a crime watch and started putting on fundraisers. [They] met with Housing and Urban Development Department officials and got them to agree to build a new community center that could house a day-care program.

Fifty teens created their own resident council, with its own teen crime watch to keep out drug dealers.

Neighbors who had not talked to one another, or who had feuded for years, began to get along and help each other out with baby sitting, shopping, transportation, and became real neighbors and friends.

At the end of five years, 80 percent of the residents had jobs. Child abuse dropped by 60 percent. School grades improved, and school disciplinary action involving the project's children dropped by three quarters.[18]

The New Model Emerging in Human Services

At Issue	The Service Model	The Living Democracy Model
Who's in charge	Professionally driven	Citizen/client driven
Contribution of professional	Professional provides answers	Professional is resource
Process	Usually diagnosing a single cause and cure	Understanding multiple causes and seeking ongoing change
Procedure	Bureaucratic	Informal
What's valued	Credentials	Experience
Communication	Largely one-way	Collaborative
Focus of problem solving	Individual deficiency	Capacities developed through interaction
Exchange	Limited to fee for service	Includes mutual benefits

A critical lesson became clear to us as we heard about this phenomenal triumph of hope over fear: the "clients" weren't alone in needing to tap their own inner capacity for positive change. For real problem solving to occur, the teachers, police, counselors, social workers, and other helpers had to reduce the stress they felt in their jobs and begin appreciating *their* roles. They had to let go of negative expectations that made them oppositional and punitive. Their positive feelings then helped to reinforce the positive expectations within the residents themselves.

The assumption that people are born with a natural yearning for mental health, and that this natural tendency can be directly accessed for positive change, is a radical idea. Yet it lies at the very heart of Living Democracy, which depends on ordinary people using their common sense and moving toward making their communities healthier.

Professionals Work with Families

Democracy depends on families that work—families in which members are learning communication skills, respectful interaction, constructive use of anger, and all the other capacities that ultimately make us effective in every aspect of our lives.

But many American families, not just the poorest of the poor, are under siege, not completely unlike those in the Modello and Homestead Gardens projects. Some are unable to withstand the pressures of drugs, failing schools, violence, and the dearth of affordable housing. As spousal and child abuse spread, for example, more and more children are taken from their parents for their own protection. By the end of this decade almost one million American children will be in foster care.[19] Yet foster care carries its own risks.

So in the mid-seventies, two psychologists in Tacoma, Washington, began to question whether removing children from abusive or dangerous homes was really the answer. In most cases, why not try to remove the risk instead of the child? They hit upon what's become a national movement, now called "family preservation."[20]

Instead of an at-risk child being taken from the home, the social worker goes into the home, spending ten to fourteen hours a week actually living the family's daily routine. The social worker becomes the family's coach, helping parents learn everything from budgeting to how to enforce clear rules, and helping family members learn how to communicate their needs and express anger constructively.

Among the originators of this approach is HOMEBUILDERS, located near Seattle. Its philosophy reminds us of Roger Mills and his team in the Modello and Homestead Gardens housing projects. HOMEBUILDERS' Daniel Johnson explained, "Ours is a model that is respectful of families. . . . Our approach is to go slower, with more respect, to treat clients as colleagues, to give them credit for their knowledge and their expertise."

HOMEBUILDERS believes "most families can learn how to handle their own problems rather than relying on social services." HOMEBUILDERS' Mary Fisher told us, "Our emphasis is on partnership."

And their efforts show results. HOMEBUILDERS works only with families who are in imminent danger of having children removed from the home, and well over 90 percent of the families they work with avoid family breakup. The savings to the community, just in sheer dollar terms, is enor-

How Well Are You Served?

List the professionals outside your job with whom you come in contact:

Rate their ability to engage in partnership with you (circle your rating):

_____ excellent	very good	good	fair	poor
_____ excellent	very good	good	fair	poor
_____ excellent	very good	good	fair	poor
_____ excellent	very good	good	fair	poor
_____ excellent	very good	good	fair	poor

Is there anything you can do—such as writing a letter or speaking directly to the person or to a superior, or even sending a copy of this chapter—to improve the partnership you have, or move you toward the one you want?

mous. The family preservation approach costs the public less than half of foster care, even though a social worker works with only two families at a time. It has now spread to thirty states.

The HOMEBUILDERS approach demystifies the role of the professional. The client does not sit meekly in the professional's office, receiving guidance. The professional addresses the real-life challenges of the family—with them—and also works to re-knit the family into the life of the community.

What's impressed us, as we've looked at the quiet revolution in human services—moving away from service delivery and toward building clients' capacities—is that often personal self-mastery includes becoming effective in the larger world.

A common perception of self-help is that its focus is inward. And indeed, some aspects of self-help explicitly discourage advocacy to change social policy. Many of the twelve-step groups, for example, have a tradition of not expressing "any opinion on outside controversial issues," which members frequently take to mean no outside involvement on their part as well. Yet Frank Riessman, director of the National Self-Help Clearinghouse, argues that despite their reluctance to admit it, twelve-step groups have had a tremendous impact on public attitudes and, eventually, on public policy. The shift by professionals and public alike to viewing alcoholism as a disease stems in part from the twelve-step movement. "Actually, the self-help approach has been in the forefront of positive, progressive social change," argues Frank.[21]

To Frank Riessman, a prime example is the Association for Retarded Persons. Formed forty years ago by parents upset about being advised to institutionalize their children, this group, by the 1970s, had helped write and pass both federal and state legislation. These laws guarantee every handicapped child an appropriate education, thus allowing more such children to remain at home with their families.

Victims' rights groups in New York City provide another case of self-helpers achieving broad public impact. Their pressure helped to pass—unanimously—a state law restricting cross-examination of rape victims about their past sexual history.[22]

SELF-HELP
BEYOND
SELF:
SHAPING
PUBLIC
POLICY
—

But the most dramatic example of a change in public policy spurred by those long discounted as handicapped may be the 1992 Americans with Disabilities Act. It's the product of perseverance and political sophistication on the part of those with disabilities. And it will enable the forty-three million Americans who suffer some kind of limitation to participate more fully and productively in public life.

During the last ten years, in virtually every part of the country, people with disabilities have begun shaking off the old assumptions that a disability means being set aside and taken care of. "There's been a 100 percent turnaround from chronic institutionalization to independent living," says Tricia Kelley, who works in San Rafael, California, at one of the 250 Independent Living Centers that have sprung up throughout the country in the last twenty years. "This change breaks through every preconception of helplessness."

As their name implies, Independent Living Centers help people with disabilities to live on their own. They offer support groups and skills training. Just as important, they coach people in securing the services they need to function on their own. These centers are not run by professionals for clients. A partnership of the two is the goal: "The majority of the staff and board of ILCs must be people with disabilities," explains Steve Brown of the Berkeley, California, Independent Living Center.

But people with disabilities are discovering that taking charge of their own lives requires more than changing attitudes. It means changing public policy.

Begun in 1987, the Connecticut Union of Disability Action Groups (CUDAG)—now sixteen groups across that state—embodies this new spirit. CUDAG meets annually to elect representatives who in turn meet monthly to coordinate statewide campaigns that benefit disabled people.

CUDAG members are discovering the rewards of public life. Hear Shelley Teed-Wargo, part of CUDAG's founding committee, describe this process: "Some of the original people we recruited six years ago have now moved into their own apartments for the first time in their lives, been able to form relationships with members of the opposite sex, gotten married. Several have full-time jobs. One of them is now a community organizer himself. There's been tremendous growth in individuals because they've entered public life."

What began as informal monthly gatherings of people with disabilities only a few years ago is now changing lives. Clients have become shapers of public policies, and in the process they are radically changing their own lives.

 Can You Create a Better Future?

Think of one problem that you or your family or your community faces—a problem for which people typically turn to professionals for answers. After reading the stories of others in this chapter, are you aware of any new understandings or resources you yourself could bring to help solve the problem? If the story of your activity during the next several years were to be added to this chapter, what might your story be?

BEYOND BOOT-STRAPS

In the emerging Living Democracy—whether in the economy or human services—we see core assumptions in flux. Whether the person is a worker on the plant floor, a student in the classroom, or a welfare recipient in a low-income housing project, the focus for generating positive change is not on filling deficiencies but on discovering and building capacities.

And beneath this shift lies an even more basic rethinking: human beings share an innate desire for self-direction, for growth, for dignity—for health. Thus, even within seriously distressed people, an innate desire for health—and some commonsense ideas about how to achieve it—are there to be tapped. Linda Warsaw, the young founder of Kids Against Crime, put it this way: "Kids like to help other kids. They love helping other children, and through our activities, they do. They see the difference they are making."

Moreover, people are discovering that we can help to heal ourselves by helping others. We gain insight into ourselves by contributing to others. And because being of use is such a deep need for most of us, practices that draw us into group problem solving also build self-respect. Self-respect then helps motivate our further learning and growth.

In this positive-feedback loop, distinctions between giver and receiver blur. We become both giver and receiver at once.

Human Services in a Democracy—Three Contrasting Views

Conservative "Bootstrap" View	Liberal "Service" View	Living Democracy View
The problem is the individual's fault.	Society is largely responsible.	Fault-finding doesn't help. Let's focus on building people's own capacities for problem solving.
The individual must take responsibility, facing the problem *without* outside, public resources. Public help only reinforces dependency.	Let's bring in professionals to diagnose the problem and prescribe solutions. People who have been damaged by the socially inflicted pain of poverty and abuse have few resources within themselves for use in problem solving.	Even in the bleakest neighborhoods, people joining together discover resources within. But building people's own capacities may also require public resources.
Where necessary, private resources—churches and charities—can help. They sustain families and communities.	Since families and other community institutions have been largely destroyed in poor neighborhoods, we can't expect them to help.	Self-help and public help can be complementary—when professionals come in not as experts to solve problems but as facilitators to help people to discover their own power.
Professional, publicly provided social services are part of the problem. They cost too much public money and enlarge government, creating self-interested professionals who thrive on continuation of the problem. They usually fail because they deny people the chance to solve their own problems.	Social problems are best solved by standardized government programs that can assure quality through oversight by professionals.	Access to public resources (funds for low-cost housing, day-care centers, and job training, for example) can help citizens solve their problems, *if* citizens (not outside experts) have a central role in shaping the programs and ensuring their effectiveness.

But how does Living Democracy within the human services differ from the long-argued conservative view that we should and can simply pull ourselves up by our bootstraps?

- Living Democracy, as it is emerging within the human services, focuses not solely on individual self-reliance but also on the capacities of people to work *together* for mutual healing and problem solving.

- Living Democracy is about creating real power, not just temporarily alleviating misery. Within the human services, it changes relationships between client and the service provider. Most important, it encourages clients to develop and wield power relationally as they grow in self-esteem and self-direction.

- In Living Democracy, government has an important role to play. Citizens properly transform government into a servant of their interests, whether it be a Modello and Homestead Gardens tenants' victory in getting government support for a day-care center or CUDAG's success in making government-enforced policies more supportive of disabled people.

Society's obligation to help support citizens with specific needs does not have to mean top-down governmental control. In Living Democracy, self-help and society's help are mutually enhancing and mutually beneficial.

8

Governing "By the People"

THE MINIMUM WAGE is the lowest hourly wage an employer can legally offer. Somewhere, some government body must set it. To Grace Trejo, a Los Angeles homemaker and first-generation American, raising the minimum wage appeared far beyond reach. In just nine months in 1987, however, Grace and other low-to-moderate-income Americans in three citizen organizations—affiliates of the Industrial Areas Foundation in Southern California—launched the Moral Minimum Wage campaign and conquered what she called "a mountain."

"Whole families were falling apart," she reported, because of the stress caused by low wages. So Grace and other regular Americans in the IAF network did research to uncover just who decides the minimum wage. In California, the answer is the Industrial Welfare Commission—just five people. Grace and her cohorts then *personalized* the impersonal, distant power of the commission. They actively educated Muriel Morse, the commission's swing vote. They took her into their homes to show her the impact of low wages on families.

In the end, with five hundred citizens crowding the hearing room, the commission voted three to two to increase the minimum wage by 27 percent. Grace remembered how she felt that day: "We really did it! That's a moment you never want to forget."[1] And soon the federal government followed California's lead.

In St. Paul, Minnesota, the citizens in each of the city's neighborhoods elect a district council. Through the Budget Priorities Process, these seventeen councils help decide how the city should spend over $65 million for capital improvements.

Every other year, representatives from the councils rank proposals from both neighborhood groups and city departments. The mayor then appoints a citizens' committee to prioritize the recommendations into a capital budget. David McDonell, who has chaired this committee, describes its makeup: "It's everyday, regular people, including widows who have never worked outside the home, construction workers, and professionals. They become very dedicated, really proud to be part of it." Finally, recommendations go to the mayor and city council. "Very rarely do they make major changes," says Ann Copeland, St. Paul's citizen participation coordinator. "So obviously, the councils have a great deal of power, the power of knowledge—of the intricacies of the city—and the power to influence lots of decisions."

These two very different stories are about politics. But not the politics most Americans know.

To most Americans, politics has become a dirty word. Mothers polled some years ago on what careers they wanted for their sons overwhelmingly agreed: they would approve of their sons becoming president of the United States. But a *politician*? Heavens, no!

 Poll Yourself

Rate your confidence in the following branches of government by circling a number from one (no confidence) to three (some confidence) to five (great confidence).

Your local government	1 2 3 4 5
Your state government	1 2 3 4 5
The president and his administration in Washington	1 2 3 4 5
The Congress	1 2 3 4 5

Today, many hands wring over the supposed apathy of Americans. Half of us don't vote. But is that really apathy? If the system is controlled by money, special interests, and the media, perhaps many people feel like suckers to go along with a game that makes them feel manipulated.

Many Americans now see big money as democracy's most formidable enemy. The title of Phil Stern's 1988 book, *The Best Congress Money Can Buy*, seemed to properly capture our feelings.[2] Indeed, it now takes $4.5 million to win a seat in Congress.[3] And even after being elected, congresspeople seem to spend more time raising money than passing legislation.

A Kettering Foundation study in 1991 captured one of the results of this system: Americans "feel as though they have been locked out of their own homes . . . evicted from their own property. . . . People know exactly who dislodged them from their rightful place in American democracy," the report observed. "They point their fingers at politicians, at powerful lobbyists, and . . . the media."[4] "It's not that people no longer have a sense of civic duty," a Seattle man said in the study. "It's that they don't have a sense of *power*."[5]

But if the majority of Americans are right that formal politics is controlled by those with money and by media that pick the issues and winners for us, what chance is there for democracy?

Understandably, more and more voices call for reform. They demand public financing of campaigns, easier voter registration, more equal access to media, clean-campaign pledges from candidates, and term limitations.

Certainly many of these reforms are needed. But would they alone lead toward Living Democracy? Democracy as a way of life in which we ordinary citizens are putting government in the service of our interests and values?

We doubt such reforms by themselves could take us beyond what we call formal democracy. In it, government fails to meet the needs of the majority of Americans—even if our representatives were elected fairly—because it remains so distant, so separate, so seemingly untouchable.

That sense of distance between citizen and government was captured for us in a debate on *The Phil Donahue Show* about the savings and loan bailout. One irate member of the audience exclaimed, "The taxpayers shouldn't pay for this; the government should!"[6]

Living Democracy, however, is not distant. It depends on citizens' knowing that we *are* the government. That the over half-million elected officials in our country and the fifteen million unelected officeholders and

What Americans Feel

Here are three commonly held views about what Americans feel. What are your views? Check them off.

	Strongly agree	Agree	No opinion	Disagree	Strongly disagree

Citizen attitudes

Americans are apathetic, or they think only about issues that directly affect them. They're too absorbed in their personal struggles to care about the general welfare.

| | ☐ | ☐ | ☐ | ☐ | ☐ |

The role of the media

The media give us what we ask for. It's the citizens who focus elections on personalities rather than issues. We Americans seem to want only sound bites; we find real discussion of the issues boring.

| | ☐ | ☐ | ☐ | ☐ | ☐ |

Special interests and reform

Many of the groups we deride as "special interests" were created by and for the people. We have them because we want them. But if we could just reform campaign financing and strengthen ethics codes, we could hold officials accountable. Then perhaps citizens would feel more confident in our government.

| | ☐ | ☐ | ☐ | ☐ | ☐ |

But the findings of the Kettering Foundation about what Americans really feel are quite different from the commonly held views. The following are their findings on these same three issues. What do you think about the results of their study?

	Strongly agree	Agree	No opinion	Disagree	Strongly disagree

Citizen attitudes

Americans care but feel powerless. We feel cut off because the way issues are presented doesn't relate them to our real concerns. Americans discover time and energy for public involvement when we see that getting involved has some chance of getting results.

	☐	☐	☐	☐	☐

The role of the media

The media gear stories toward the sensational. We Americans want the media to help us in sorting out complex issues. We'd even like a chance to interact among ourselves about these issues, not just have information pushed on us. Right now, the few avenues we have for expressing our views widely seem mere show, not sincere openings for our voices to be heard and our views to be considered by our fellow citizens.

	☐	☐	☐	☐	☐

	Strongly agree	Agree	No opinion	Disagree	Strongly disagree

Special interests and reform

The handful of "public interest" groups in Washington
that try to represent the
views of ordinary people are
no match for the huge conglomerates whose big money
seems to have stolen our
politics from us. We want
clean elections as well as
election officials who are not
beholden to big money. And
we want more—we want on-
going, back-and-forth relationships with our elected
officials, so that we can
share in the development of
our public policies and hold
our officials accountable.

	Strongly agree	Agree	No opinion	Disagree	Strongly disagree
	☐	☐	☐	☐	☐

Source: Adapted from *Citizens and Politics,* prepared for the Kettering Foundation by the Harwood Group, 1991.

government employees work for us. And we, in turn, are responsible for holding them accountable.

So Living Democracy demands more than a change in the election rules. It demands a change in culture—in people's expectations of government and of themselves. Such a profound change comes only as our experience of government changes.

In this chapter we'll explore efforts to alter the very culture of political life—the expectations of all of us, both officials and citizens, about the appropriate role for citizens.

In the section titled "Acting from Our Authority as Citizens," we high-light examples of independent citizens' organizations that have shaped their communities' futures, set statewide policies, and even achieved national influence.

In the section titled "Moving Government Closer to Citizens," we showcase localities that are creating new official positions for citizens—narrowing the gap between government and citizen.

What's to Come

Acting from Our Authority as Citizens

- Citizens plan their communities
- Citizens set values that guide life-and-death choices
- Citizens become lobbyists
- Citizens learn to hold government accountable

Moving Government Closer to Citizens

- City governments create official roles for citizens
- Cities help neighborhoods get organized
- Citizen organizations get direct access to public funds
- Police learn to work with—and listen to—citizens

How do citizens discover their capacity to help develop sound governmental policies? And to hold officials accountable to citizens' interests?

Acting on the authority we have as citizens begins close to home. After all, how can we feel connected to Washington if we feel disenfranchised in our own neighborhoods and cities? And adding up the impact of decisions that take place below the federal level about schools, zoning, welfare, labor law, penal codes, pollution control, and so on, it's obvious that the power we often think is in Washington is actually much closer at hand.

Throughout this book we show everyday citizens going beyond the usual roles—donor to a cause, for example, or protestor of a decision—in order

ACTING FROM OUR AUTHORITY AS CITIZENS

to shape specific public policies, from school reform to the laws protecting the interests of people with disabilities.

In this section we'll dig deeper, focusing on citizens engaged in long-term community planning, as well as citizens establishing the values that guide public choices. We'll see others learning new ways to lobby and to keep officials accountable to their interests on all the issues they care about most. And finally, we'll hear from those who see citizens as essential "coaches" in helping government govern.

Citizens Become Community Planners

Alarm over government-as-usual's incapacity to meet mounting challenges—from failing schools to worsening crime and a shrinking industrial base—is forcing some cities to turn to citizens to break the problem-solving paralysis. Some call it community *visioning*. Some call it consensus building. But the point is to bring citizens into the long-range planning process for their communities. It's happening in dozens of cities and towns.

"Traditionally, authorities devise the plan, sell it to the public, and then try to implement it," explains Tyler Norris of the National Civic League (NCL). But it just doesn't work. "Implementation gets blocked or never happens, because people resist what they had no part in creating." NCL's Civic Assistance Program facilitates a different process, says Tyler. At each stage—defining the problem, devising solutions, and implementing them—stakeholders in the community are involved, including those who are usually left out of decision making.

"Then, 'selling' the plan becomes unnecessary," says Tyler, "because people feel 'it's my plan,' because they've been involved all along."

For Ron Thomas of Community Design Exchange in Seattle, the outstanding example of bringing citizens into the planning process is Roanoke, Virginia.[7] Its commitment to citizen-based planning extends back more than a decade. Ron, who was a consultant to the Roanoke planning process, explains: "In 1980, we developed a problem-solving and skill-building program called Roanoke Neighborhood Partnership, working with a series of neighborhoods. We trained citizens in problem solving and collaboration. Each year, it's expanded to new neighborhoods, so now nearly everybody is involved." As a result, Roanoke city planner Evie Gunter told us, citizen involvement in planning is "becoming a cultural

You as Planner

Have you ever driven through your community and thought to yourself:

- Why did the city do that?

- Why don't they build a _____?

- We really need a _____!

- Why not provide a _____?

- We need less money spent on_____ and more money spent on _____!

- We could save money if only _____.

In other words, do you have some ideas about what your community needs?

Do you ever see opportunities to have your voice heard about what your community needs? If not, why not? If you do, are you willing to take advantage of those opportunities?

Who is responsible for planning your community?

Who do you think should be responsible?

What role would you like to play in determining your community's future?

With whom could you talk, what action could you take, to move toward assuming the role you wish to play in planning the future of your community?

norm." And neighborhood boards are being created to provide continuing channels for citizen input.

In Phoenix, a similar process called Futures Forum took sixteen months, ultimately involving thirty-five hundred residents and almost half a million dollars. The final report called for hundreds of steps by government and industry—from electing neighborhood planners so citizens have more say in land use, to increasing taxes on gasoline and putting bike racks on city buses. The process created six "action groups" charged with implementation. This is key, says Tyler Norris. "The stakeholders have to know from the beginning that they're responsible not just for coming up with a plan but for *making it happen*."

Now the city administrators in Phoenix are evaluated on whether they're achieving the goals of the Futures Forum. Several Forum recommendations are now part of the city's official plan. The action groups have become "another layer of local governance," according to political scientists involved in the process. They "complement the more traditional, business-dominated group structures. . . ."[8]

What Can Citizen Involvement *Really* Accomplish? Chattanooga, Tennessee, may boast the greatest practical outcomes of a citizen-involvement process.

In the early 1980s, when the city was hit with a rash of plant closings, the layoffs hurt the city badly. Public infrastructure deteriorated fast. Schools were failing. And racial tensions ran high.

So about fifty citizens, aware that the old ways of decision making were failing, gathered to study how other cities had been successful in "turning themselves around," as Chattanooga native Eleanor Cooper puts it. The group formed Chattanooga Venture, which encouraged the city to begin an inclusive, community-wide process of setting goals. "For the first time across the city people came together to say what they wanted their city to be," says Eleanor, who became head of Chattanooga Venture.

In 1984, this twenty-week visioning process produced thirty-four goals for the city, some of them addressing immediate needs—a shelter for abused women, for example. They also included such long-term, ambitious targets as creating a riverfront park. Yet by 1992, a remarkable 85 percent of the goals had been met, and millions of new dollars had been invested in the community.

Just as important, Chattanooga Venture had become an ongoing all-community institution—a multiracial, cross-class organization to involve citizens in achieving these goals.

To do this, Venture has trained citizens to facilitate community dialogues. It has "incubated" new nonprofits that now serve the community. It has helped organize dozens of new neighborhood associations and link them in an all-city Neighborhood Network. In 1992, it sponsored a city-wide meeting to begin forming an agenda for school reform, expecting several hundred to attend. Instead, fifteen hundred participants generated two thousand suggestions. And in 1993, Venture brought citizens together again to establish a new set of goals.

These stories demonstrate how citizens are learning to make hard choices among competing claims for their resources. But nothing could be harder, we believe, than tackling the crisis of health care funding.

Citizens Grapple with Life-and-Death Choices

When the newspapers tell us of poor patients dying for lack of emergency attention, and of terminally ill patients kept alive against their wishes at enormous expense, more and more Americans feel we can no longer avoid America's health care crisis. We pay a greater share of our national wealth for health care, but get less for it, than any other major industrial country.

Over the last decade, in at least fourteen states, citizens have begun to claim their role in determining health policy.[9] The movement began in Oregon when the 1980 recession hit and tens of thousands of citizens lost their medical benefits. With limited resources, everyone was asking how the state should respond. No one had answers. Taking the initiative, the state's health council pulled together a conference from which two key questions emerged:

> Can today's invisible rationing of health care [by ability to pay] be made explicit and then consistent with community values?

> How does society rank curative care compared to preventive service?

Experts couldn't make these choices, the conference decided, because they have to do with society's fundamental values. Only citizens themselves could. So a number of participants in the conference launched a new non-profit organization—Oregon Health Decisions (OHD). OHD recruited thirty community volunteers—including homemakers, businesspeople, county officials, nurses, physicians, social workers, retirees, teachers, ministers, and school board members—to involve other citizens in grappling with these questions. After some training, the volunteers' job was to get their neighbors talking. During the 1980s they helped facilitate hundreds of discussions involving thousands of Oregonians. By 1990, the years of in-depth public talk had paid off. The legislature created the Oregon Health Services Commission, officially required to use community meetings to identify the values that must guide the allocation of health care resources.

Who Should Decide?

Do you agree with the intent of the Oregon Health Services Commission?
Should rationing health care and containing health costs be determined by:

Medical experts?	Yes___	No___
Government officials?	Yes___	No___
Religious and ethical leaders?	Yes___	No___
Ability to pay?	Yes___	No___
All the members of a community?	Yes___	No___

Through this process, citizens gained confidence. They came to believe that by combining the efforts of technical experts and a responsive community, Oregon could rationally create a priority list to guide the use of limited health dollars. Nowhere had such a listing ever been attempted. In early 1991, the Oregon Health Services Commission released a citizen-generated ranking of 709 "condition/treatment pairs." Twenty thousand hours of citizens' volunteer effort—discovering community consensus on values and weighing the difficult trade-offs—went into producing the list. Once fully implemented, the plan will save enough health dollars to expand by 50 percent the state's Medicaid roles, reaching 120,000 additional women and children.

In conversations about rising health care costs colliding with limited resources, it's tempting to "weasel out" with a vague "well, society must decide." But that's not good enough, says Michael Garland, co-founder and first executive director of Oregon Health Decisions. There must be a way for citizens to determine the values so that society can decide. Oregon citizens are showing us one way.

Small, Rural Communities Decide Their Health Care, Too. "Living in small communities my whole life," Ramona Bishop told us, "I've noticed that when problems occur, everyone takes sides. It's the 'High Noon' approach to problem solving. But a new process gave us a way to look at our health care challenges as a community and decide what to do about them."

Your Voice in Health Care Policy

Health policies involve fundamental choices between competing values. It's difficult to decide broad policies that boil down to life-and-death decisions in individual cases. How would you feel about helping to set guidelines for how your state's public health monies will be spent, knowing that life-and-death choices must be made?

Could you do it? Should you do it?

What opportunities do you now have to make your voice heard, your values influential, in the allocation of health care in your community?

What opportunities should you and your neighbors have to influence the distribution of health care and health costs?

What steps can you take toward creating the opportunities you think you and your neighbors should have?

Ramona lives in Harney County, Oregon—a small, isolated, high desert community. In 1988, the county hospital was in debt and the only local doctor was about to retire. Over seven thousand residents faced the prospect of not having a health facility closer than 130 miles.

Just three years later a district-owned hospital is flourishing. Four doctors now serve the community, along with trained emergency "first responders." What made the difference?

"Direct citizen involvement in health care planning," according to Paul McGinnis, director of the Mountain States Health Corporation. This nonprofit group worked with Harney County residents to turn crisis into opportunity. "We try to get people away from blaming the Feds, or whomever, and to take the responsibility for controlling their own destiny," Paul told us. The process goes like this:

First, the community hires a local person to serve as part-time "community encourager"—linking health care representatives and local citizens. Ramona Bishop, a sheep rancher, took the job in Harney County.

After intensive training in group skills, health care issues and economics, the encourager's job is organizing residents to form a

Community Health Council—a cross section of Harney's residents from retailer to rancher to teacher. Members agree to gather together their own sector of the community to generate ideas and opinions. They talk with family and friends until they arrive at a "consensus list"—those health care issues citizens care most about.

At a town meeting, residents then prioritize these issues and set their goals. The council then divides into research groups to evaluate options for meeting these goals. It then returns its findings to the community groups for discussion.

By not hiring outside consultants to do the research, but rather doing it themselves, citizens gain a deep understanding of the health care crisis and their options. They learn to calculate the economic *benefit* from a health care facility in terms of jobs and goods and services purchased, as well as the tax burden. (One rural county, for example, found that it could invest $1.5 million each year in its hospital and still come out even.[10])

In just three years, Harney County citizens achieved every one of the goals they had set for themselves, but the impact on Harney County didn't end with this success. The project has lived on by being replicated, Ramona told us. "Through this process the community members learned new thinking patterns which they've transferred to school issues and to a newly formed economic development organization," she explained. "It [the citizen dialogue process] was used to pass a school bond measure. It has kind of circled through our community."

Harney County's experience is not unique. More than twenty other rural communities, from Alabama to Washington, have successfully completed the same process.

Citizen Lobbyists

In health care and many other areas, citizens are designing policy. But another critically important role for citizens is lobbying to *influence* policy. But "lobbyist," to most Americans, is even lower on the sleaze scale than "politician." Lobbyists, after all, are usually seen as the hired hands of big corporations and other special interests.

Some citizen organizations, however, are demonstrating the potential of another type of lobbyist—the citizen-lobbyist. We don't mean the staff paid by public interest organizations. We mean citizens learning how to influence decision making and hold others accountable. We mean everyday people standing before legislative bodies.

"In KFTC [Kentuckians for the Commonwealth], we baffle legislators all the time," Jean True told us, laughing. "They can't believe regular citizens would be up there testifying. One week, it's one person; the next week, somebody else. The legislators are used to working with professional lobbyists who are paid to be there all the time. We baffle them! Always different people testifying. There's *power* there. It resides in our membership.

"We've had lots of bills passed, and we've affected even more," she said. "We even got it written into law that one of our [KFTC] members has to be included in a state program to get industry to find ways to not produce hazardous waste in the first place, rather than hauling it off later. We've been an important force in fighting for that concept—source reduction of hazardous waste."

Citizen lobbying efforts by the IAF affiliates in Texas have shifted public funds to poor barrios on the border, and state health dollars have been redirected to the indigent. Citizen lobbying efforts by ACORN, National People's Action, and others prevented the gutting of the Community Reinvestment Act in 1991.

Holding Officials Accountable. Lobbying for what you want means holding public officers accountable for what they promise. Citizens are devising ingenious new strategies for doing so. We encountered one example on a brisk fall evening in 1991.

We entered a large auditorium in Santa Rosa, California, where six hundred people crowded the room. The air was electric—these were serious people. Placards with the names of local churches dotted the room. Behind us stood a group of Hispanic farm workers, looking both exhausted and eager. Near them was a Quaker congregation, mostly white and middle-aged. And not far away were representatives of a mostly African-American church. All were members of the Sonoma County Faith-based Community Organizing Project.

Their gathering had at least two goals. One was to decide the focus of their efforts for the coming year—the culmination of months of what they called a "listening process." The second was to formally hold county

✎ What Do You Want from Your Officials?

If you could give marks to your local government officials, what *criteria* would you use to grade their performance?

Write down what you think should be important about the jobs of the following:

Your town or city council _____

Your school board _____

Your police _____

Your housing officials_____

Your public health officials_____

Your street and sanitation officials _____

Your traffic planners _____

Your welfare and social service officials _____

Since you are a taxpayer, these are your employees. Do you have any opportunity to let them know what you think about the jobs they are performing for you?

officials accountable to the demands these citizens had made throughout the year.

On stage were local government officials looking a bit uncomfortable. They were to undergo their first performance evaluation by their real "superiors"—the regular taxpaying citizens.

Six-foot-high "report cards" were propped up in the center of the stage, each spelling out in large letters the grounds on which these officials would be marked. As leaders in the Organizing Project called out and entered a letter grade on each count, the crowd was delighted. The officials received straight As, except for one "incomplete."

These citizens had succeeded in securing the local government's cooperation in meeting virtually all of their goals during the year. What we witnessed that evening was an example of what many active citizens now call accountability sessions.

One type of accountability process, with numerous follow-up sessions, is planned long in advance. A case in point is the 1991 annual meeting in Brockton, Massachusetts, of the Brockton Interfaith Community (BIC). This coalition of thirteen congregations worked for many months to prepare for having the city's two mayoral candidates attend their meeting. Their own listening process resulted in a list of very specific demands—what they called the Rebuild the City Plan. BIC's goal was to get both candidates that evening to commit—very specifically—to the plan, which involved everything from expanding affordable housing to using funds confiscated in drug raids to support crime watch groups.

A standing-room-only crowd came to the meeting to hear the candidates not speak but *respond*—respond to plans created by the citizenry. Both candidates pledged to act on BIC's agenda, in some cases competing with each other as to whose record was more consistent with it. Perhaps most important, both candidates agreed to meet on a bimonthly basis with BIC leadership and to arrange meetings with city department heads.

It's in these follow-up meetings that the original commitments become useful. Whoever is elected, BIC can call on the mayor to uphold prior commitments. By ensuring that the promises were made publicly and highlighted in the local press, these citizens have devised a powerful tool to exert continuing power in public life.

Citizens Enforce New Policy

It's one thing to get policy passed and quite another to see it happen. The citizen organizations ACORN and NPA, for example, played key roles in

Could You Help Your Officials Govern?

Are there views you now hold that your elected officials ought to hear?

With which officials do you wish you could speak?

Can you voice your views by yourself? Or are they better voiced in collaboration with other like-minded citizens?

Are there people with whom you should join to develop shared views and advance those views together?

creating the national Community Reinvestment Act. But without their members' *ongoing pressure* to expose banks' noncompliance, the law would have produced few resources for low-income communities.

Similarly, Kentuckians for the Commonwealth moved the state to go beyond cleanup to actually reduce pollution at its source. Then, Jean True told us, "we did our *own* survey of major polluters throughout the state, to find out how many had been contacted by the Kentucky Partners [the state oversight committee] or by the Environmental Protection Agency. We got lots of publicity from that survey when we found that too many companies had not been contacted." KFTC helped bring policy off the books and into reality.

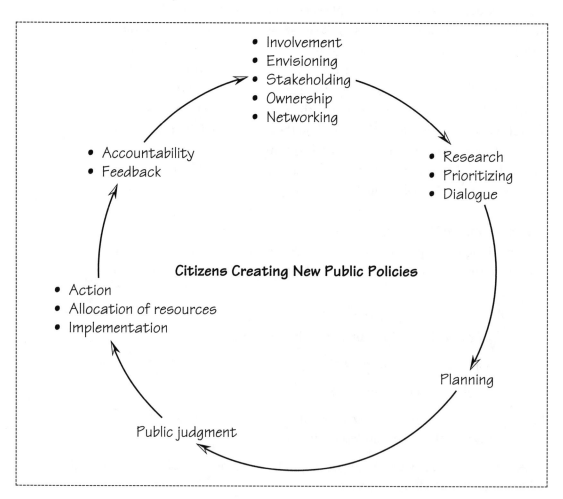

- Involvement
- Envisioning
- Stakeholding
- Ownership
- Networking

- Accountability
- Feedback

- Research
- Prioritizing
- Dialogue

Citizens Creating New Public Policies

- Action
- Allocation of resources
- Implementation

Planning

Public judgment

Citizens as Public Policymakers

Issues	Citizens' impact
Government accountability	In "accountability sessions," citizens periodically "grade" public officials in public meetings for their follow-through on specific citizen demands.
Corporate accountability	In Kentucky, citizens get their own water testing officially recognized for the purpose of monitoring corporate compliance with environmental regulation.
Human services	In Oregon, citizens prioritize the medical procedures they are willing to fund.
Media	Citizens influence the 1984 Federal Cable Television Law allowing local governments to require cable license holders to provide public access.
Education and school governance	In dozens of school districts, parents, teachers, and community members are succeeding in decentralizing authority.

In a similar vein, Jean told us how KFTC had won a role for citizens' participation in water testing: "One big problem we've had is the pollution from mining activities. That stuff is sometimes dumped into water at night or on weekends when inspectors are not around. Then the inspectors won't write it up—if they don't see any signs in the water.

"Now, thanks to our efforts, the state recognizes *citizen* testing and monitoring. Our samples and videotaping are now treated as valid evidence of violations." Through KFTC's efforts, citizens have become part of policy enforcement.

And in San Antonio, organizer Tom Holler was emphatic that the role of Communities Organized for Public Service (COPS) in solving public problems goes well beyond pushing for favored policies. He cited its efforts with the Housing Trust Fund: "Our efforts set up the fund to finance low- and moderate-income housing. Then our efforts got it funded. Now there's a lot of internal fighting. So the mayor said to COPS, 'Come back and show me how to structure the board so that it will be accountable.' That's governance!"

Tom articulated what we heard from many citizens discovering their power: "City governments don't know how to govern. They may be able to keep things going. But they don't know how to bring people together, how to create something new." That's what Tom sees citizens doing.

Citizens Are Needed to Create Something New. In 1990, Shelby County Interfaith (SCI) in Memphis, Tennessee—an unusual, city-wide biracial coalition—held 437 house meetings involving six thousand people in order to create its "municipal agenda." "We then got thirty-five thousand signatures—thirty-five thousand people saying these are the things we want for our city," said SCI member Susan Penn.

SCI's agenda ranged from affordable housing initiatives to neighborhood boards for dispute resolution and decentralizing school decision making. SCI then succeeded in electing a school board and city council on which every member had committed to the SCI agenda. Additionally, both candidates for mayor pledged support.

But SCI did not sit back and wait for the board, the council, and the mayor to act on its agenda. Before the elections, they secured promises from candidates that they would join SCI in half-day retreats. The retreats would tackle the really important question: just how can these goals be *achieved?*

"So at the school board retreat," recalls SCI organizer Gerald Taylor, "we agreed on two goals: reducing class size and what we call 'independent public schools'—what others call school-based management. SCI also went to the full school board hearing. It was unanimous. All nine voted for school-based decision making."

After the vote, SCI began intensive face-to-face meetings with the teachers' union, principals, school staffs, and students. It developed 110 teams of five people each, trained to conduct what SCI calls relational meetings. "The teams visit the school," explained Gerald, "to discuss what their school should look like. Every school will have to develop its own framework for how it will operate as an independent school. The teams also asked students to be part of the visioning process by completing this sentence: 'I think the perfect school would be . . .'

"SCI expects to visit schools and interview five thousand teachers, auxiliary staff, and students," Gerald reported with justifiable satisfaction.

SCI—an organization of fifty-eight congregations and associations representing thirty-five thousand households from every economic stratum of Memphis—is drawing both officials and average citizens into a new way of governing. A new way of *self*-governing. "It's a wonderful process of doing politics a different way," said Susan Penn. "I get to sit across the table from my mayor or school board member. Now we start as equals. We get to know personal stories. We share our visions."

Citizens Create an Ongoing Place at the Table. Citizens like those of SCI in Memphis or KFTC are gaining an ongoing place in the decision-making process. Tim McCluskey, organizer with Valley Interfaith in South Texas, sums it up: "We want an ongoing place at the table so we're not always starting from scratch. We are transforming the political culture. Public officials don't make decisions unless they interact with us."

And Ernie Cortes, who supervises almost twenty church-based community organizations in the Southwest for the IAF (with which COPS, SCI, and Valley Interfaith, for example, are affiliated), puts it this way: "Our goal is not just to elect different candidates, but to get all candidates to start thinking differently—to change the culture of all politicians so they respond to the questions and agenda that we set."

So far we've explored ways citizens are creating new roles for themselves in governance. They are acting from their authority as citizens, not in any official capacity.

But as our culture begins to upgrade its notions of what regular citizens have to offer, some cities are creating new structures of government that *officially* recognize citizens' capacities and incorporate their voices. It's happening in at least two hundred cities as different as Portland and Birmingham. There's no blueprint. Each is experimenting with its own channels for official citizen participation—channels that enhance, rather

MOVING GOVERNMENT CLOSER TO CITIZENS

than just add another layer to, municipal decision making. These cities are trying to move government closer to the citizen.

Here we look at five cities—Seattle, St. Paul, Dayton, Birmingham, and Portland—that are experimenting with new public bodies to more directly involve citizens in self-government. Their experiments become laboratories of Living Democracy. For a quick survey of how these cities are innovating, look at the following chart showing the five cities' citizen participation bodies. In most cases, new city offices at the bottom link with elected councils dispersed throughout the city.

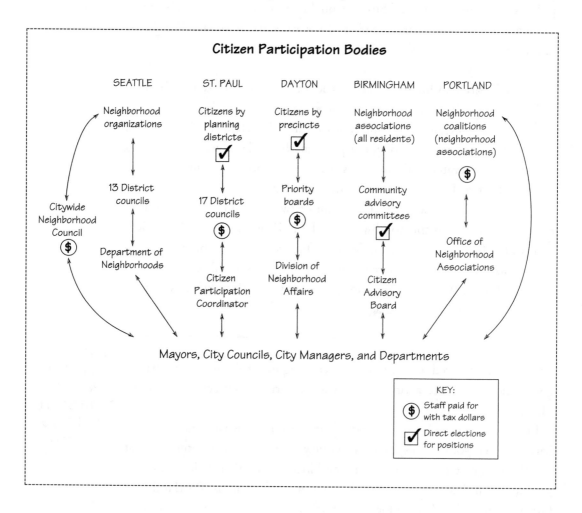

Citizen Participation Bodies

A City Involves Its Citizens

"I used to be an organizer," Jim Diers told us. "And we were always beating up on the city, and we always felt the city was beating up on us. . . . But we were always in a very reactive mode." Jim Diers now heads Seattle's new Department of Neighborhoods. "What this program attempts to do is give neighborhoods tools so that they can be much more *proactive.*"[11]

Jim's department, and the district council system it supports, emerged out of intensive citizen input beginning in 1987. Today, Seattle's mayor continues to lead the way. He's African-American, and half of the department's staff of sixty-eight are people of color—double the all-Seattle proportion—thus reinforcing the program's stated intent to involve those citizens who have previously been kept out.

The Department of Neighborhoods helped put in place thirteen district councils, corresponding to boundaries determined by neighborhood leaders. Membership is open to any community organization or business group. Seattle has over two hundred neighborhood organizations, some seventy-five years old, but historically they rarely collaborated. Seattle hopes its new district councils provide a forum to change that.

In some neighborhoods, particularly poor ones, however, few organizations exist to represent the citizens. So, Jim told us, his department's goal is also to provide special help to those low-income neighborhoods that are not well organized.

Your Views on District Councils

As you read about Seattle's district councils, ask yourself whether you want something like them in your city.

Do you feel that the distribution of city resources going to various neighborhoods in your city should be evened out, or that resources should be shifted disproportionately toward certain distressed areas? If so, would district councils be the way to do that?

What advantages might neighborhood-based district councils bring to your city?

We talked with Ellen Stewart, one of the people with whom Jim had worked in a previously unorganized neighborhood. Ellen told us she "was really not a joiner, but needed some sense of connection," so she went to Jim's office for help. She wanted to know how she and her friends could activate a community council in her neighborhood. "Using Jim's suggestions and reading materials," she said, "we got six people as a working group to plan a town meeting at the local school. After talks and speeches, we broke into small groups to identify neighborhood issues and needs. Group leaders wrote it all down. It was a good meeting, a *really* good meeting. There were over a hundred people! We evolved into a board meeting every other month, and a public meeting on alternate months."

Ellen explained how, from that first town meeting, the council became a catalyst for change. Previously, Ellen had not known there was any public housing in her neighborhood, but through her new community council she learned about its problems. She and her neighbors decided to assist Jackson Park Village residents to get a grant for a drug program. Ellen explained, "We got a three-bedroom unit in the project turned into an after-school center, and the Jackson Park Villagers hired a coordinator for a recreation program. Parents started an arts and homework program. And they were able to hook up with the local community center, which had never done *anything* for the low-income projects. So it really was the beginning of some wonderful things."

Ellen and Jim agree that the Department of Neighborhoods has been important both in Jim's help on the first town meeting and in the district council system's providing a structure to support residents who want to make things happen.

Citizen Groups Gain Access to City Funds

In Seattle, representatives of community groups now oversee $1.5 million each year in grants to neighborhoods, to be matched by the neighborhood organizations, either in cash or labor.

In a typical year, 125 matching-grant projects get funded, most in low- and moderate-income neighborhoods. With matching grants, citizens have taken on drugs and crime among youth, brought parents into their children's schools, created a homework center for underachieving children, built dozens of playgrounds, reforested ravines, created new parks, covered graffiti with beautiful murals, and much more.

On What Would You Spend City Money?

If you had access to city tax dollars for your neighborhood, what would you spend them on? What would be your three highest priorities?

1. _____

2. _____

3. _____

Who do you feel should make the decisions about how public money gets spent in your neighborhood?

_____

Do you believe your neighbors would be willing to decide the allocation of tax dollars in your neighborhood if they felt their voices would be heard and respected?

Yes_____   No_____   Your Reasons: _____

_____

Seattle's citizens also have a channel for directly affecting how tax dollars are spent. It's called the Neighborhood Budget Priorities Process. "Neighborhood organizations conduct surveys or community meetings to find out what people want in the budget, *before it's made up*," Jim Diers told us. In this process, the city gets about five hundred budget requests each year from neighborhood organizations. Typically, seventy-five percent are approved.

Little City Halls Bring Services into Neighborhoods

Seattle has also brought government closer to people—literally. A "little city hall" now sits in each district. "Officially called Neighborhood Service Centers, they help citizens access city services, including citizens who are intimidated by a big bureaucracy," Jim explained. The centers are also available for community meetings (this is where Ellen Stewart's first meeting took place). And most provide computers that community groups can use to produce flyers, newsletters, and mailing lists.

But Is New Power Being Generated?

Seattle's new district councils are unusual hybrids. They are officially recognized by the city to carry out certain tasks (like neighborhood-based budgeting), but their membership comes from non-governmental community groups. Through them, citizens may be developing new power, based on numbers of people, growing expertise, and relational self-interest. But one critical question remains: can a city government genuinely promote citizen-owned organizations—organizations that are not co-opted by the city but remain independent? At least some in Seattle believe they can; Ellen Stewart was quite adamant on this point: "The city people are encouraging a grassroots movement, and that is risky. We go down and testify at city council and at the budget priorities process and elsewhere, and sometimes we testify *against* the city. The whole purpose of our neighborhood movement is to hold the city accountable.

"I admire the city for creating little monsters [laughter] because they're helping groups that conflict, or may conflict, with their views. They are putting trust in people and saying that the people of this city have so much to contribute. And they are not dictating what or how we have to contribute. The city often walks into the unknown, and I really admire them for that."

A Service Center for You?

Write down your answers to the questions below.

Think of a few interactions you may have with public officials in a typical year. Would Seattle's concept of neighborhood service centers make your interactions easier?_____ Better? _____

Would such centers be likely to save public money? _____

Are they worthwhile, regardless of the cost? _____

Who in your city should research the advantages and disadvantages of decentralized service centers? _____

_____

What role could you take to get them to do that?_____

_____

Directly Elected Citizen Councils

Two decades before Seattle's innovations, St. Paul, Minnesota, developed its own district council system. But unlike in Seattle, where community groups send representatives to the councils, St. Paul's citizens *directly elect* members to its seventeen neighborhood district councils. Also unlike Seattle's system, each council is funded by the city, with its budget based on the size and financial needs of the community.

According to Jerry Jenkins, St. Paul's former Citizen Participation Coordinator, the system grew out of a widely felt need to move beyond an us-versus-them mentality. In 1972, the mayor appointed a blue-ribbon committee that produced a booklet called *Making Democracy Work*. The gist of its conclusions was that "to reestablish confidence in democratic government, we need to get back together through participatory planning," according to Jerry. "The city's planners wanted some way to actually talk to the folks they were planning for." Other needs motivated the change as well, says Jerry. "The city felt a need for a better communication system to send messages out to neighborhoods. . . . They also needed a systematized way for citizens to send messages back to city hall."

Think About Your City

How much divisiveness and deadlock is there in your local government?

How much confidence do citizens place in your local government?

How much interaction do you see between city officials and the people they represent?

Is planning accomplished, and are city services delivered, in a vacuum—without much input from citizens?

St. Paul's district councils serve at least three functions. First, they're an ongoing channel for citizen influence in all the city's major decisions affecting the neighborhoods. Second, every two years they involve citizens in choosing capital improvements for their neighborhoods. And, third, they sponsor citizen-initiated projects.

In these roles, the district councils have forced the city council to change its position more than once on big issues. Ann Copeland, Citizen Participation Coordinator, described this example:

> The University of Minnesota proposed a separate, elevated busway between St. Paul and Minneapolis. People were very upset with it. So citizens drastically affected the way it was built. There are no tremendous elevated bridges that were first proposed, and the parking isn't in a residential neighborhood. People don't mind what has been planned since the citizens got involved and changed the plans. And besides, they saved the taxpayers a lot of money because the new design is drastically less expensive than what was originally proposed.

People who are active see the difference these councils can make. They do have a lot of clout!

See How They Run

Despite America's overall disillusionment with government, many of us might consider running for positions on local councils. Fully 20 percent of us, according to a National Civic League poll, would consider competing for public posts—and of those people, most would run for city council or school board.[a]

If your city had district councils like St. Paul's, would you consider running for a position on one of them? Why or why not?

a. "Interest in Running for Office," a poll by the George H. Gallup International Institute on behalf of the National Civic League, Denver, Colo., 1990.

City Hall and Citizens: Can They Get *Too* Close? In Dayton, Ohio, thirty to thirty-five citizens elected by precinct sit on each of six priority boards, with a seventh board for the downtown business district.

Unlike St. Paul's councils, which get city funds to hire staff if they wish, each priority board in Dayton is staffed by at least three city employees. "The downside," argues Dean Lovelace, who worked with the boards for a decade, "is that the staff sees the city manager as boss. City hall will try to influence the results of priority board meetings. I left when the city put pressure on me to get my board to vote in a certain way."

Despite the control, Dean observes, "Priority boards make up their own minds anyway. Many of these people are critical thinkers. Half the seats are contested every two years. There really is good grassroots participation, pretty intense."

Here's how Dean assesses the impact: "Dayton is different because of the priority boards. Community representatives know what's going on in city hall and in their neighborhoods. Before, just a few people knew what was happening inside city hall; now three hundred to four hundred people know *intimately* what's happening. There's real power in opening up and letting folks know what's going on." Here Dean stresses the power of knowledge—the information that citizens gain through the system.

"I see myself as constructively critical of the priority boards system," Dean said. "For two years Dayton has been battling over a site for landfill in a black community. All kinds of citizens and all the priority boards are against the landfill, but the mayor is for it because the landfill company will give the city $26 million over ten years. A thousand people protested at city hall last week, but the city council will vote four to one against the people next week.

"Imagine! One hundred and twelve acres of landfill in a stable black community inside the corporate limits of Dayton! So people are cynical about priority boards because it can't stop this.

"Yet despite the problems, the process is highly valued," he continued. That's because the boards play formally mandated roles in planning, zoning, and other decisions. And they have a hand in allocating the city capital budget and federal grants. Each board meets monthly with the largest city agencies.

For Cilla Bosnak, superintendent of Dayton's Division of Neighborhood Affairs, the importance of priority boards is that they enable citizens to make the tough trade-offs that self-government is all about. She reported:

Last night the city task force concerned with all the city's capital expenditures met to consider proposals. It's made up of half city administrators and half priority board people.

Parks, Planning, and Fire submitted their plans for the next five years. Citizens who sit on the task force are getting the perfect opportunity to say, "Why do you need a $24,000 kitchen for the fire station? What value does it add to the quality of life in the neighborhood? Is it more important than the roof? What's the trade-off?" That may not be terribly exciting, but ask a citizen, "Should we hire a police officer or pave a street? Which is more important?" *Then* you get to the heart, the guts, of what governing yourself is all about."

With Which Do You Agree?

Common criticism	Cilla Bosnak's response
Priority Boards co-opt citizens, getting them to go along with what officials think.	"Citizen participation is just part of what government provides. People haven't been co-opted. Actually, it's the other way around: the system has been co-opted instead."

From Ninety-Nine Neighborhoods to the City Council. Birmingham, Alabama, has developed a very different approach to citizen participation. The city's ninety-nine neighborhoods elect officers to serve on twenty-three community-level boards. The community boards each send one person to the citywide Citizen Advisory Board, which meets regularly with top city officials. Its committees mirror the city council's, so that they can monitor the council's work very closely. This 99–23–1 system produces results similar to those we found in Seattle, St. Paul, and Dayton. But people in Birmingham underscore three changes in their city.

First, since the system was introduced in 1974, "every issue that affects a neighborhood really gets discussed at the neighborhood level first," Benjamin Greene, an assistant to the mayor, told us. "Any developer, for example, must make contact with the citizen structure before they even contact the city."

Second, because Birmingham was determined to bring young people into the process, in 1990 they lowered the voting age to sixteen for the citizen participation bodies. "Candidates campaigned in high schools like they did in their own neighborhoods," Benjamin explained. "This gets more youth involved . . . and lays the groundwork for more participation by youth later."

And the third result of this southern city's innovation is that resources have been significantly shifted. Benjamin, an African American, told us that he'd been there "before, during, and after" the system got under way. "I was from one of those areas that in the past did not have a pipeline to city government. Now people generally feel that they do have a pipeline." And, in fact, poor neighborhoods of color, devastated by years of neglect of basic city services, have received major infusions of capital improvements under the system.

Many people in Birmingham stressed that the process also serves as a training ground, bringing citizens into city government. "Four of the nine present members of the city council," Benjamin noted, "were at one time officers in the neighborhood citizen participation program."

Beyond Demands: Citizens Bring Solutions. Since 1978, Portland, Oregon, has been an innovator in promoting a strong role for citizens in self-government. That year the city amended its official city code to acknowledge a place for neighborhood associations in making the city work for them. Today, Portland distributes $1.5 million directly to seven independent, nonprofit organizations, with their own staffs and boards of directors. Their job is to encourage and support citizen participation and neighborhood crime prevention. The associations get funding from private sources as well.

"Citizen participation isn't something we do to enhance the way we do city business. It's not an add-on. It's the way we do business," says Rachel Jacky, who headed the Portland Office of Neighborhood Associations.

Over time, Portland's system of citizen participation degenerated into a lot of paper shuffling, Rachel told us, and some city departments weren't responsive enough to citizens' priorities.

So instead of just coming up with a laundry list of needs, the neighborhood association will now devise a comprehensive plan. "Portland is getting away from the customer service model in which the citizens simply make requests to government," Rachel explained. "That's passé. That's over with. Now everyone brings their piece of the solution to the table."

Now the city's goal is helping neighborhood associations come up with a coordinated plan, not just of needs but also of ways to meet them. That will mean everything from whom to call in city government and how to get private funding, to how to mobilize volunteer community resources. To gear up to this next stage means a lot of training, says Rachel. "That's what many citizens are looking forward to."

 Four Rewarding Roles for Citizens

Citizens are learning four rewarding roles—forming policy, budgeting, implementing, and evaluating—in order to govern themselves better. In each role, regular Americans are redefining the meaning of democracy as they discover their own capacities for solving their problems. Here are a few examples:

KEY GOVERNMENT FUNCTION			
Forming policy	**Budgeting**	**Implementing**	**Evaluating**
Moral Minimum Wage Campaign (California) Oregon Health Decisions (Portland, Oregon) Chattanooga Venture (Chattanooga, TN) Community policing (Baltimore, MD)	Neighborhood Budget Process (Seattle, Washington) Budget Priorities Process (St. Paul, MN)	Kentucky Partners Program— environmental protection (Kentucky) Shelby County Interfaith— education and jobs (Memphis, Tennessee)	Sonoma County Faith-Based Organizing Project— accountability sessions (Santa Rosa, CA) Brockton Interfaith sessions with public officials (Brockton, MA)
GUIDING PHILOSOPHY			
Citizens shape values and vision.	Taxpayers are in charge of public resources.	Civil servants are our employees.	The government must answer to us.
THE RESULTS			
Responsive, democratic policies and programs—Living Democracy			

Police Listen to and Work with Citizens

In this chapter we've been looking at how citizens are changing their relationship to government, and vice versa. For many citizens, however, the biggest challenge is reconceiving citizens' link to law enforcement. For policing is the most intimidating of government functions—the most distant and, especially for many people of color, the most unaccountable.[12]

The Baltimore County Police Department is widely recognized for initiating what is now called community policing in 1981, when citizens' fears had intensified in response to two terrifying murders. The chief of police brought on forty-five new officers. But instead of receiving standard training, these officers learned collaborative problem solving, conflict resolution, and how to gather and analyze information.

Community policing means more foot patrols and fewer squad cars. It means expanding the new training to all officers. "Our training includes how to interact with people, and how to work with and get help from different agencies. Now the entire Baltimore County Police Department goes through problem solving courses."

What do the police do when they see a neighborhood or housing project that has serious problems? Garden Village, a low- to-moderate-income housing complex, provides one example. "The people in Garden Village were living in terror," said Baltimore's Police Chief Cornelius Behan, "and their relationship with the government had so deteriorated that they had stopped reporting crimes."[13] But the police knew that without a citizen organization to work with they could do little. So, Officer Mark Steindler told us what they did: "We stayed in the background as much as possible. We even asked the president of another community organization to come in and donate a lot of time. We stayed in the background so it didn't look like we were controlling or running the show. And we weren't; *they* actually were, and they run it now."

Wannetta Thompson, president of what became the Garden Village Community Association, told us about her experience with community policing. "In June a year ago, we had a lot of crime in Garden Village, and it was increasing." So when the community policing unit wanted to try their approach, Wannetta said, "a few of us were willing to listen." She described what happened:

Our first meeting was June 28, 1991. The police talked to us about our concerns. They talked about developing a "tot lot" for the little kids. They talked about street cleaning. And dealing with gun control and missing kids. They *really listened* to our concerns. That is what we needed.

Gangs were definitely coming in. But with the police being here—walking through, knocking on doors (it was fantastic!)—the gangs really couldn't start up here. Between all of us, parents and everybody watching, and the police presence, the gangs had nowhere to go. They drifted away as fast as they were getting ready to come in.

Community Policing: Do You Need It?

Community policing can challenge some fundamental notions about what's required to maintain law and order.

Since you pay taxes, the police are your employees. Does it make sense to you for police to invest their time and energy developing closer relationships with people who live in high-crime areas—where their principal job, quite frankly, is to control crime?

Would *your* neighborhood be better served by community policing?

Where in your city do you think community policing would be most useful? Least useful?

What can you do to make known your views on community policing? Or to begin a dialogue in your community about new approaches to police work?

Roughly four hundred cities are following Baltimore's lead, or at least are experimenting with community policing. In 1992, when crime rates dropped in New York City for the first time in thirty-six years, the mayor and police commissioner credited the progress to community policing, which quadrupled the number of police officers walking beats.[14] Nationwide, roughly twenty thousand neighborhood crime watch groups, with eight to ten million volunteers, are collaborating with the police to make their neighborhoods safer.[15] The early results show that bringing citizens and their governments—in this case, even the police—closer together and having them listen to each other, can pay big dividends in the form of citizen safety and government effectiveness.

Official Citizen Participation Versus Independent Citizens' Organizations

Throughout our conversations with the people we've featured in this chapter, we've asked whether government-sponsored participation can undercut independent citizen organizing. Living democracy needs *both* more independent citizen organizations and more official citizen voice in decentralized structures of government. The latter need not detract from the former. In fact, government made more accessible through neighborhood-level councils can encourage more independent citizen action. That's the way it has worked in Seattle, Jim Diers told us. And both St. Paul's district councils and Dayton's priority boards, for example, have spun off independent, nonprofit community organizations.

But this clean distinction between independent citizen action and government-sponsored participation gets blurry when money enters the picture. Are community groups independent if they receive public funds? Can financial links compromise independence?

Yes, they can. Critics have charged that sometimes funds are taken away from a St. Paul district council because they "don't please the establishment." For us, the answer to whether public funds (or for that matter, private foundation or corporate funds) can compromise a citizen organization comes back to the question of *culture*—people's expectations about what's right and their willingness to stand up for it.

Rachel Jacky headed the Office of Neighborhood Associations in Portland. She tells a story of a citizens' organization, funded with city dollars, that challenged the city's desire to locate industry in fragile wetlands. The battle went to court and citizen pressure took the case all the way to the Supreme Court. The citizens won. Yet the city wouldn't consider withdrawing funds from the group, Rachel told us. In fact, "the city officials who were beaten ended up with grudging respect for citizens' expertise and how they amassed the technical expertise needed to win."

Rachel adds, "Yes, some strings are attached to groups' getting public funds in Portland. Getting public funds makes you responsible for getting the word out about things affecting your neighborhood. Also, it means you cannot be exclusive." In Seattle, a stipulation of being recognized by the city is that the district council cannot exclude any organization that seeks membership.

Thus for us, whether the two forms of citizen engagement—official and unofficial, inside and outside government—offer real opportunities for citizen influence depends less on a specific structure than on whether a "culture of democracy" is evolving. In a Living Democracy, responsibility and decision making are shared two-way and expected.

"My Faith in Democracy Got Stronger"

Through both independent citizen action and governmental bodies that draw citizens into decision making, communities across America are bringing democracy to life and addressing tough problems. In this chapter we've seen everyday citizens reject the notion of politics as a spectator sport, deciding instead that true democracy includes them in the game of governance. While their confidence in "politics as usual" is probably as low as the next person's, they don't feel the same way about democracy.

"My faith in democracy got stronger during the last decade," said Michael Garland, the first executive director of Oregon Health Decisions. Experience is teaching millions of Americans to appreciate the crucial role of citizen.

 Addressing Issues in Your Community

Pause for a moment to think of all the ways you are personally affected by decisions your local government makes—from the school board's decisions determining the size and curricula of schools to the housing and planning department's choices influencing the availability of affordable housing. What decisions do you care most about? Have the people in this chapter offered you any ideas your community could use to address issues of concern to you?

Think of people you know and organizations you take part in—your congregation, PTA, scout troup, tenant association, union, Rotary club, or community organization. What suggestions might you bring to them about how to bring democracy to life in your community?

9

Educating Real-World Problem Solvers

WHEN I CAME TO THIS SCHOOL, it was hands-on. It was more active, and my grades went up. Everything just made sense to me. It was fun to come here. At my old school we just listened to the teacher talk all day. Here we work in groups and we can talk to our friends in class. We learn through writing plays and doing projects. It's a whole different experience.

—Zawadi Powell
Senior, Central Park East
Secondary School
Harlem, New York

Everyone here thinks of it as *our* school because we make things happen here. I think that our school's process encourages people to participate more in democracy in our country when they are older because they are used to it here.

—Kate Madden
Freshman, ACS Public School
Ithaca, New York

These students are succeeding. Their schools are succeeding. But the dominant debate about how to fix our failing schools has yet to hear their voices.

Proposed "fixes" for schools in trouble have too often centered on national standards, higher teacher salaries, tighter security, more discipline,

Think About Your Schools

Write down your answers to the following questions:

- What's your impression of the quality of the schools in your community?
  _____

- What progress is being made to improve them?_____
  _____

- What additional changes would you like to see?_____
  _____

voucher systems, and more required time and courses in school. For the most part, these are a call to do *more*, or do *better*, what our schools have always tried to do.

And for that reason, these solutions are doomed. The world has changed radically. *More*, or even *better*, is not enough. In order to prepare young people for effective living in the modern world, today's successful schools are involving everyone who has a stake in education—students, parents, teachers, community residents, taxpayers, all of us. They are discovering the value of using democratic approaches in preparing students who will have to *think* for a living.

From the ground up, they are building on a long tradition of democratic schooling to reinvent education appropriate to our twenty-first century needs.[1]

In this chapter we peer into schools and classrooms that work and ask why they are so successful. We explore profound changes in school governance that are expanding the "ownership" of education. And we witness schools re-embedding themselves in the life of the community. We discover that at the very heart of their success is the creation of *a culture of shared responsibility*—the essence of Living Democracy.

The Problem with America's Schools

The world is changing, but America's schools are not meeting the needs that are flowing from these changes.

CHANGES IN TODAY'S WORLD	NEEDS THAT FLOW FROM THESE CHANGES	INSTEAD OF MEETING THESE NEEDS, OUR SCHOOLS . . .
Greater Diversity: More cultures and races interacting	Appreciation of diversity	Isolate students individually and from community life
Heightened interdependence	Understanding of relational self-interest and power	Seldom reward collaboration
	Interaction skills	Offer little training in teamwork and conflict resolution
Spreading Alienation: Growth of huge, distant, impersonal institutions	Opportunities for meaningful face-to-face relationships	Are large-scale and hierarchical; they separate, atomize, isolate
Growing magnitude and severity of problems	Skills to negotiate interests, hold others accountable, and solve problems	Provide little training in problem-solving skills
Decline of community institutions and family life	Schools as centers of community life	Remain islands, separate from community life
Accelerating change in: Technological development, information output and processing	Knowing how to learn and how to teach ourselves	Emphasize routine tasks, repetition, and retention of facts and figures

HOW DEMO-
CRATIC
IDEAS ARE
MAKING
SUCCESS-
FUL
SCHOOLS
—

Zawadi Powell's inner-city school suffers from all the problems of urban life. It's surrounded by poverty, drugs, and crime. In fact, Central Park East Secondary School (CPESS) should be failing like much of its East Harlem neighborhood, but it isn't. Why not?

The school's founding in 1984 grew out of district-wide changes that began in the mid-1970s. A farsighted district superintendent, concerned about growing numbers of dropouts and worsening school problems, allowed teachers and parents to innovate. Over time, says Deborah Meier, co-director of CPESS, new approaches to teaching emerged, including differing "styles of leadership, forms of governance, tone, and climate."[2] Pragmatic educators, embracing a trial-and-error approach, set out to create a learning community of *collaborators*—teachers, students, parents, and administrators. They decided their primary goal was not simply data-filled students but what CPESS teacher David Smith calls "independent thinkers"—young adults who are capable of shouldering responsibility and contributing creatively to our society for the rest of their lives.

Four Keys to Our Future

As we walked through the doors of CPESS, we immediately began to understand. Outside, in the hustle and bustle of New York's Harlem, we had been assaulted by graffiti and the urban ugliness typical of America's inner cities. But once inside CPESS, we relaxed. The building looked old but clean. The halls and classrooms were busy, not rowdy. Soon we learned

What's to Come

- How democratic ideas are creating successful schools and effective classrooms

- How teachers and parents are regaining "ownership" in education

- How schools are reconnecting to the life of the community

- How a new culture in democratic schools revitalizes rule-weary institutions four essential lessons—four keys to the future—that CPESS can share with all concerned Americans.

The First Key: Caring Relationships Create a Culture of Mutual Responsibility. CPESS co-director Debbie Meier believes no one can learn responsibility toward others when those others are anonymous. And big schools, often containing thousands of students, impose anonymity.

But if small schools are essential for building meaningful relationships, what can we do with America's enormous public school buildings? Just as the Empire State Building houses many corporations, says Debbie, so one building can house several schools. In CPESS's school district, fully fifty schools now inhabit nineteen buildings. CPESS itself will top out at fewer than five hundred students.

Small classes, in which students and teachers can get to know and appreciate each other, also seem out of reach, especially in a poor inner-city school like CPESS. Yet there are only eighteen students in a typical CPESS class, a feat accomplished in part by virtually doing away with administrators. Almost every adult at CPESS is a teacher.

Continuity of relationships is also consciously cultivated. Teachers stay with the same students for two years. And every teacher is also an advisor, meeting with the same eighteen students three to four hours each week. "My advisor is someone to help me organize my life and my class time, someone to support me and help me grow in every way, someone to make sure I don't get lazy and slack off," says Zawadi Powell, explaining to us why the daily advisory group is such an important part of her school life.

The Second Key: Shared Decision Making Creates Common Ownership. CPESS students learn decision making by doing it.

They assist each other in carrying out projects that make up the heart of the curriculum. And in their last two years they are responsible—with support—for designing their own educational program. They must demonstrate mastery in fourteen areas that make up the graduation requirements. One student serves on each senior's four-member committee that determines eligibility to graduate.

Students also share responsibility for discipline. "When some students stole money from other students," Zawadi said, "we felt we should have the power to deal with it. And we were given it."

Teachers at CPESS also shoulder more responsibility than in traditional schools. "The direction of the school, the curriculum, the assessment, are all in the hands of the teachers," David Smith explained. "I'm not just a cog that can be replaced." Teachers, like students, work collaboratively. In teams, they develop their own courses.

The Third Key: Learning Is Meaningful. A typical high school chops up the curriculum into fifty-minute periods of disconnected information. But at CPESS the curriculum is synthesized into just two blocks: humanities and science/math. Students stay long enough in each—two hours—to allow real depth. In David Smith's two-year combined seventh- and eighth-grade humanities class, one year the central question was: what is power through the focus of American history?

"We designed questions that were open-ended, with no right answer, so the students returned to the questions over a long period of time," David explained. "The class read about the American Revolution and the Civil War, focusing on those who were originally left out of the constitution and how they pushed themselves back in."

But regardless of the topic, what CPESS calls "the essential questions" guide student projects that usually cover several disciplines at once.

These questions "become part of your mentality," Zawadi revealed. "They are very important in thinking people who plan to be problem solvers." Continually asking such questions develops what CPESS calls "habits of mind" for lifetime learning.

Student progress at CPESS is judged not by multiple-choice exams but by the completion of collaboratively designed projects that demonstrate real mastery. In David's humanities class on the Civil War, for example, stu-

Some Essential Questions Asked at the Central Park East Secondary School

How do we know what we know? What viewpoints are we hearing, seeing, reading?

How are things connected to each other?

What difference does it make?

dents put together their own declaration of secession and then prepared and delivered a speech that Lincoln might have given to explain why he would go to war to save the Union.

The Fourth Key: Learning Is Connected with the World Outside of School. Part of the teacher-advisor's job is to get to know each student's family and include the family in supporting the student's learning. Class projects take advantage of New York City's vast learning resources, and each student contributes two hours of work each week in agencies that serve their community. "You start realizing the problems in the world and the role you can play in solving them," Zawadi explained.

In a city where only 50 percent of high schoolers graduate in four years, at CPESS it's over 70 percent. And of its first graduating class, almost all are college bound (Zawadi herself is on her way to Brown University).

Learning Democracy by Doing It

Even in its brief history, Harlem's CPESS holds intriguing lessons about educating for democracy. But another secondary public school, this one in Ithaca, New York, has two decades of experience in democratic education.

The Alternative Community School (ACS) has weathered many of the storms of public education in America: taxpayer revolts, budget cuts, mediocre (or even hostile) superintendents, and teacher burnout. Launched in the early 1970s with just sixty kids, ACS now includes grades six through twelve and has 260 students, with another fifty eager students on a waiting list every year.

Even browsing the ACS bulletin boards, as we did one bright May morning, the distinctly democratic character of the school is hard to miss. Most prominent was the agenda of the next All-School Meeting (ASM), where all students, faculty, and administrators gather to make important decisions. Nearby hung a cheery, step-by-step guide on how to bring a proposal before the All-School Meeting. Next to it was a teacher's proposal to make student participation in governing the school a required part of the curriculum. From outside came the laughter of students preparing for mud sliding and other fun as part of the one non-business All-School Meeting planned by the students each nine-week cycle.

Talking with the school's principal, Dave Lehman, we tried to understand what makes ACS work: "A sense of community is at the heart of any democratically run organization," Dave told us, echoing Deborah Meier's view at CPESS in Harlem. "Our community is built on what we call 'family groups,'" Dave declared. "These are ten or so students and a teacher who meet together at least twice a week. Our family groups ensure that no student will get lost in the shuffle. But there's an upper limit on the number of people who can be part of a school community. I think it's somewhere between 200 and 250."

Ninth grader Kate Madden told us, "You know everyone's name, and that helps give you a sense of community." And, adds Dave Lehman, "They know they're cared about."

At ACS, decisions aren't handed down from the principal. Four participatory bodies make the school's decisions. They involve students and teachers as well as members of the community.

"Do even major policy decisions go through these participatory bodies?" we wanted to know. The answer: "Absolutely, including requirements for graduation." Some years ago, students voted to *increase* the minimum requirements for graduation in order to make more room for "community studies"—their term for learning-by-doing in what might be called career

---

Democratic Decision Making at ACS

Who makes the decisions?

- The weekly **All-School Meeting (ASM),** made up of all students and staff. The student Agenda Committee is responsible for receiving proposals put before the ASM, preparing the agendas, and running the meeting.

- The **Advisory Board,** which includes four representatives each from the students, staff, parents, and community.

- Fifteen or so **student committees**, facilitated by faculty. They include the Review Board (or the disciplinary committee), the Student Rights and Responsibilities Committee (the "appeals" committee), and the Café ACS (which helps prepare and serve lunch).

- The weekly **staff meeting** of teachers and administrators.

explorations or mini-apprenticeships. Then, in 1990, students voted to add a community service requirement.

Students also initiated the proposal to require a special senior project—something each senior would present at the graduation ceremony. The students said they wanted to make their school "a cut above."

"The only role in which I have absolute authority is in staff evaluation," said Dave. "And here, too, I get a lot of feedback from students. A student committee collects students' views of their teachers' performance."

At ACS, students do not determine their own grades, but they are nonetheless key decision makers in the classroom. "The teacher presents the plan of what she or he wants to accomplish in the course, then asks the students, 'What do *you* want? How will we evaluate ourselves?' Students participate in helping to structure the course, in setting goals and criteria for themselves," Dave explained.

The school is so successful that not only has it attracted a long waiting list in its small city, but New York State's Board of Regents—not known for its flexibility—recently released ACS from several state regulations so that it might innovate further. And Dave is now a much sought-after advisor to other schools wanting to improve by using the enthusiastic cooperation of their students.

Dave Lehman stresses that what sustains ACS is more than a simple commitment to a democratic ideal—to the belief that you only learn democracy by doing it. "What also sustains us is that we experience democracy *working*," he says.

"I remember when our central administrator gave me a long list of changes I had to make," Dave continues. "I felt overwhelmed. How could I do it, given all our different options and course offerings? Instead of just believing it was *my* problem to solve, I took it to the All-School Meeting. I asked: how do *we* deal with it? A lot of new ideas came out. We pushed on, and we figured out together how to meet the demands without sacrificing our program.

"Our democratic process gets us through a lot of crises. It solves problems for us. People become believers. Sure, it takes a lot of talk, but it works."

Sharing Common Discoveries from the Ground Up

ACS in Ithaca and CPESS in East Harlem are special but not unique. Both schools confirm key lessons from highly successful, ground-up (as opposed

Four Common Discoveries: What Is Working in Today's Schools

From decades of experience in thousands of American schools, four lessons stand out:

1. **Building caring, collaborative relationships creates an environment for successful learning.** In Chapter Four, we challenged the common view of power as a one-way force. We said the source of *creative power* lies in relationships. It follows that successful schools and classrooms deliberately build collaborative, caring relationships. The creative power of students, teachers, and staff grows; the impersonal, competitive environment gives way to a community of common purpose.

2. **Students' interests shape the learning process.** The work is set up around the students, not around the teacher. And students learn by doing, not just listening.

3. **The community becomes a resource.** Student projects take on meaning because they are linked to real community concerns.

4. **In the process, academic learning is not sacrificed, but enhanced.** Educators who experience the results of democratic schools see no trade-off between educating for democracy and academic learning. Students discover that in democratic settings they are *more* likely, not less, to come to value traditional fields of study.

to nationally-mandated) school reforms. These improvements now involve thousands of schools nationwide, linked through a dozen or more networks.[3] Their experience suggests a rich, but still largely invisible, heritage on which America can build. Schools *can* restore excitement to learning when they become sites for developing our democratic public lives.

LIVING DEMOCRACY IN THE CLASSROOMS

Now we'll move from a focus on entire schools to explore what democratic *classrooms* look and feel like. Then we'll turn to the larger questions of democratic school governance and the relationship between school and community.

What's to Come

In successful classrooms, there is:

- Learning with a purpose

- Training for effective teamwork

- Democratic discipline

- Commitment to diversity as an asset

Kids with a Purpose: Project Learning

Educators throughout the country are asking: How can learning the basics—from reading and writing to math and science—become connected to the issues that really matter to students? How can excellent education be a by-product of their interests? Teachers associated with the Institute for Democracy and Education (IDE) express it this way: How can they and their students "make a difference now, not in some far-off future?"

Their answer is called *project learning*. When asked to describe project learning, teachers associated with IDE tell us it is:

- Hands-on—kids doing, not just listening.

- The work belongs to the kids; it's what they want to do.

- It ends with a product—something real—for someone other than the teacher.

- It's evolutionary; it may change its focus as the work goes on.

- Kids get a sense of fulfillment from it ("Hey, I did this!").[4]

Project learning responds to the increasingly appreciated truth that we retain about 10 percent of what we hear but about 90 percent of what we *do*. Five cases will give you a sense of what project learning is all about.

Case One: Sixth Graders Test the Town's Water Quality. Bill Elasky teaches a sixth grade in Amesville, Ohio. A few years ago, Bill's class read the book *Who Really Killed Cock Robin?*, all about a boy named Tony who tests the water in a nearby river. The children were intrigued. Not long afterward, it so happened, an oil company accidentally dumped solvent in the town creek.

The Environmental Protection Agency managed the cleanup, but Bill's sixth graders decided they "didn't trust the EPA." After much discussion, the class declared itself the "Amesville Sixth-Grade Water Chemists" and decided to use some of their class money on a water testing kit. Seeking advice from the local university and other expert sources, they set out to test the creek water themselves—and succeeded.

In the process, they learned to divide into teams, assign tasks, plan sampling and testing times, write letters, and digest a good deal of basic ecology and chemistry. They learned to make charts and maps. And they learned such arts of democracy as active listening, public speaking, negotiation, and compromise. They also learned strategic planning. "We learned we had to put one smart kid in each group," they told us. The class also produced a successful ad campaign to "sell" their testing services to local residents. After discovering an unhealthy bacteria count in the school secretary's cistern, they produced a public service announcement on the care of cisterns.

Some adults in Amesville were stunned at the students' initiative. So the sixth graders announced, "We think what we are doing is important and fun. The importance of this project is to let people know what pollutants are in the water. The fun is that we know we are helping others. You may think we are too young. Well, we are young. But we are trying our very best and it works. So put your trust in us."[5]

Case Two: Students Provide Voter Information. In Little Hocking, Ohio, teacher Kim Wile also wanted to try project learning—this time with an eighth-grade class and with more of an emphasis on social science. But how to begin? She knew the children's own interests had to motivate the project or it could not work. So when a conversation in reading class turned to the presidential primaries and a girl asked why people don't vote, Kim seized the moment. Students came up with ideas and recorded them on the board. Still, they wanted to know more and decided to prepare a voter survey. It went to four hundred people in their small town and became a springboard for action. The overwhelming reason the people of Little Hocking gave for not voting was that they did not know enough about the candidates or the issues. The students felt that national candidates got enough coverage, but not local candidates. So they set out to do something about it.

First, they decided to interview each candidate for county office and put together a pamphlet for voters. "I came to realize that nothing is more natural in a teenager's hand than a telephone," said Kim Wile.[6]

Naming themselves VIPs—Voter Information Persons—students volunteered to use their lunch hours and after-school time to type up the interviews. Their booklet, *Let Your Vote Be Counted*, went to 575 voters in the county. "The students' writing reverberated into further action," Kim explained. They volunteered to baby-sit for parents so they could vote; they composed ten public service announcements, which were broadcast on two local stations; and they convinced the local pizza parlors to include a notice about the upcoming election with each delivered pizza. The town of Little Hocking reported increased voter turnout, and the kids reported that they "felt proud to think that we played an important role in this." (Plus, Kim believes a large portion of her students will find their way to the polls when *they* reach voting age.) They've experienced Living Democracy.

Case Three: Teens Take on the Teen Pregnancy Crisis. The possibilities for building curricula based on community needs are nearly endless. Another high school class in Ohio took on the problem of teen pregnancy. They educated themselves by interviewing dozens of people in the community—from doctors and correctional officers to a teen mother. Then they approached the school board themselves for funds and published a booklet so well done that the local medical center, as well as the area schools, distributed it.

Their teacher, Nancy Corbett, admitted, "I tilted my head in disbelief" watching the students conduct themselves in interviews at the medical center. "These were the same young people I faced daily in the classroom, yawning over *Wuthering Heights*," Nancy marveled. "Student behavior in so many cases in this project showed me a maturity I hadn't thought possible in high school teens. We learned that democracy can really work—in a classroom or in a school board meeting."[7]

Case Four: Students Shape Environmental Policy. In the three cases above, project learning amounts to an activity completed in a relatively short time. But project learning can also involve the long-term collaboration of schools and public agencies.

In Fort Myers, Florida, you'll find the High School Environmental Education Seminar class—nicknamed the Monday Group. It all began in the early sixties when students organized a successful highway litter pickup. Then the students hit on what they thought was a nifty idea: hanging the county commissioners in effigy for their lack of environmental concern. That's when it dawned on teacher Bill Hammond that despite their exceptional environmental knowledge, these young people "did not know how to use the democratic process." Out of this realization came the Monday Group, with its goal of "helping students acquire and refine skills through practical experience in addressing significant community problems."

Principals from five area schools—four public and one private—sent some of their most promising students, as well as some of their most troubled ones, to participate in what became an all-day, every-other-week seminar on environmental concerns. It has continued for the past twenty-three years.

One Monday Group project saved an endangered swamp—the Six Mile Cypress, a 2,500-acre cypress stand on the edge of Fort Myers—from developers. Carefully prepared, the students convinced the county commissioners to place a referendum on the ballot asking Lee County taxpayers to foot the bill to acquire the swamp. The students educated the public, and the referendum passed with the highest plurality ever on a county tax issue.

After their success, the students realized their work was still not done. The County Parks and Recreation Department, it seemed, had no staff to plan the newly acquired park. So the Monday Group took on the challenge of designing a master plan for the Six Mile Cypress Swamp. These high school students became the technical assistance arm of the County Parks and Recreation Department. Each year's class continues to take on a new community problem or issue.

The Monday Group students not only learn natural sciences but key arts of effective public action. Bill Hammond, the initiator of the Monday Group, stresses that the students' "operating rules" flow from the "principles of diversity, change, and interdependence," which can be observed in the natural world. Instructors act as facilitators, committed to ensuring that students enjoy "equal access to all viewpoints and positions."[8] In other words, real dialogue is promoted and creative controversy is encouraged.

The Class Commandments of the Monday Group

- **Take only positive positions.** *Be for a solution rather than being against proposed solutions. Share your vision for solving the problem.*

- **Do your homework.** *Read on the subject, interview experts, study until you know enough that others view you as an expert or at least well informed.*

- **Eliminate stereotyping—individualize.** *It is too easy to lump others together. He or she is a "developer," "environmentalist," "politician." Stereotypes prevent real understanding—instead treat everyone as an individual who really matters.*

- **Keep a balanced view—empathize.** *Examine all sides of an issue. Try to see the issue from the viewpoint and feelings of others who may not agree with you. Try to "walk in their shoes" by talking to them to understand why they see things differently than you do.*

- **Probe the force field.** *Know who is involved in the issue. Design your action plans and strategies to accommodate their interests if possible. When you encounter a "block," back off, reconsider your options, and implement your revised plan.*

- **Eliminate scapegoating—accept responsibility.** *When you don't succeed, don't blame others. Accept that you and your team did not do everything needed. So look at the process again, tune it up, and recycle through it. Each time you start from a stronger, more knowledgeable position than the last effort.*

- **Recycle—BE PERSISTENT.** *Try, try again! Never, never, never give up! (Winston Churchill). Difficult problems do not usually happen overnight. It often takes time, sometimes even years of persistent action, to solve them.*

Source: Bill Hammond, "The Monday Group: From Awareness to Action," Secondary Schools Activity Guide, Project WILD, Salina Star Route, Boulder, Colo. 80302, 1983. Reprinted with permission.

Case Five: Kids as Planners. Every five years in Maine, each governmental unit—from school district to city building department—is required to project the need for its services for the next five years. To Marvin Rosenblum, a veteran educator, youth are a "municipal resource" to do the vital tasks involved in that planning. So he helped organize Kids as Planners.

In one project, grade school students use satellite photographs and computers to identify the borders of the city of Bath. By foot, they figure out the meaning of each color of the satellite photograph and then determine the area's physical characteristics. "A young person walking in [to a planning meeting] with that kind of data is making a major contribution to the town and saving the town significant expense," notes Marvin, who now works with the Maine Office of Community Development.[9]

Other students in Kids as Planners have worked closely with a developer to make sure construction near a pond would not destroy community access. Still others do what Marvin calls "garbology"—studying the waste stream to find out what can be recycled. "Why not *practice* civics instead of just learning about it?" he asks.

These five cases suggest the far-reaching implications of project learning, just one effective practice in democratic classrooms. These young people are offering practical benefits to their communities, while gaining knowledge and skills. Project learning connects the learning process to their interests and needs.

Learning Teamwork for Lifelong Effectiveness

Project learning means making decisions *with* others—teamwork. It involves virtually all the arts of democracy we describe in Part Three. But in most classrooms, teamwork is virtually forbidden. Lecturing is still the norm—in fact, it still accounts for 90 percent of instruction in America's schools. As several leading advocates of cooperative education put it, "At a time when being able to interact effectively with other people is so vital in marriages, in families, on jobs, and in committees, schools insist that students don't talk to each other, don't work together, don't pay attention to or care about the work of other students."[10]

The evidence is in, and it's overwhelming: More than five hundred research studies now report that students learn better when they work cooperatively.[11]

And this truth is starting to catch on. What's often called *cooperative learning* is gaining currency among educators. Typically, this phrase is used to describe any process in which small groups, instead of individual students, are responsible for completing tasks. But working in groups is *not enough*, argue researchers at the Cooperative Learning Center at the University of Minnesota. Students learn better in groups than they do working individually only when certain key conditions are met.[12]

On the accompanying chart, we contrast the features of effective team learning with the traditional notion of group learning in which students are

Two Approaches to Group Learning: A Comparison

TRADITIONAL LEARNING GROUPS	EFFECTIVE LEARNING TEAMS
No interdependence.	Positive interdependence (members need each others' contributions).
Little face-to-face interaction.	Lots of face-to-face interaction.
No individual accountability.	Individual accountability.
Homogeneous.	Mixed membership: gender, race, aptitude.
One appointed leader.	Shared leadership.
Responsible only for self.	Responsible for each other.
Only the task is emphasized.	Both the task and maintaining the group are emphasized.
Teacher ignores groups.	Teacher observes and supports.
No reflection or evaluation by group.	Group reflects and evaluates its process regularly.
Interaction skills assumed or ignored.	Interaction skills taught directly.

Source: Adapted from David W. Johnson, Roger T. Johnson, Edythe Johnson Holubec, and Patricia Roy, "What Is the Difference?" in *Circles of Learning*, Association for Supervision and Curriculum Development, Alexandria, Va., 1984.

simply assigned to groups with little structure or guidance. As this chart suggests, effective team learning requires attending to the structure and process of the group.

Cooperation is itself a set of *learned* skills, the Cooperative Learning Center's research clearly shows. For cooperation to work, teachers must teach these skills with all the deliberateness they use to convey academic content. The Center develops curricula for successfully teaching a wide range of interactive skills, including decision making and the creative use of conflict. In one classroom, first graders learn eight skills throughout the year, including "sharing ideas and materials" and "giving directions without being bossy."[13] These skills develop the democratic arts of listening and negotiation, essential in a Living Democracy.

Democratic Discipline

Teachers are learning that even very young children can not only help make the rules but enforce them, too. Instituting democratic discipline means the students themselves hold class meetings to reason through the rules needed to make the classroom work well.[14]

For eighteen years at Schaefer Elementary School in Tappan, New York, children have taken responsibility for their school by serving on the Due Process Board. They don't make decisions, but they do issue opinions about the fairness of the treatment a child receives. The Due Process Board can also hear cases brought by one student against another. In these cases it can even determine consequences.

Here's just one example of the kinds of challenges these elementary students have resolved effectively: A few years ago a youngster was caught drawing swastikas on the books of Jewish students. Students brought him before the Due Process Board. The offender, Raymond, "seemed unable to tell them why he had been doing this," explained principal JoAnn Shaheen. So the board finally decided the only reason someone would do this is that they didn't understand Nazi mentality and its consequences. When Raymond admitted he didn't understand, a Jewish child who had lost his grandparents in the Holocaust volunteered to help Raymond research and write a paper on Hitler and Nazism. "Months later," JoAnn told us, "when a little first grader was drawing swastikas, it was Raymond who came to my office to ask if he might teach him about Nazism."[15]

"The mistake we make in this country," JoAnn Shaheen concludes, "is that we keep thinking kids need to be older to take on the big ideas—justice, fairness, equality—the landmark ideas of our country." But JoAnn's experience tells her something quite different: "You can teach fairness to seven- and eight-year-olds like you can never do later."

Diversity Becomes an Asset

By the year 2000, one in three Americans will be a person of color. And the last decade of this century finds our country with an influx of new Americans as large as the migrations we experienced during the century's first decade.

If our schools spread the message that diversity is only a *problem* to be coped with, our children will also see it that way. But to create a function-

Key Elements of Democratic Classrooms

Teaching methods change
Dialogue replaces one-way instruction.

Learning is student motivated.

Teamwork is taught.

The community becomes a text
Problem solving is in the real world.

Students see the impact of their learning.

The curriculum expands and deepens
Skills of active citizenship are taught.

It builds on the diverse cultures of students, using diversity as an asset.

A culture of democracy grows
Students shape rules and help enforce them.

Both students and teachers are accountable for learning success.

Caring, collaborative relationships replace anonymity.

ing democracy in the midst of such rich diversity, young people must be encouraged to find value in that diversity. Classrooms with children of diverse cultures and languages present opportunities as well as challenges. In a democratic classroom, differences among students offer the possibility of sharing family histories, knowledge, and culture that add life to the study of geography, social studies, the arts, languages, and humanities.

"The democratic classroom assumes that *everybody* brings differences to it—and that includes the 'mainstream' kids," says education professor Terry O'Connor. When classes use student input in planning and working on the curriculum, "the classroom becomes as good as the sum of all its members, rather than as weak as its weakest link," he adds.

Language differences can be among the learning tools. At the public elementary Fratney School in Milwaukee, all students—not just those of Hispanic origin—become bilingual in Spanish and English. Native speakers in each tongue become teachers and learners. And at Theodore Roosevelt High School in the Bronx, Hispanic students teach Spanish to their teachers and other school staff.[16]

How You Can Spread the Influence of Good Ideas

Check off the democratic themes that seem best for your local schools.

☐ Project learning

☐ Teamwork

☐ Democratic discipline

☐ Treating diversity as an asset

Will you introduce these ideas at a PTA meeting? In a discussion with the principal of your school? With one or more teachers? With students you know?

Will you send this chapter to members of your school board or the head of your local teacher's union?

What about talking over these ideas with your children?

For information on reprinting this chapter, please contact the Jossey-Bass Inc., Publishers Permissions Department (see the copyright page in the front of the book for details).

Ethnic diversity is but one type of difference among children that can be treated either as a problem or an opportunity. Differences of learning ability are another. Earlier we introduced you to the Amesville Sixth-Grade Water Chemists. Placing children with varying abilities on the same teams changed their class dynamic. One student described the impact this way: "It used to be that there were two groups in our grade: the tough kids and the smart kids. And we sat in different parts of the room and didn't do anything together. Like even on the playground, we didn't play together. When we were together, we fought. But not this year. . . . Right, we play together and everything. 'Cause in class we're all working together on projects and helping each other and you can't tell who's smart or who's tough or whatever. . . . Yeah, we're like a real team, you know?"[17]

As adults in the real world, we're required to relate to people of varying abilities at work, in our families, and in our communities. How can we prepare our young people for effective participation in such a world if we segregate them during twelve of their most formative years?

LARGE-SCALE CHANGE: WHO OWNS THE SCHOOLS?

At the beginning of this chapter we focused on democratic *schools*. And in the last few pages we've looked at *the classroom*—at the students' experience of practicing Living Democracy as they take responsibility for their own learning. But each classroom and school exists within a larger culture—within the school district and the larger community. Can democratic learning in the classroom be sustained within a larger structure that remains authoritarian? Of course not.

Across the United States, invisible to most of us, bold democratic experiments are under way. They may or may not use the language of Living Democracy, but in fact their aim is to democratize the culture in which our children learn: to bring all the stakeholders—teachers, parents, students, administrators, community members—into the decision-making process. Many promising—and some quite dramatic—reforms began in the 1980s.

That American schools are failing so utterly is itself igniting courage. "People ask me if this reform is going to work," one Chicago elementary principal told us. "I don't know," she said, "but I do know that nothing was working that we were doing before." In Chicago, as in many cities, desperation, not mere necessity, has become the mother of democratic invention in education.

Schools Shuck Top-Heavy Bureaucracy

In 1991, Denver teachers signed a new contract after sixty hours of public hearings and innumerable meetings. The contract announced "a new way of doing business in the Denver Public Schools. The heart of this new world was collaborative decision making."[18] Denver—like public school districts in Dade County, Florida; Rochester, New York; Chicago, Illinois, and dozens of other cities—decided to decentralize decision making. Now *school-based management* replaces top-down authority.

Although the decision-making structures vary from city to city, in each case reformers are reacting to fifty years of increasingly centralized authority. Over the last five decades, the average size of American school districts has grown ninefold. Top-heavy bureaucracies have assumed ever-greater power over the management of schools, from instruction to tenure. By the 1980s, in Rochester, New York, there was one administrator for every eight teachers. "That means there are more school administrators in New York state than in all of Western Europe," bemoans Adam Urbanski, the outspoken president of Rochester's teachers' union.

For Adam, reform means flipping the decision-making pyramid upside down. Before Rochester's reform, everyone—students, teachers, principals, superintendent—answered to those above, those one step higher up the pyramid. And parents were left out altogether. Instead, Adam wants to see educators and administrators accountable to those "below"—those they serve.

But an inverted pyramid may not be the best metaphor. The democratic breakthroughs now spreading authority down and throughout America's school systems are creating accountability that flows in *both* directions. The principals we met, for example, are accountable not only to those "above" in the central office but also to teachers and parents and students.

In some cases, the impact of these changes is immediate. Take principal Madeleine Maraldi's school, where 90 percent of the students are poor. When the reform process began, their reading scores ranked in the bottom fifth of Chicago's schools. Freed to design her own budget, Madeleine now allows each child to buy a book at a bookstore five times a year for the class library. "When we bring the children out to a public place, they see adults purchasing books. This is best thing we could have done. And it's so simple!" the principal declared. After all, a child who gets to purchase a book is likely to value it—and read it. Allowing children to enter the world of adults who treasure books, and to make their own choices, was just one of several innovations that in a year moved her students from the bottom fifth to the top quarter in citywide reading scores.[19]

Empowering Teachers

Most students believe teachers have lots of power. But, in truth, the factory model of education allots teachers very little. They just work the learning assembly line. Screw on some science here, attach a little math there, pound in a little history, and out comes a shiny new graduate. Teachers aren't co-creators of a process; they are simply conveyors of mandated data.

But all this is changing as schools incorporate democratic practices. In Chicago, teachers now help hire and fire principals, as well as help determine curricula, through their representatives on the new local school councils. In Rochester, school-based management teams—with teachers in the majority—interview the applicants for every principal's job and recommend three top candidates to the superintendent, who makes the final decision.

Rochester's reform emphasizes the transformation of teachers into professionals—not factory hands—who are then entrusted to develop their own curricula and participate in school governance. Teachers are free to develop interactive, student-motivated approaches that truly engage the students.

Democratic reform begins what some call a shift in focus, from *what is taught* to *whether students are learning*. The consequences of such a shift are threefold: First, teachers are freed from very long lists of requirements. They can personalize their teaching, to discover what actually works. And second, holding teachers accountable for their students' learning means taking seriously the training and evaluation of teachers. That's why Rochester created a Peer Assistance and Review Program, in which experienced professionals serve as "lead teachers." They are mentors for both new and failing teachers, and they help develop curricula and training programs. "Some of our best teachers are responsible for improving their colleagues or getting them out," reports Adam Urbanski in Rochester.

Third, teachers are increasingly expected to attend to the *whole* child, not just the learner in the classroom. For example, Rochester's reform explicitly expands the role of the teacher to become the student's counselor as well. Its Homebase Guidance Program assigns a diverse group of twenty students to each Homebase teacher. "The same teacher provides a consistent focal point in each student's day, every day, every year the child is in school," states the official program design. The goal is a caring adult for each student—even if the teacher has to go to the student's home.

For many teachers, assuming such responsibility was not what they bargained for when they decided on a career in teaching. Some in Rochester were downright scared to go into the poor neighborhoods of their students. "I guess I had a certain amount of reservation about this, as well as fear, because no one ever taught me how to do this," teacher Walter Jahnkhe admitted.

Adam Urbanski says, "Empowerment is not enough. Enabling is necessary." What he is getting at is that teachers, like the rest of us, have to *learn* democracy. Because we grow up in a hierarchical, authoritarian culture, we don't get to practice the arts of democracy—active listening and negotiating, for example, or creative conflict.

Teachers in Dade County, Florida, discovered this quickly. When team decision making came to Myrtle Grove Elementary School, teacher Carla Rippingill said it was like having a committee drive the principal's car: "We all got our driver's license, but no one told us how to drive."[20]

In Part Three we explore some of the arts of public life such training must address as we create a Living Democracy. We hope you'll want to learn them, employ them, and share them.

Parents Gain a Voice

The growing evidence is undeniable: involved parents, especially at the grade school level, contribute enormously to a school's success. In Fort Worth, Texas, Morningside Middle School powerfully confirms this truth.

Three years ago, Morningside's academic performance ranked twentieth—at the very bottom of the city's schools. Morningside serves a very poor community plagued by drugs and violence. "Far more than half the families are on welfare," principal Odessa Ravin told us. "There was lots of apathy. More than 70 percent of the kids were labeled 'at risk.' We had no parent volunteers at all."

Then school officials and community people, working with the citizen organization Allied Communities of Tarrant (ACT), decided to stop just worrying and start doing something. They hoped that by turning parents into true stakeholders in their children's school, they could ignite positive change.

Soon they discovered that just having a teacher visit a parent didn't produce much. Many parents felt intimidated by their first experience of having a professional in their living rooms. Odessa explained how they made the process work: "We set up teams. We grabbed a few parents and trained them. Teams with one parent and one teacher visited over 75 percent of the kids' homes in one year. We talked about what was happening with their child, with the school, and how they could gain access to us. We told them there was training available for them, and that they could serve as volunteer receptionists or lunch room monitors. Now—from nothing, from not being involved at all—parents fill twenty-five advisory posts."

This proud principal recited several measures of dramatic change that took place in only three years: Morningside now ranks third in the city's test scores. Almost 90 percent of students now pass the state writing skills test, compared to only one-third just three years ago. And police visits to the school, which were as frequent as two or three a day, are now virtually zero all during the school year. And it's not unusual for 200 parents to attend a PTA meeting.

During this same period, Morningside established a school-based management team—with three parents, three teachers, one non-parent community member, and the principal. "But parental involvement is more important than anything else for our success," Odessa Ravin is convinced.

She stressed not just the effect on students but the impact on parents when they get involved. "What parents get out of this is enabling. We African Americans sometimes come to believe that because we are poor in material goods, we are poor in spirit. That we have little to offer. Involved parents learn to break this equation, to see how *much* they have to offer."

In this chapter, we've moved from how children learn to how schools are governed. We've shown how, when parents gain a say in the life of the school, they are enabled to contribute to their children's success. Moreover, in successful schools, the school and the community re-link. Each becomes a resource for the other.

SCHOOLS RECON-NECTING TO THE COMMUNITY
—

The Town as Text

In many of the classrooms successfully engaging young people, the community itself becomes a learning lab. Remember Marvin Rosenblum, the instigator of Maine's Kids as Planners? He argues that "there really are very few subjects that could not be appropriately learned in the community itself. History, geography, social studies, architecture, the arts, the sciences are all part of a look at a complete community."[21]

Using the "town as text" provides rich opportunities for civic learning, but the current language of community service often confuses public discussion of these opportunities. Hundreds of schools, and even whole school systems in Atlanta and Detroit, now mandate community service. In 1992, Maryland became the first state to require it.[22]

Unfortunately, the language of service carries the notion of charity, of "doing for" the less fortunate. Little wonder that in Bethlehem, Pennsylvania, a group of parents sued the school board over mandatory community service.[23] How could anyone justify coerced altruism, they asked? Isn't that a contradiction?

Yes, it is. What's appropriate is not for schools to require acts of charity but for schools to provide opportunities for community-based learning, just as Marvin is doing.

Elementary, junior high, and high schools, as well as more and more colleges and universities, are developing learning programs in the civic arts that involve students in the community. At Rutgers University in New Jersey, a civic education course is now as necessary to graduate as English. The course requires teamwork and experiential learning, with community involvement as one option. And a number of small colleges—Franklin College in Indiana and Tusculum College in Tennessee, for example—are working creatively to make civic education integral to their missions.

At the University of Pennsylvania, students are not just sent down from the ivory tower to do good work in the impoverished community. The university has slowly built partnerships with community groups, labor unions, schools, and local government. These partnerships activate students, faculty, and the community members to address some of the most daunting problems of inner city poverty.

Town as text also suggests the possibility of students experiencing the real world of work. At ACS Public School in Ithaca, New York, junior high

Community Service Versus Civic Arts Learning

	Community Service	Civic Arts Learning
Primary value for students	Making students "better people"—more altruistic and empathetic	Learning the arts of public life and building knowledge
Program direction	School faculty and staff	A partnership between school and community
Function	Service to others	Collaborative community problem solving

school students work in such places as a veterinarian's office, a lawyer's office, or city hall. And high school students earn math credit by doing bookkeeping and accounting at the local credit union, or English credit by writing at the local newspaper, or art credit by working with a potter in an actual potter's studio.

Neighborhoods Reclaim the Schools

"Historically, most neighborhoods grew up around a school," Jim Diers, head of Seattle's Department of Neighborhoods, reminded us. And recreating the school as a center of neighborhood life is what motivated Seattle's Community Schools Program. In Chapter Eight you read about the strides Seattle is making to renew democracy in its neighborhoods. Schools, Jim says, are playing a key role. Here's how:

Many schools are now open at night for lots of community activities. School parking lots have even been torn up and turned into community gardens. Neighbors have created urban wildlife sanctuaries around schools. School and community interests have joined together to rebuild playgrounds for the benefit of both.

Some neighborhoods have started involvement projects for parents. Many community schools have youth recreation programs, computer cen-

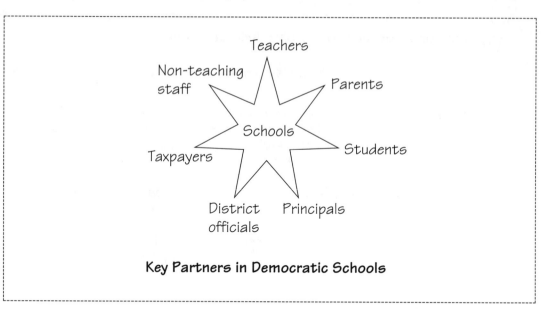

Key Partners in Democratic Schools

ters for people who need to learn, adult training programs, homework centers, dropout learning centers, urban gardening programs, and so on.

On the other side of the continent, Philadelphia offers rich lessons on what it means to reconnect schools with the life of the community. Through partnerships with the University of Pennsylvania, mentioned above, nine public schools in poverty-stricken west Philadelphia are now open for a wide variety of community uses, including Saturday and evening classes for adults. The goal is schools open twenty-four hours a day, year-round. Because schools belong to "all the members of a community," they can become "catalytic hubs" for addressing community problems and guiding renewal, argues Professor Ira Harkavy, a founder of Philadelphia's program.[24]

Businesses Create New Links to Schools

Businesses are also discovering possibilities for constructive ties to schools, beyond charitable handouts. Here are just three examples:

- Polaroid offers teachers a paid "sabbatical" with the company. The company gains from the new perspectives the teacher brings to the job; the teacher gets recharged and acquires new skills.[25]

- Several corporations in Chicago have offered their companies' trainers to local school councils that need help preparing new decision makers.

- In Baltimore, the business community has been a full partner with citizen organizations and educators in designing strategies to improve the city's schools. Every student with a 95 percent high school attendance record is guaranteed three job interviews among the 150 participating businesses. Those not offered jobs get additional training and more job referrals.[26]

Before leaving our discussion of democratic schooling, we want to repeat a core theme of this book: democracy is not just about changing the rules; it's also about changing the culture—our attitudes, values, and expectations.

In Rochester, Marc Tucker, who works at a think tank that focuses on schools, put it this way: the aim is to transform a school system that is "overwhelmingly bureaucratic, and hostile to fresh ideas," into one that welcomes them.[27]

America's traditional authoritarian culture can be comfortable, even as it fails. But Living Democracy requires more. Teacher Kim Wile from Little Hocking, Ohio, claims, "Actually, it is much easier to be [the one] in control of the class. Democracy can be an untidy and challenging business. I felt quite comfortable in the traditional role of the directive teacher. It is far more nerve-racking to take the back seat and let the students take the reigns of control, but it is entirely worth the effort, because the rewards of watching the students' pride, excitement, and growth are so great."[28]

With greater self-determination for teachers, parents, principals, and students comes greater responsibility—and accountability. Within these promising, diverse reforms, that theme is constant. Principals and teachers who gain greater freedom to make choices as professionals, rather than

A NEW, REVITALIZED SCHOOL CULTURE

- Bureaucracy
- Authority
- Hierarchy

⟹

- Self-determination
- Freedom

⟹

- Mutual responsibility
- Accountability

The Democratic Shift in Values

Taking Action to Change Schools

Based not on pipe dreams but on what you have seen is already under way, how can you make change happen? What are your sources of power to ignite change? Recall all the many sources of power we've cited that often go untapped. Your ideas can be a source of power for change, too. What ideas in this chapter do you want to talk about with others? Write them down.

_____

_____

_____

_____

_____

With whom can you share your ideas?_____

_____

_____

_____

_____

What meeting can you attend—or pull together—in order to build interest and a common vision? _____

_____

_____

_____

_____

What first step can you resolve to take during the next week? _____

_____

_____

_____

_____

being on an education assembly line, must also make themselves accountable for *results*. (In the first year of education reform, for example, about a
third of Chicago's principals lost their jobs.) And parents can no longer
simply blame the schools. Their participation appears essential to success.
Students, too, can no longer slip by, content to memorize, repeat, and forget what the teacher said. They must demonstrate mastery through projects
they directly shape.

Throughout this chapter, we've seen how democratic practices link freedom with responsibility in some of America's most effective schools. Here's
how Principal William R. Renauart in South Miami describes the effect on
his school: "We would never go back to the old authoritarian ways of doing
things. . . . Just like Eastern Europe, we have tasted the exhilaration of freedom and the creative urge that goes with it. It takes time to learn to make
freedom improve your life, but after four years of school-based management, life is better. We will never go back."[29]

PART THREE

Living Democracy: The Practical Tools

I N THIS FINAL SECTION, comprising Chapters Ten through Thirteen, we probe the heart and soul of democracy. We answer two key questions: What are the skills we need in order to interact with each other in public life—so that we can solve our problems effectively? And how can we build the qualities of character that will create the kind of public culture America so desperately needs?

Culture? Qualities of character? Good Lord, where are we going on this journey?

Please give us a moment to explain the concept of public culture by looking elsewhere, outside the United States.

From 1989 onward, we Americans marveled at the staggering pace of change throughout Eastern Europe and the Soviet Union. Communism's political institutions—seemingly as rigid and immovable as the mammoth steel and cement structures that housed them—simply collapsed. Command economies gave way to the market. Secret police were disbanded. And the world celebrated when democracy seemed to be breaking out all over.

Yet as the 1990s wore on, and the euphoria wore off, it became clear that behind these highly visible structural changes, the reality of people's daily lives was *not* altering nearly so quickly—at least, not in positive ways. Not only did these societies appear unable to solve their problems, several dissolved into bloody conflict. The formal institutions could change dramatically, but that was not enough. Something else was needed.

But what is that something else? It's amorphous, to be sure. It's not near-ly as clear-cut or visible as the structures of government or the rules of an economy. Nevertheless, that something else may be just as important to democracy as the rules on the books.

We call what's needed the *culture of democracy.* Sometimes we think of it as "the spirit of a truly free people."

To a large extent, the culture of democracy is a set of expectations. How will we behave toward each other? What can we expect from our fellow cit-izens? What do officials expect from us? What norms are most important to us? What are the unspoken rules that we just assume will be followed in our daily interactions with ordinary people and with those in authority?

In Part Two we visited people from all walks of life who are changing the culture of their institutions—from workplaces and newspapers to ser-vice agencies and schools. They're helping to shape a democratic culture that offers them much greater rewards.

Compared to Americans who work in authoritarian settings, they are different people, these Americans learning to live their democracy. They have different skills, different values, different expectations. They seem to have a different spirit, and, yes, they have developed different qualities of character.

We suspect that what's most important about them is that *they know how to get things done* in their public lives. That effectiveness and its rewards help to build and strengthen the personal qualities that, in turn, make them even more effective.

So we welcome you to continue with us on this unique journey. Explore the skills—the arts of democracy—that are required for this enhanced effectiveness in public life. In Chapter Ten we discuss the skills most often used in one-on-one interactions: active listening, creative conflict, media-tion, and negotiation. Chapter Eleven focuses on skills most often used in group settings: political imagination, public dialogue, public judgment, cel-ebration and appreciation, evaluation and reflection, and mentoring. In each of these chapters on the democratic arts, we suggest practical guide-lines to help you develop these skills and provide real-life examples of how these skills have been put to good use.

Then, in Chapter Twelve, we'll explore the Democratic Self. Here we reflect on those qualities of character you may choose to cultivate in order to enhance your life. And finally, in Chapter Thirteen, we'll close with thoughts about what it means to abandon the search for any fixed model of the "good society" and embrace instead a Living Democracy—one ever-evolving as more and more ordinary Americans develop the capacity to shape our society according to our values.

10

Mastering the Arts of Democracy: One-on-One Skills

YOU'VE MET MANY PEOPLE in these pages. Their lives are becoming more satisfying, because they are learning how to move from hopelessness to effective problem solving. For them, a new way of thinking is becoming a new way of being.

What You Already Know

What lessons has your life taught you about the skills needed to be effective in public life? Before reading our list, what skills of public life do you think make people effective? What five come to mind first? Write them down.

_____

_____

What lessons did you learn from your family? At school? In the workplace?

_____

_____

_____

Were these lessons implicit or deliberately taught?
Do you believe that skills for effectiveness in public life can be learned?

But to translate understanding into action requires that we hone new skills. We call the skills that make possible effective public life *the arts of democracy.* Here we'll highlight just ten of the democratic arts we've seen people practicing to achieve breakthroughs in public life.

We've chosen the term *art* quite deliberately. Art to us sounds pretty important. It's something people take seriously, and that's exactly the point. We want to elevate the notion of democratic practice to something that is highly valued, prized—something that is actively sought by all of us.

Yes, but we know some people are put off by the notion of art, as in, "I could never be an artist; I don't have what it takes." So we need to explain further.

Art doesn't *have* to suggest something exclusive, something at which only the talented few can succeed. Developing an art is possible for each of us, but—and we want to underline this—it can't be learned by rote or formula. In any art, individuals add their own twists. Plus, we like the idea of an art because its practice calls on not just one but many of our faculties.

Most important, an art can be learned. Being born with certain talents—manual dexterity, great vocal cords, or perfect pitch, for example—is not enough. Artistry develops over time. And in art there is no end point to the learning. The same is true of a Living Democracy. It has no end. It is always in flux, fluid, in development.

We Learn by Doing

Like sports or the art of dance, we learn the arts of Living Democracy by *doing* them and by reflecting on our doing. Practicing the democratic arts means participating in democratic decision making and action.

After all, human beings are innately social creatures—meaning that we're obviously dependent on each other. But we're not born *effective* social creatures. While virtually all of us have the potential to listen, to communicate well, to envision a better society, to imagine ourselves in the shoes of others, to resolve conflict, and so forth, we do not all realize that potential. Realizing that potential requires deliberate learning.

But how? In this chapter we highlight just a few of the many capacities— the democratic arts—that we see regular people in all walks of life actively cultivating in order to make a difference. We can't give you, in this one book, a detailed, step-by-step training manual. But we *can* help you understand the importance of each art in your life. And we can help you choose

Ten Arts of Democracy

ART ONE:
Active listening—encouraging the speaker and searching for meaning

ART TWO:
Creative conflict—confronting others in ways that produce growth

ART THREE:
Mediation—facilitating interaction to help people in conflict hear each other

ART FOUR:
Negotiation—problem solving that meets some key interests of all involved

ART FIVE:
Political imagination—reimaging our futures according to our values

ART SIX:
Public dialogue—public talk on matters that concern us all

ART SEVEN:
Public judgment—public decision making that allows citizens to make choices they are willing to help implement

ART EIGHT:
Celebration and appreciation—expressing joy and appreciation for what we learn as well as what we achieve

ART NINE:
Evaluation and reflection—assessing and incorporating the lessons we learn through action

ART TEN:
Mentoring—supportively guiding others in learning these arts of public life

the next steps you can take to achieve ends you care about deeply.

In this chapter, we begin with four arts that we often—though not exclusively—practice one-on-one. In the next chapter we turn to group skills.

 Democratic Art One: Active Listening

HALLMARKS

✓ Stays engaged

✓ Is supportive of the speakers' efforts whether or not there's agreement

✓ Searches for underlying meaning

✓ Is nonjudgmental

BENEFITS

✓ Uncovers deeper interests

✓ Permits the discovery of mutual interests

✓ Spurs creativity

✓ Changes the speaker as well as the listener

✓ Creates positive bonds

SOME 'HOW-TO'S'

✓ Reach out for the ideas of others

✓ Sometimes, just be quiet

✓ Be encouraging and feed back what you hear

✓ Ask probing questions

✓ Take in more than the words

✓ Make the speaker comfortable

The first step in old-style politics or old-style management is drawing up one's manifesto, plan, or agenda and then selling it to others.

In contrast, the first art of Living Democracy is *simply listening*.

But is it really so simple? Listening and really hearing is an art that most of us must actively learn. It is the basis of any successful organization, whether it be a business, a community group, or even our family.

Active Listening Uncovers Mutual Interests. At its most complete, active listening suggests putting oneself in another's shoes, seeing the world—

How often have you been asked—by a colleague at work, your spouse, or even a canvasser at your doorstep—to sign on to somebody else's agenda before first being asked about your own concerns?

If you disagreed with their position, did you feel free to offer another view? How did their approach make you feel?

even if for just a fleeting moment—from their vantage point. This carries several benefits. First, we can then perceive another's interests fully. That's critical in finding the links to our own interests. And if both parties are to agree on action, common ground is key.

Earlier we recounted how COPS (Communities Organized for Public Service), a citizen organization in San Antonio, reacted to its frustration at high unemployment rates among Hispanics. COPS members were upset because the city's biggest employers were bringing in outsiders to fill local jobs. COPS might have simply staged an angry protest. Instead, they invited corporate leaders to the table. COPS members *listened*. They listened to the concerns of those they might have seen only as adversaries. They listened to the companies' CEOs tell them of their own frustrations in not being able to find qualified employees locally. COPS members discovered a common interest with the business leaders: improving the city's job training efforts. From there, as Tom Holler described, COPS went on to develop an innovative redesign of the city's job training programs, which the city council passed unanimously.

Active Listening Spurs Creativity. Active listening spurs creativity because it opens us to new ways of seeing. That's why English professor Peter Elbow at the University of Massachusetts uses active listening as a teaching tool. He calls it "The Believing Game." Peter believes that our culture overemphasizes the importance of critical thinking, looking for flaws in any argument. The problem with using only this approach is that it can make even the best idea look bad. A creative idea with far-reaching advantages may be ignored because it contradicts conventional wisdom, or is poorly stated. To see its virtues, Peter argues, we must make a conscious,

The Believing Game

Play it when a proposal or idea gets roundly rejected before anyone has taken the time to explore it fully.

Rules:

1. Everyone tries as hard as possible to believe in the proposal, even briefly. As they listen nonjudgmentally, they look for possible *strengths* only.

2. Participants offer only positive elaborations—ways to bolster the idea. No criticism!

3. Don't try to evaluate an idea until people have been able to bolster it with the believing game.

Sometimes you have to play the believing game with yourself on your *own* ideas.

Source: Adapted from Peter Elbow, "Methodical Belief," in *Embracing Contraries* (New York: Oxford University Press, 1985) and "Believing Game," appendix essay in *Writing Without Teachers* (New York: Oxford University Press, 1973). Used with permission.

---

disciplined effort to *pretend* it is the best proposal, and then see what we notice.

What's required is a special kind of active listening—the temporary suspension of disbelief. We drop our tendency to first identify all the problems, freeing our creative input.

Peter uses this approach to enhance his teaching. But he encourages any group to try something similar.[1]

Active Listening Changes the Speaker. In private life, when we go to a friend for advice and that friend simply listens, we're often amazed to discover it is we ourselves who have the answers. We've had them all along. But formulating our ideas in order to make ourselves clear to someone else enables us to "see" those answers for the first time.

The same possibility exists in public life. In North Carolina, for example, the Listening Project bases its community improvement work on hundreds of in-depth, one-on-one interviews with people in their homes. Instead of quick, check-off surveys, organizers ask open-ended questions about people's values and concerns. In one home, a middle-aged white man complained that the biggest problem he saw was the noisy black teenagers who hung out on the streets and caused trouble.

On a simple survey, that one comment might have gotten him labeled a racist. But the organizers just listened. They didn't argue. As the man talked, he began to reflect as well. By the end of the interview, he himself had restated—and re-understood—the problem in his neighborhood as the lack of decent recreational and job opportunities for young people.[2]

So while we think of listening as passive, at best having some impact on the listener, this story suggests much more. The very act of being truly listened to can change the speaker's own understanding.

Active Listening Creates Positive Bonds. Because being listened to is such a powerful experience—in all the ways we just mentioned and more—it creates strong bonds among people. In Chapter Four we described a growing appreciation of the power of such bonds—relationships of trust—in public life. These relationships help sustain our commitment to tasks over time, and help us survive the disappointments that all rewarding effort entails.

Active Listening How-To's

Here are some steps you can take to ensure that your listening becomes more active.

Reach Out for the Ideas of Others. Americans often think that social change occurs when someone "who cares" comes up with a plan and then mobilizes others to make the change. But over and over again in our research we found that this is not what happens in the most effective organizations.

In Nashville, Tennessee, to give one example, a congregation-based effort, associated with the IAF, began with almost two years of listening. By this we mean the pastors and others (who were committed to working throughout the city to unite citizens across race and class lines) didn't begin by mapping out the issues *they* cared about most. They began by simply listening to the concerns of their colleagues, parishioners, and neighbors, listening to understand why *others* might want to be part of such an effort. They expanded that listening process to include dozens of "house meetings" to listen to the concerns of diverse congregations and housing project

How Well Do You Listen?

Are there people with whom you communicate—either in your private life or in your public life—whom you wish you understood better? In your most honest judgment, is something about your communication and listening perhaps partially responsible for the less-than-full understanding?

Do people sometimes tell you that you don't listen well enough, that you don't really hear them? Do you feel there's some merit to that complaint?

Are you conscious of what you actually do in conversations that encourages other people to communicate more or less fully? Please list here your principle listening behaviors (interrupting, using encouraging sounds and expressions, and so on).

_____

_____

_____

Now you can do your own assessment of your listening skills. You've just searched your heart for instances in which you desire to listen better, for listening problems others have brought to your attention, and for the level of your conscious awareness of listening skills in your everyday life. What do your answers say to you about your listening skills? (Rate yourself from one to five.)

How good a listener are you? (1 = poor; 5 = excellent.)

1   2   3   4   5

How comfortable do other people feel talking to you?
(1 = not at all comfortable; 5 = very comfortable.)

1   2   3   4   5

What is your diagnosis of the skill development (if any) you need?

_____

_____

_____

residents, among others. Out of this lengthy listening process TNT (Tying Nashvillians Together) was born.

Sometimes, Just Be Quiet. The most simple, and maybe most difficult, how-to of active listening is how to keep quiet. Most of us want to be heard more than we want to listen. It feels like this is the only way to protect our interests. Actually, talking can undermine our interests, since our interests are often tied to the other person's feeling positive and heard.

So one skill in active listening is the habit of pausing after the other person speaks. Get comfortable with a little space there. The pause will allow you to be sure that the other person has finished. It will allow you to compose a more thoughtful question or a more balanced and calm response.

Seeing Yourself as an Active Listener

Think of three scenes—with your colleague at work, for example, or with your child, or with a friend—that are likely to occur within the next week in which you want to listen very, very well. Write them down.

1. _____

2. _____

3. _____

Imagine yourself in each scene. What do you see yourself doing differently now in order to actively listen?

1. _____

2. _____

3. _____

How will you know you've succeeded?

1. _____

2. _____

3. _____

Be Encouraging and Feed Back What You Hear. Most of us have a hard time talking without an audience. If you as a listener want someone to talk, demonstrate that you are taking it all in. Make eye contact. Lean toward the speaker, never away. Nod your encouragement. Add "uh-huh" or other encouraging expressions as often as is comfortable. And take the time to summarize what you're hearing. Only then do your listeners know they're being heard. Check in to see whether the speaker thinks you "got it."

Ask Probing Questions. Juanita Mitchell of the Metropolitan Organization (TMO) in Houston stresses another aspect of active listening. It involves asking questions that encourage the speaker to reflect on his and her own words. "We help people go deeper," Juanita told us. "We ask, what do you mean? What do you really mean? We get people to think about the words they use."

Take in More Than the Words. Disciplining oneself to talk less and to pause more allows you to become a better observer. Communication is about a lot more than the words spoken, as we all know. The speaker's facial expression, tone of voice, and body language (positioning and movement) all communicate feelings that we can take it in. We're not suggesting that it is always possible to read these expressions accurately, but we can register them and weigh them in light of everything else we know about the speaker.

Make Sure the Speaker Is Comfortable. Joe Szakos is a low-key, highly effective citizen organizer with Kentuckians for the Commonwealth (KFTC). He told us: "If you want people to talk, you can't just invite them to a meeting to discuss an issue you think is important." Then he emphasized to us: "You have to go sit on their porch. You have to sit with them and drink coffee, not worrying about what the agenda is. What they care most about may not even come up on the first sit." In other words, it's important to go to a place where people feel most at ease and aware of their feelings.

At home or on the job, effective listeners go to where people feel most comfortable, and they take in more than the words. Effective listeners reach out to the ideas of others; they ask probing questions and feed back what they hear. And sometimes they're just quiet.

Democratic Art Two: Creative Conflict

HALLMARK

✓ Constructive, honest confrontation.

BENEFITS

✓ Demonstrates that diverse stakeholders are involved.

✓ Uncovers interests.

✓ Can deepen understanding.

✓ Generates more options.

✓ Can build group confidence.

SOME 'HOW-TO'S'

✓ Value and incorporate diversity.

✓ Create an environment "safe" for difference.

✓ Leave labels at the door.

✓ Agree to disagree when there's no common ground.

✓ Focus on the present and on solutions.

✓ Allow some "venting" but limit reactions.

✓ Use self-discipline in expressions of anger.

✓ Be well prepared.

✓ Make no permanent enemies.

✓ Model the "surfacing" of conflict.

"To live is to have conflict," a leader in Allied Communities of Tarrant (ACT) told us when we visited him in Fort Worth. "If you don't have problems, you're not doing anything. This is what we're teaching our children. Friction means fire—and fire is power."

Is his view typical? Hardly. Most Americans abhor conflict. Whether in politics or at work, school, or home, most of us learn to see conflict as negative—as something to avoid. Typically, an employer promotes a subordinate for being "a good team player" who "doesn't make waves." A principal believes his good teachers are those who maintain orderly classrooms without noise and—above all—without conflict. A parent praises his teenager for being "a good kid" who "never gives me problems." Entire minority communities are cursed or praised according to whether they "cause trouble," or are seen as "peaceful, good folk."

Quickly, without hesitation, list the first six words that come to mind when you think about the word *conflict*.

1. _____   4. _____

2. _____   5. _____

3. _____   6. _____

When we ask Americans what comes to mind when they hear the word conflict, we receive answers like "tension," "power grabs," "nastiness," "fights," "win-lose," "war," and "anger." This limited perspective understandably leads to a version of the "flight or fight" response: either avoid conflict or be prepared to "duke it out."

There is hope, however, in this limited picture. Millions of Americans, including many of those introduced in this book, are acknowledging that neither fight nor flight is a very successful strategy.

Instead, many people are experimenting with techniques for negotiating conflict constructively, as books like *Getting to Yes* soar to the top of the best-seller list.[3] But before we Americans make the effort to learn new skills, we have to uproot our own prejudices, fully grasping the *positive* functions of conflict.

Conflict Demonstrates that Diverse Stakeholders Are Involved. If there's no conflict, it might just mean that important perspectives have been excluded from the decision-making table.

Conflict Can Uncover Interests. Conflict can shake us out of our narrowly defined interest, as we see the consequences of our views through the eyes of those who disagree.

Conflict Can Deepen Our Understanding of a Problem. Considering several definitions of a problem—and the consequences of different solutions—helps sharpen our understanding of even the most complex issues.

Conflict Can Provide More Options for Action. Conflict avoids one of the most common mistakes in problem solving—leaping to a premature commitment to one solution. Conflict gives us more choices.

Conflict Can Be About Learning Instead of "Winning or Losing." Every difference, discomfort, or disagreement can be used to better know ourselves and others. Conflict provides clues to prejudices, needs, values, and goals—all information we need to successfully interact with others.

Conflict Can Build Group Confidence. Groups that successfully use conflict for learning come to believe in themselves more strongly. With confidence in their ability to use conflict well, they can take more risks. Healthy conflict can get us more engaged in the problem-solving process—deepening our sense of ownership, both of the process and, eventually, the solution. As Belle Zars, a member of a social justice group in West Virginia, told us: "It's good just to know that any time you get change you get conflict." Further, adds Belle, "I've learned that any time we have a good rip-roaring fight, the quality of our decisions is much better. Heat isn't necessarily bad."

Conflict will not go away. Yet, think how much energy and time we waste trying to avoid it or engaging in destructive battles. Simply perceiving conflict as both inevitable and useful—even essential—to healthy public discussion is the first step in turning it from a curse to a creative tool.

How do we create positive conflict, conflict with all its potential benefits?

Creative Conflict How-To's

Here are some pointers to help you accept and embrace conflict as a healthy part of public interaction. First, positive conflict requires that we welcome diversity, in all its forms.

Value and Incorporate Diversity. By the 1990s, nothing could be more PC—politically correct—than to swear allegiance to the principle of diversity. It's one of the biggest "shoulds" of our time. Living Democracy, how-

How Well Do You Handle Conflict?

Rate your ability to handle conflict by circling a number from one to five.

Poorly—I get very
upset; I run from
conflict; I blow up.

Very well—I can
use conflict
constructively.

1   2   3   4   5

Most of us can easily think of conflicts in our lives, even in the last week or two. Think of three conflictual situations that have occurred in your life recently:

1. _____

2. _____

3. _____

Did any of these conflicts bring benefits? What were they? _____

_____

_____

Could they have been more beneficial? More creative? How?_____

_____

_____

For each of these situations, is there anything you wish you had done differently? _____

_____

_____

ever, approaches diversity from another angle: diversity can produce better results. If it helps spur creative conflict, diversity contributes all of the benefits we just listed. From more perspectives come more understanding, more creativity, and more commitment to implementation.

So appreciating diversity is not a moralistic "should. " It creates better solutions. That's Ken Galdston's experience. As you may recall from Chapter Five, Ken works with the Merrimack Valley Project in Massachusetts, which includes both unions and churches, each with very different styles of action.

> I see the way the church people challenge the union people and vice versa. That's good. An example is when two companies announced they were closing. Hundreds of jobs were at stake. This brought church, union, and chamber of commerce people together.
>
> Once it was clear that the plant closures couldn't be reversed, we decided to ask for job-retraining money from the companies. The union people were ready to write it off. They didn't trust the companies. They wanted to jump on the companies for bad faith. But the church people were inclined to give the companies a timetable and to just see how it went. They said, 'We can be more principled.' If we'd just taken this go-slow approach or just had the jump-the-gun approach, it wouldn't have worked. In the end, the *combination* worked. We got $55,000 from the company for retraining 140 workers, and that leveraged other funds.

Jean True of Kentuckians for the Commonwealth put this lesson quite simply: "The best decisions are those made with the most input by the most people."

Create an Environment "Safe" for Difference. Making conflict constructive begins by creating environments in which people feel free to dissent, to offer opposing views. Conflict by which we grow is "open, public, and often very noisy," writes educational philosopher Parker Palmer. What blocks such creative conflict is fear, he says. "It is fear of exposure, of appearing ignorant, of being ridiculed." People feel safe to expose their ignorance only when we work to communicate that "every attempt at truth, no matter how off the mark," contributes to the search.[4]

Recently we heard about a marvelously successful high school history teacher, very popular with his students. "That's a brilliant wrong answer!" he's been known to say to a student who ventured beyond his or her own sure knowledge. This teacher was creating a public environment free from fear of embarrassment. He was preparing young people who will be able to deal with differences without fear that being wrong will bring humiliation.

Even about what appears to be a no-compromise issue—abortion—some advocates on both sides have tired of battling. They've worked hard to create an environment safe for differences.

Beginning in 1991, abortion rights advocates and those opposed in Milwaukee came together in what turned into half- or even full-day meetings every four to six weeks. Initially, what made the meetings possible were commitments to keep the encounters safe. Everyone agreed: no media coverage, and "the only agenda would be to have a dialogue," Maggi Cage, one of the conveners, told us.

Agree to Leave Labels at the Door. Participants in the abortion discussion arrived at certain rules to foster active listening. For one, they agreed to ban the use of clichés, labels, and rhetoric. Without the distraction of defending themselves against each other's labels, they could see beneath differences to discover that they all, as Maggi explained, do have a shared interest. It's a "common desire to prevent unwanted pregnancies." Stereotypes broke down; trust grew. Out of this dialogue came ideas for "sexuality education" for youth, which the group later presented to legislators.

Agree to Disagree, Then Explore Common Ground. In St. Louis, representatives from the two abortion camps took a very different approach. While the Milwaukee participants believed it was important to really listen to each others' views on abortion before finding common ground, in St. Louis they "decided to table the abortion issue and talk about everything else in between," said Jean Cavender of Reproductive Health Services. Since most of the participants were providers of services to women and children, they found that "everything else in between" covered quite a lot of ground—including common ground.

So even in the most divisive battles, participants can deliberately create conditions allowing all sides to discover their shared interests. The idea is catching on in the abortion debate; such groups are now forming in several other cities.[5]

Keep the Focus on the Present—and on Solutions. In Berkeley, California, a zoning plan had been stalled for years. Labor union members and other workers wanted zoning in order to keep high-paying manufacturing jobs. But environmentalists and some residents applauded the exit of polluting industries. How could such opposing interests ever converge?

Planning Commission member Babette Jee agreed to chair a subcommittee on the West Berkeley Plan, but only with the understanding that she would bring every interested party to the table. And she did, in a series of face-to-face meetings that continued over many months.

"At first the meetings were a little tense," she told us, "because people were complaining about the past.... So we made people talk about the present and a little about the future. We would focus not just on the rhetorical or political point of view, but a real situation: 'practically speaking, how do we deal with this problem?'"

Discipline Expressions of Anger. Meeting facilitators encouraged participants in the West Berkeley Plan to get their competing feelings out on the table but to resist reacting to inflammatory statements or "under-your-breath" jabs. They encouraged people not to interrupt each other and to reflect back on a speaker's interests before stating competing interests. After a while, participants realized that they didn't need to be abrasive to be heard.

The process generated a plan that none had started with but that held to the highest environmental standards while still protecting good jobs. By the end, "Almost anyone in the group could articulate the other's side," Babette Jee marveled. When it came time for the city council to vote on the plan, thirty or forty citizens testified—*all in favor.* "Speaker after speaker got up, basically supporting the proposition, not because it was exactly what they wanted, but because it supports the entire group of people," said one of the participants.

The outcome of this creative conflict surprised even the participants. They learned that creative conflict requires disciplining anger if we hope to be effective.

Undisciplined anger can cause others to shut down: their fear response renders them unable to perceive the *reasons* for the anger. So its intent backfires. Rather than the hoped-for change, undisciplined anger provokes greater resistance to change.

After much work before the 1991 election, Shelby County Interfaith in Memphis had finally gotten a meeting with the mayor. Hear Gerald Taylor tell it: "In the middle of the mayor's remarks, some of our members snickered. This offense gave the mayor an excuse to try to end the meeting. A small-scale confrontation blew up into a large one. And it took us some time to get back on track toward our goals.

"In the evaluation we did after the meeting, everyone in the group agreed: the snickering gave the mayor an opening to deflect the meeting from our agenda. We still ended the meeting better positioned than when we began, but we all learned from that."

Here, the group's internal evaluation session encouraged SCI members to reinforce their commitment to disciplining their expression of anger.

And there's another drawback in undisciplined anger: It often strikes the wrong target.

An Easy Question . . .

Can you think of two or three times recently when you have felt anger? Write them down.

_____

_____

_____

And a Tougher Question . . .

If you're not satisfied with how you handled your anger, what would your improved behavior have looked like?

_____

_____

_____

Take, for instance, the temptation to rail against a government or corporate official about something his or her bureaucracy is doing. If you make the person feel personally blamed, you may have alienated a potential ally. Citizens in Seattle, upset about a development proposed for a wooded ravine in their neighborhood, invited a city planner to a block meeting. These neighbors decided not to attack the planner for the city's role, but to listen instead. They read between the lines of her remarks and discovered that she was actually sympathetic to their cause. They built on that relationship and ultimately triumphed. Disciplining anger is critical to constructive confrontation.

Be Well Prepared. Jean True of Kentuckians for the Commonwealth described why discipline is so important in, say, testifying before the legislature or state agencies: "They'll bait you. They'll try to get you mad. Then they'll turn around and make you look like a fool. They'll say, 'oh, she's not rational. She's too emotional. We can't invite *her* to meetings.' They also tend to pick on certain people they know are more vulnerable."

That's why, Jean told us, the training KFTC provides is so important. It prepares people to keep calm, to not react to baiting, to prepare themselves mentally beforehand.

Make No Permanent Enemies. Many of the most effective citizens we've met have learned that in public life it doesn't pay to create permanent foes, whether in the workplace, school, or citizens' organization. Someone who opposes you on one issue might become your greatest asset on the next.

Model the "Surfacing" of Conflict. No group can deal creatively with conflict if its participants refuse to acknowledge it. So Rick Surpin, cofounder of the Bronx worker-owned home care service you read about in Chapter Five, works to model the "surfacing of conflict, so that the group can deal with it." And Rick describes the payoff: "If body language shows something different than what people are saying, I used to have to make sure that the real feeling came out. Now, others are starting to do it. People will put out more of what they're thinking. Some number of people will— even if only a few. This creates space for a broader middle to speak. It starts the ball rolling. It was like pulling teeth in the beginning. Now that isn't

Using Creative Conflict in Your Life

Which one of the how-to's of creative conflict do you most need to practice during the coming week?

_____

Now, develop a plan of action: what *specifically* are you going to do in order to practice creative conflict during the next week?

_____

_____

_____

_____

What benefits do you expect? How will you know if you've succeeded (or at least made progress)?

_____

_____

_____

_____

necessary." Rick was pleased at that. "A belief that conflict should be out on the table is part of our culture now," Rick told us.

Too often in public life, as well as in private, people in conflict feel reluctant to confront each other directly. They may fear embarrassment. They may fear the other person's anger. They may fear they won't be heard, or treated fairly. So they tell everyone *else* about their conflict. Or those in conflict simply lock horns. They attack. And their anger and fear of not being heard makes them unable to listen. In either mode, there's little hope for positively resolving conflict. Mediation may be needed.

Democratic Art Three: Mediation

HALLMARK

✓ A skilled, neutral listener helps those in conflict "hear" each other.

BENEFITS

✓ Avoids destructive conflict.

✓ Makes problem solving more possible.

✓ Reduces the likelihood of unproductive conflict in the future.

✓ Enhances personal dignity and mutual respect.

SOME 'HOW-TO'S'

✓ Someone who's neutral—the mediator—invites those in conflict to state their views.

✓ The mediator listens in order to bring differences to the surface.

✓ The mediator doesn't judge, but asks questions to uncover common interests.

✓ The mediator stresses points in common that the disputants may not see.

✓ Disputants search for a solution that meets some interests of both parties.

Mediation is a fancy word for a simple process—a neutral listener plays a facilitating role. Its power lies in people feeling they've had a chance to express themselves fully in a safe context. Feeling heard, in and of itself, often reduces the intensity of people's anger. It taps many of the benefits of active listening, including hearing oneself perhaps for the first time. New options can emerge.

Mediation How-To's

For this art of democracy we've woven the how-to's into two stories about Americans learning mediation skills. Do these stories suggest ways mediation could improve problem solving in your workplace, organization, school, or family?

San Francisco's Community Boards Resolve Conflicts. In 1976, in a racially mixed, working-class neighborhood in San Francisco, several residents decided that many problems creating stress and bad blood couldn't be addressed simply by calling in the police. In fact, bringing in the police was deepening the antagonism.

These citizens looked for a better way to resolve conflict, be it barking dogs, vandalism, petty theft, fender-benders, lousy service, whatever. Volunteers set out to train residents to mediate conflicts among neighbors. And the Community Board Program was born with this motto: "Neighbors helping neighbors resolve conflicts that keep us apart."[6]

Today, the Community Boards' full-time staff trains and oversees the work of three hundred volunteer conciliators, ranging in age from fourteen to seventy. Over a third are people of color. Its volunteer mediators handle and settle more cases in San Francisco than the municipal court.

"I think it's not so much that these programs do problem resolution, but they allow for problem *reformation*," explained Terry Amsler, who heads the Community Boards. "They help people get off their stuckness, off the conflict, into 'what are the bigger positives we can shoot for by doing it together?' . . . It's not how we resolve the problem, it's how do we talk enough to establish a relationship."

Terry explained the four steps in mediation that allow this problem-reformation:

Disputants introduce themselves and tell their stories to the mediation panel. The sense of being heard "brings out the best in people," reports staff person Rita Adrian. "It's the fact that people who, not getting paid, give so much sympathetic attention to them . . . and take everything they say so seriously. That's incredibly disarming," she says.

The mediation panel responds. The panel then praises the disputants for being willing to conciliate. It summarizes the nature of the dispute and stresses the common points of agreement, which often the disputants have not noticed.

How Good a Mediator Are You?

Rate yourself as a mediator from one (terrible) to five (terrific).

Terrible. I get too involved.   Terrific. People trust me
Or I don't know how.   to listen and be neutral.

1   2   3   4   5

Think of three times recently when you have witnessed conflict between others.

1. _____

2. _____

3. _____

Now think of three times in the near future when you are likely to be present while people are in conflict.

1. _____

2. _____

3. _____

Can you imagine yourself as a neutral mediator in these conflicts? What do you need in order to strengthen your ability to play a mediating role?

_____

_____

_____

_____

_____

_____

_____

_____

Disputants turn their chairs and talk directly to each other, while the mediation panel listens attentively. Sometimes the mediators might intervene to say: "Please repeat back what you heard the other person say." But the main goal is to give people the time just to talk to each other, Terry told us, so they begin to break down "the evil, mean monster" picture they've created of each other.

The disputants and the mediation panel then talk together to come up with "win-win" solutions. The point, says Terry, is to "satisfy to some degree the self-interest—if not all the issues—of the parties."

The resolution arrived at then gets committed to paper and all parties sign what is a moral, though not legally binding, agreement. In a few weeks, Community Boards follow up to see how things are going and to offer any additional assistance if necessary.

Eighty percent of the time, neighborhood mediations resolve problems to the satisfaction of all parties. Considering that a third of the cases involve violence or threats of violence, Terry says he's pleased.

Analyzing Disputes and Your Role in Them

Think of the three disputes you listed earlier that you have observed in the recent past. Could a mediator have helped?

In each case, who might have served as a mediator? Where would the best mediation have occurred? When? How?

Answers to these questions—who, where, when, and how—add up to your analysis of what mediation might offer in each of these conflicts.

Now what about your role in mediation? What could you have done to facilitate the reaching of a constructive agreement?

The impact of Community Boards goes far beyond the prevention of violence and neighborhood tension. The volunteer mediators—one-third of whom first became involved as disputants themselves—learn skills that enrich the community. "Volunteers from Community Boards marshal parade routes and facilitate community meetings," Terry observes. "[They are] a resource to the community in many ways."

Students Learn Mediation Skills and Reduce Violence. In the early 1980s, San Francisco's Community Boards became one of the trailblazers in the movement to teach dispute resolution and to train children to mediate conflict among their peers.[7] Since then, a half-dozen other centers around the country have also developed training programs in positive conflict resolution for school children.[8] Most require that the young, would-be mediators receive ten to fifteen hours of training in how to resolve the disputes they see developing among other kids.

Now, from Sacramento to Iowa and New York, some two thousand schools are involved. In the Community Boards' approach, the young disputants must agree to four key rules: (1) agree to solve the problem; (2) tell the truth; (3) don't interrupt; and (4) no name-calling.

New York's Board of Education, jointly with the organization Educators for Social Responsibility, launched the Resolving Conflict Creatively program in 1985. It now involves forty thousand students in over one hundred schools. At P.S. 321, for example, fourth and fifth graders elect students who receive special training to negotiate their classmates' disputes.[9] Sporting special T-shirts and working in pairs, the youngsters patrol the playground and lunchroom. If they see fighting or arguing, they ask, "Can we help?" If the disputants agree to mediation, they follow steps similar to the four that San Francisco's Community Board Program uses.

The results are striking: young mediators have dramatically decreased the discipline problems in their schools. At a middle school in Tucson, Arizona, for example, peer mediation cut the number of physical fights by half in just three months.[10]

These two developments—one community based, one school based—provide guidelines for successful mediation. They suggest that mediation could become part of our public culture, and aid our private lives as well.

☑ **Democratic Art Four: Negotiation**

HALLMARK

✓ Problem solving that meets some key needs of each party.

BENEFITS

✓ Makes resolution more possible.

✓ Maintains the dignity of all parties.

✓ Makes it more likely that agreements will be upheld.

✓ Prepares the ground for future problem solving.

SOME 'HOW-TO'S'

✓ Know your interests so well, you know what you can compromise.

✓ Focus on crucial interests; don't bogged down in debate over means.

✓ Search for common interests; work to narrow differences.

✓ Maintain respectful communication—it's in your interest.

✓ Take the pressure off and keep talking.

Every day, we're involved in negotiation, whether it's with our spouse about who will do the grocery shopping, with a colleague about how to share tasks, as part of a parents' group dealing with a rigid school principal, or as part of a citizens' organization getting banks to invest in our neighborhood. If we negotiate well, we ensure that agreements will be honored and that they meet some needs of everybody involved. Plus, we can feel confident we're preparing the ground for resolving any future problems.

Negotiation How-To's

To achieve these benefits, what does effective negotiation require? It requires all the other arts we've mentioned, such as active listening and constructive conflict, and more.

Know Your Interests Well. One obstacle to effective negotiation is a fear of compromise (fear of being "had"). To overcome it, we must reflect ahead of time. If we're clear on our real interests, we know what we can compromise without sacrificing that interest.

Consider a citizens' organization asking for the school board's commitment to an annual community-wide survey evaluating the school's performance—a "community report card." Before meeting with the board, members decide they would be willing to compromise on *when* the survey would first be introduced and whether the school would allocate funds for mailing it. But, members agree, the community-wide school evaluation itself is not negotiable.

Focus on Interests, Not the Means to Achieve Them. A related danger is getting sidetracked in disputes about the *ways* to achieve a goal, instead of remaining focused on the goal itself. In this case, the citizens know that their goal is a genuine evaluation process in which all citizens could participate. They remain open to suggestions about *how* that evaluation might best be done.

How Good a Negotiator Are You?

During the next month, what three issues are you likely to have to negotiate?

1. _____

2. _____

3. _____

What will be the likely result? Whose needs will be met? Will the outcome bode well for future disputes?

1. _____

2. _____

3. _____

You're the best judge of your effectiveness at negotiation. For each of the above situations you'll face during the next month, how effective are you likely to be?

☐ Not effective   ☐ Slightly effective   ☐ Moderately effective   ☐ Very effective

Search for Common Interests; Work to Narrow Differences. In the school-evaluation example, the citizens' group can ask itself, what might be the *school board's* interest in annual school evaluations by the community? The citizens would look for ways to demonstrate the value to the board—such as a higher profile for the school, identification of problems before they become intractable, a greater sense of ownership by the community.

Maintain Respectful Communication—It's in Your Interest. Sometimes you can't achieve what you *most* want. But if you've maintained respectful give-and-take, you leave the door open for identifying a different, more feasible objective. When the Merrimack Valley Project in Massachusetts realized it couldn't save the jobs it wanted, for example, members and staff were able to negotiate funds for retraining because they had maintained good communication with the company throughout the negotiation.

Take the Pressure Off and Keep Talking. A dramatic labor dispute offers another lesson about effective negotiation. In April 1989, seventeen hundred members of the United Mine Workers of America struck the Pittston Coal Group. The ensuing struggle was bitter: it lasted nine months and involved sympathy strikes reaching ten other states and affecting forty-six thousand additional workers.

Finally, the secretary of labor appointed long-time mediator Bill Usery. Bill pledged to bring Pittston's CEO and the union president face to face. But his approach was not typical of adversarial, labor-management wrangles. When asked how he managed to arrive at a "win-win" contract, he explained that it was by breaking out of the formal negotiation process: "For seven days and into the nights, I kept them [labor and management] talking to each other, not even asking them to make a proposal. We talked about concepts. How would they see the best relationship working? How could they best achieve the productivity they wanted? . . . For seven days—for ten to fifteen hours at a time—we just kept them talking to each other, and relaxing, and hearing one another and understanding one another. Then we broke for two days, and we came back. . . . We tried to back away, to look at it anew with a better understanding of one another."

This process of just talking, without pressure to take positions, broke through feelings that Bill described as "total mistrust" and "animosity" between the two sides. Bill kept both sides talking, but in such a way that they didn't fear that a mistaken remark could kill them. The process led to a settlement both sides could accept.[11]

So the next time you lock horns with someone, take a tip from the mine workers: call a moratorium for a few days. Just be together without trying to find out the answer. See whether a resolution comes more easily when you resume.

Before going on, you might wish to pause here and review the four democratic arts introduced in this chapter.

Applying the How-To's of Negotiation

In the last exercise, you listed some situations that may occur during the next month that will call on your negotiating smarts. Now that you've reviewed some how-to's of good negotiation, which will be the most important to success in the upcoming negotiations you anticipate?

_____

_____

_____

_____

_____

What can you do to practice each of these how-to's and improve upon your ability?

_____

_____

_____

_____

_____

11

Mastering the Arts of Democracy: Group Skills

N EXT WE TURN TO THOSE ARTS OF DEMOCRACY that we practice more frequently in group settings. But for many of us, the very thought of group settings is off-putting. We have sat—bored and frustrated—through too many bad meetings. If Living Democracy means more meetings, you may be thinking, then it's not for me!

But perhaps the problem is not with bad meetings but with meeting badly. In our research for this book, we have observed meetings that left participants feeling energized, not depleted. People walked out with a sense of solid accomplishment. They'd even had fun. Such meetings almost never happen spontaneously. But learning how to create them isn't difficult, even though as youngsters few of us ever had the chance to learn. (If you'd like suggested reading on the mechanics of great meetings, please write to us.)

Now to the six arts of democracy that can vastly enrich our satisfaction in any group endeavor.

✔ **Democratic Art Five: Political Imagination**

HALLMARK

✔ Reimaging current reality to more nearly match our values and needs.

BENEFITS

✔ Spurs creativity.

✔ Motivates action.

✔ Releases and focuses positive energy.

✔ Enables goal setting.

SOME 'HOW-TO'S'

✔ Contrast the world as it is with the world as you wish it to be. Be concrete.

✔ Learn to hold both images in your consciousness at once—to avoid either cynicism or naiveté.

✔ Try cultural expressions such as art.

When today's world can look so grim, when all the evils of our time—poverty, violence, and environmental decay—are worsening, how is it possible to envision positive alternatives?

Yet, without an image of where we want to go, we're not likely to get there. Thus *political imagination* is a primary art of Living Democracy. It's the ability to suspend the givens of today's social and political order in order to envision new possibilities. It's the capacity to reimage the world. Political imagination is what philosopher Peter Kropotkin was getting at in his advice to students in the last century: "Think about the kind of world you want to live and work in. What do you need to build that world? Demand that your teachers teach you that."[1]

Political Imagination How-To's

Here are some guidelines to assist you in imagining the world you can help to build.

Contrast the World as It Is with the World as You Wish It to Be. From business groups to community-based organizations, people are experimenting with exercises in political imagination. Training and workshop facilitators ask participants to describe the world—or community, or

Reimaging Your Community

Without reading about how others have responded, please list the first five to ten values you want to see in your community:

1. _____
2. _____
3. _____
4. _____
5. _____
6. _____
7. _____
8. _____
9. _____
10. _____

Now list the actual values you see expressed by and in your community:

1. _____
2. _____
3. _____
4. _____
5. _____
6. _____
7. _____
8. _____
9. _____
10. _____

workplace—in which they wish to live. Such exercises can be much more than wishful thinking when they remind participants that the world is not static; it is remade daily by our choices.

Learn to Hold Both Images in Your Consciousness at Once. The exercise opens a discussion of the contrast between the world as it is and the world as we wish it to be. Living in the tension between the two—avoiding both cynicism and naiveté—is what makes people effective in public life. In the citizen training offered by the Industrial Areas Foundation, learning to hold both realities in us at once is an important theme.

Try Cultural Expressions Such as Art. Art is a powerful vehicle for sparking political imagination. In the northern California community of Ukiah, residents temporarily transformed their city hall into a gallery. People of all ages were asked to offer their visual images of what they want their community to look like a decade hence. The result: a map of the future with a sense of differences and shared values. A similar process has been repeated in hundreds of towns and cities across America.

Once we understand where we wish to go, Living Democracy involves us with others whose visions are not the same as ours. Dialogue is then required.

Democratic Art Six: Public Dialogue

HALLMARKS

✓ Public talk on matters that affect all of us.

✓ Talk in which differences are valued.

BENEFITS

✓ Reveals interests.

✓ Expands and deepens knowledge.

✓ Generates more creative alternatives.

SOME 'HOW-TO'S'

✓ Use face-to-face discussion.

✓ Use a neutral facilitator, where feasible.

✓ Use resource materials with diverse perspectives.

✓ Probe beneath positions to explore values.

✓ Sometimes start small; let trust build gradually.

What we call public dialogue our friend and political philosopher, Benjamin Barber, calls "public talk." "It is not about the world; it is talk that makes and remakes the world," he writes.[2] Public dialogue is how citizens learn to incorporate varied interests and come to public judgment. At its fullest, it means creating an ongoing conversation about public matters in which differences are valued because they help us explore underlying assumptions and new sources of information.

In stark contrast, today's public talk is dominated by media broadcasts in which even the sound bites are shrinking. Political campaigns have become more fundraising machines than forums for face-to-face discussion. And Annie's small-town café—serving up community gab along with hot coffee—has been replaced by Dunkin Donuts and suburban sprawl.

Igniting an Envisioning Process

To think about the value of an envisioning process for your community, workplace, or school, make believe you are preparing a fifteen-minute talk on the importance of political imagination to help create positive change. What will you tell your audience?

Now imagine a process to help your fellow citizens create a community that more nearly matches their values. Who should be involved? How might they become involved? What would be necessary to make people feel their views will be heard? What role might community and religious leaders and organizations play? And what result would you find most satisfying?

Where and how do we engage in public dialogue? Some Americans are coming up with innovative answers, from issue-focused talk shows to community problem-solving meetings.

In our chapter on making the media our voice, we cited El Paso's televised issue discussions. Ismael Legarreta, an engineer for a steel company, was one of many who discovered that these discussions met a real need for people who rarely had opportunities to talk about important concerns.

Public Dialogue How-To's

Here are ways some everyday citizens have initiated public dialogue.

Use Face-to-Face Discussion. "When we looked around, we saw there were plenty of places to go to fight with each other. What we wanted to do was just talk to each other," said Glenn Gross of the Connecticut Environment Round Table. So Glenn and his colleagues created a "study circle" on environmental issues. "Our real goal is not just to talk to each other, but to get other people out in the world talking to each other."[3]

Study circles that Glenn mentioned are hardly new. The term is borrowed from Sweden, where study circles are a way of life: today over three hundred thousand study circles meet in that small country.[4] Today, Americans, too—in workplaces, union halls, schools, communities, and places of worship—are experimenting with these loosely structured discussion groups.

Use a Neutral Facilitator and Use Resource Materials with Diverse Perspectives. In one type of study group, diverse participants read a common set of background materials, offering a variety of perspectives on one issue. Then they come together with a neutral facilitator to share their reactions and "to work through" their differences. They often gain a deeper understanding and, in some cases, a course of action.

Thinking About Your Public Dialogue

Think back to the last time you had an in-depth conversation about a matter of public importance. Jot down responses to the following questions:

How did it feel? _____

Was there sufficient give-and-take? _____

_____

Did anyone's views change or develop? _____

_____

Did participants gain from the experience? _____

_____

If you're missing real public talk in your life, what is one opportunity open to you now to really engage in conversation and learn from others?_____

_____

In Maine, Sarah Campbell is communications director of that state's Council of Churches. During the Gulf War, the council agonized over an appropriate response. Since its member organizations held "varying points of view," wrote Sarah, "a public position on the war was out of the question." Instead, we defined our role as facilitator and educator, she explained. The council used the Study Circle Resource Center's booklet *Crisis in the Gulf* to initiate discussion groups.[5]

Probe Beneath Positions to Explore Values. In El Paso, Ismael Legarreta explained to us how being involved in discussion groups changed his way of relating to people: "You start looking at what people *are*. People say things, and even though they might not make sense, you start learning why they're saying them, where they came from, what their environment was, how they grew up. And you're not judging. What you're trying to do is find out what makes them say the things they say."

Sometimes Start Small; Let Trust Build Gradually. Dan Kemmis is the mayor of Missoula, Montana. He had long been frustrated by the divisiveness of Missoula's political culture. In the 1980s Dan and the head of the chamber of commerce took a bold step: each agreed to invite two other people to talk about how to do things differently.

Start a Study Circle

Is there an issue in your workplace, school, or community that study circles could address? Perhaps it's school reform, health care, or drug abuse.

Two national organizations, the Study Circles Resource Center and the Kettering Foundation's National Issues Forums, could offer you help. They develop materials on critical national issues—from AIDS to homelessness to the Arab-Israeli conflict—for use by study circles and discussion groups. Their booklets and study guides contrast different perspectives and encourage participants to engage their differences. They also offer guidance on how to generate study groups. Please see Resources at the end of the book for the address of the National Issues Forums and the Study Circles Resource Center.

Eventually their group grew to twenty-four, with members hand-picked to represent both sides of the ideological fence. It called itself the Missoula Roundtable. To join the group, each person had to agree to honor one basic covenant: "Although they would disagree about much, the goal was a better way of doing public business, a better way of listening to each other, and to say things so they could be heard," Dan told us. "It was hard. It took time."

Confidence grew slowly. But eventually, group members moved past their differences and took on a major issue together. The issue, a proposal to build a ski resort, "had all the elements that normally would have guaranteed years of divisiveness," said Dan. Instead, the Roundtable asked citizens to come and talk to them from both sides of the issue. They asked that everyone approach the issue in a way that "does the least harm to the community."

The two sides agreed that there must at least be a way to collect the data in a less adversarial way. So instead of having two sides amassing contradictory data, they made one effort. In the end, the data itself settled the issue.

The Roundtable languished when Dan ran for mayor against the chamber of commerce director. But when Dan became mayor he reconvened it as the Mayor's Roundtable. He's tried to balance the group by gender and income, as well as by ideology. "It's invaluable," he says enthusiastically. "I can bring big and divisive issues to the Roundtable and people must think about what's good for Missoula, as well as their own positions."[6]

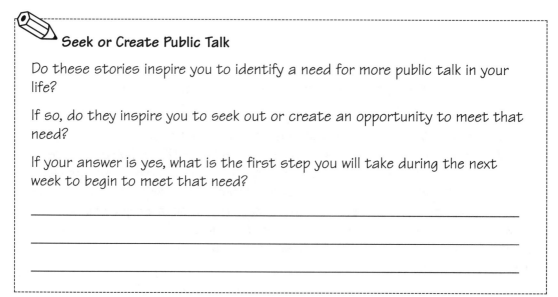

Seek or Create Public Talk

Do these stories inspire you to identify a need for more public talk in your life?

If so, do they inspire you to seek out or create an opportunity to meet that need?

If your answer is yes, what is the first step you will take during the next week to begin to meet that need?

_____

_____

_____

✔ **Democratic Art Seven: Public Judgment**

HALLMARK

✓ Discriminating reason, arrived at through talk and reflection.

BENEFITS

✓ Better solutions.

✓ Greater willingness to accept tough trade-offs.

SOME 'HOW-TO'S'

✓ Learn to accept the consequences of one's choices.

✓ Explore the values that underlie alternative choices.

✓ Try deliberation by randomly selected groups of citizens.

Public talk of the type just described makes possible what many call *public judgment*.

Public judgment is not public opinion. What gets polled in surveys as public opinion usually registers our knee-jerk reactions—our undigested private thoughts about issues and controversies. Public judgment is something quite different. It emerges only in hearing other points of view, thinking through the clash of values. It is the difficult, rewarding process people in Connecticut and Montana went through in our examples earlier.

Public judgment involves dialogue, of course. But it is distinguished by a willingness to *make choices*—even tough choices.

Public Judgment How-To's

Here are several lessons from Americans who are learning how to come to public judgment.

Learn to Accept the Consequences of Our Choices. In his book, *Coming to Public Judgment*, Daniel Yankelovitch argues that a key measure of high-quality public opinion is not how much information we citizens have under our belts. Rather, "the quality of public opinion [should] be considered good," he writes, "when the public accepts responsibility for the consequences of its views, and poor when the public, for whatever reason, is unprepared to do so."[7] Citizens' demanding more public services but refusing to pay the taxes to cover them is a prime example of his point.

Forming Public Judgment

Where do you help to formulate public judgment? At work? At school? In your community? Where you worship? With a community or volunteer organization?

_____

_____

_____

Where else? _____

_____

_____

Think about a public decision that got made without you but was important to you or your family.

How might you have contributed to the formation of public judgment on this issue? _____

_____

_____

_____

_____

What is the first step you could take within the next week to join, or to put in place, a process of forming public judgment on this issue for the future?

_____

_____

_____

_____

In 1988, the Maverick Institute, along with the University of Arizona's 4-H, involved 360 young people, aged twelve to eighteen, in small group talk about pressing social issues. The process clearly affected the teenagers: in one county, after thoroughly discussing alternative perspectives, the young people's willingness to increase taxes to pay for public improvements changed from a slight majority in favor to a seven-to-one majority in favor.[8]

How do people come to accept tough trade-offs? Only as we ourselves weigh alternatives, so that the choices are *ours*, not trade-offs forced upon us by others.

Explore the Values That Underlie Alternative Choices. The Oregon Health Decisions movement we described in Chapter Eight offers a powerful example of how ordinary citizens began by exploring underlying values, which then guided their discussion about health care. After agreeing on one core, shared value—that access to basic health care is a commitment that citizens make to one another through democratic government—these Oregon citizens were then able to make difficult choices about how to allocate public funds.

Try Deliberation by Randomly Selected Groups of Citizens. Some Americans who refuse to accept the shrinking of political debate into ten-second sound bites are responding with citizen juries. In citizen juries, randomly chosen citizens join together to study an issue and make public their findings.

An example from the 1992 elections gives a taste of their potential. That year, the League of Women Voters sponsored citizen juries in both Philadelphia and Pittsburgh. Two groups of eighteen average citizens were selected by random telephone survey. The juries studied the two senate candidates' records, held two days of hearings with knowledgeable witnesses, and on the third day questioned the candidates. They released their findings, along with their reasoning, believing their deliberations offered other citizens a real service.[9]

Citizen juries are no substitute for the ongoing practice of developing public judgment we've seen in citizen organizations featured throughout this book. But they do, along with many other models, offer an enrichment of public deliberation. They can demonstrate the distinct contribution that citizens can make to evaluating public issues.

Democratic Art Eight: Celebration and Appreciation

HALLMARK

✓ Celebration and appreciation integrated into the daily practices of public life.

BENEFITS

✓ Sustains and recharges.

✓ Builds loyalty and strengthens relationships.

SOME 'HOW-TO'S'

✓ Celebrate the learning as much as the winning.

✓ Create a celebratory spirit.

✓ Show appreciation of your adversaries as well as your allies.

Too many organizations and businesses feel that they can't take time to celebrate and express appreciation. There's just too much to *do*. They see celebration and appreciation as "extras" that can happen *after* all the work gets done. But in the most effective organizations, celebration and appreciation are integral to their very purpose.

Celebration and Appreciation How-To's

Here are just a few suggestions from citizens who are learning the importance of celebration and appreciation.

Celebrate the Learning, Not Just the Winning. We don't always get what we want. But out of every effort comes learning to be appreciated. After one citizen group's legislative campaign failed, we noticed that their newsletter celebrated how much their members had learned about both the issue and the citizen lobbying process. So by "celebration" we don't necessarily mean throwing a party. We also mean acknowledging and expressing satisfaction in what has been accomplished, even when an intended target is not met.

Create a Celebratory Spirit. Colored balloons. Noisemakers. Streamers. Amusing props. Live music. All these features create a mood of celebration, even in a public gathering dealing with deadly serious problems. Each time we've attended public meetings held by the Sonoma County Faith-Based

Organizing Project, for example, our moods are lifted as soon as we enter the auditorium. These techniques infuse their meetings with a spirit of celebration, despite the fact that this group faces such difficult issues as affordable housing and school reform.

What are they celebrating? Not just a victorious moment. One feels that we—all of us in these meetings—are celebrating the power of citizens to come together with a common vision. (And that power is not lost on the public officials present.) We're celebrating the hard work required to pull off the event. We're celebrating the power of hope over fear.

And it works. After two hours, members walk out feeling new energy, not drained from another boring meeting.

Show Appreciation of Your Adversaries as Well as Your Allies. Many of the groups you've read about in this book thrive because of the unpaid efforts of volunteers. Feeling appreciated can substitute for a lot of nonexistent paychecks. The most successful groups that we know acknowledge their volunteers at events in which the particular contribution of each individual is described. As members hear what others do, appreciation becomes a means of building a sense of interdependence within the group.

But the tough part is showing appreciation of our adversaries. Recall the earlier advice to make no permanent enemies. It was one how-to of creative conflict. Sometime in the future, you may need your present adversary's good will. Members of Kentuckians for the Commonwealth, at the close of one legislative session, passed out buttons to legislators whom they had been battling all year. The buttons read "I survived the 1990 legislative session!" In this gesture, KFTC members expressed their good will and appreciation for their adversaries' hard work. At another point, KFTC set up a lemonade and cookies stand for legislators near the state rotunda. The message of appreciation was mixed but good-spirited: "The lobbyists take you out for expensive meals. Come have some lemonade with us!"

Gestures like these, along with letters and calls of thanks (even when you disagree with the person), do not signal weakness. You'll establish your credibility as a person or group with strength, who knows you'll be around for the long haul.

Democratic Art Nine: Evaluation and Reflection

HALLMARK

✓ Public and private assessments of lessons learned through action.

BENEFITS

✓ Helps participants to improve their practice of all the other arts of democracy.

✓ Develops group and individual memory.

SOME 'HOW-TO'S'

✓ Create a new habit: immediately after each public action, discuss what worked, what didn't, and what lessons were learned.

✓ Encourage self-evaluation.

✓ Record lessons, so that history becomes a basis for ongoing learning.

✓ Reflect by digging deeper; it complements public evaluation.

Unfortunately, human beings have short memories. We tend to focus on the challenges of today, often failing to see or appreciate the distance we've traveled. This human tendency underscores the importance of the art of reflection and evaluation.

The most effective organizations and workplaces use every meeting, every discussion, every significant public event as an opportunity for learning—in part by immediately evaluating what went on. How, for example, did the event help them move toward their goals? An in-depth evaluation reviews the overall strategy and the effectiveness of the individual participants. It also examines any changes in the development and distribution of power.

Evaluation and Reflection How-To's

Here are several suggestions for how to make evaluation and reflection part of the culture of your organization or business.

Group Evaluation

The structure of a good evaluation can be elegantly simple. A few basic questions can become powerful tools of change. For example:

How do you *feel* about what happened? (Answers can be in one-word descriptions of emotions: upset, happy, relieved, angry, energized. No intellectualizing allowed.)

What worked?

What didn't work?

What could we do better?

Make an Evaluation of Each Meeting or Public Action a Habit. A good evaluation is far from a rote exercise. It deeply probes not only what we learned but *how we might change* based on what we've learned.

In the Youth Action Program (YAP) in New York City, both the staff and the trainees get together every Friday for an evaluation. Christopher Hatcher, who joined YAP to learn the building trades and escape inner-city poverty, told us that he appreciates the evaluation because "everybody has time to talk. Everybody listens." There's praise and there's criticism. The leadership is knowingly creating camaraderie in the group. At YAP, terms like *good* or *bad* are avoided in evaluations. The staff is acutely aware of the low self-esteem these young inner-city residents carry into the program. Staff person Richard Green explained that these kids are too often called *bad*. "We don't want to continue that," he says. "So we simply talk about specific behaviors and note whether they are occurring 'more frequently' or 'less frequently.'"

Encourage Self-Evaluation. In the most effective evaluations, citizen groups that are concerned about building the leadership strengths of their members are careful not to let criticism demoralize people. At Brockton Interfaith Community in Massachusetts, organizer Scott Spencer explained to us that after any "action" they always begin by encouraging participants first to evaluate their *own* performance before anyone else makes a critical

Evaluation, Reflection, and You

Write down the tools you use (such as discussions, a journal, or letters) to contribute to your ongoing learning by consciously:

Evaluating _____

Reflecting _____

Building memory of lessons learned _____

Where could you strengthen your practice of these arts? How might you do this? _____

_____

_____

What benefits could you expect if you did this? _____

_____

_____

What is one first step you will take in the next week to improve your practice of these arts? _____

_____

_____

comment. Acknowledging one's own mistakes is easier for most of us than hearing others' criticisms. The approach also fosters self-awareness.

Record Lessons So That History Becomes a Basis for Ongoing Learning. In most organizations and institutions, participants know little about the experiences of those who've gone before them. To create *group memory,* participants create records from which others can draw over time. Without them, members can't learn from group experience or feel rooted in the efforts of others. Kentuckians for the Commonwealth, for example, celebrated its tenth anniversary by publishing its own history as a handsome hardback book.[10] And Cooperative Home Care Associates (CHCA) has recorded its group memory for others who are starting worker-owned and -managed enterprises. There's no blueprint to follow, CHCA stresses, but it wants to provide a "sense of history."[11]

Reflect by Digging Deeper; It Complements Public Evaluation. By *reflection* we mean deeper thought—sitting back and asking, What did I learn from all this? Why am I doing it? What do I need to learn to become more effective in the future? While we can be aided by the penetrating questions of others, our most important insights come when we take the time to be alone, in order to listen to ourselves and record how we perceive our own growth.

Ken Galdston at the Merrimack Valley Project describes how his group encourages reflection: "We do one-on-one meetings with people about where they are going with their lives. At the Leadership Retreat, we reflect on their self-interest. What's the fit between their stated self-interest—things like personal growth and family—and how they are spending their time? We try to help people bring them into alignment."

 Democratic Art Ten: Mentoring

HALLMARK

✓ Encouragement and guidance to motivate learning.

BENEFITS

✓ Makes learning possible, regardless of the starting point.

✓ Motivates.

✓ Builds self-esteem and feelings of accomplishment for all.

SOME 'HOW-TO'S'

✓ Model the arts.

✓ Supportively "push."

✓ Break learning down into small steps.

✓ Team up newcomers with old-timers.

In conversations with hundreds of people who are learning the arts and skills of Living Democracy, the concept of mentoring came up often. We learned to think of a mentor as an on-the-scene guide or coach. This is a person who asks the leading questions, offers suggestions and feedback, and also demonstrates the skills being learned.

Mentoring How-To's

The following examples suggest guidelines for using mentoring to help individuals and groups develop new skills in the practice of Living Democracy.

Model the Arts. Jeanne Gauna of the Southwest Organizing Project (SWOP) is convinced that people learn the art of positive conflict by seeing it in action: "We teach it by doing, by modeling. We encourage people to see the value of different points of view. A lot of it has to do with facilitation of our meetings. We show facilitators how to point out the value of differing views—to say 'that's a good point. He's right. That's another good point,' even when the points seem radically opposed."

Supportively "Push." Preschool teacher Dulcie Giadone described how mentoring—with some friendly pushing—allowed her to become president of HART, an influential citizens' organization in Hartford, Connecticut. "The organizers keep pestering you," she told us. "'The meeting two weeks from now—would you chair it?' Jim [a staff person] would come early to the meeting and go over everything with you. He would always support you. It took me one year to handle the meeting completely on my own."

Elena Hanggi, who moved from homemaker to head one of the nation's largest citizen organizations, ACORN, used her own story to explain the importance of being pushed: "The first time, I literally had to be shoved to the podium to speak to the city council. The staff organizer knew that I could do it. I even knew that I could do it, but I *still* was afraid. If all that stands in the way is fear, sometimes you need others to help you get past that fear."

Break Learning Down into Small Steps. Mentors guide people, training them step-by-step in the new skills they need. "We teach people facilitation [of meetings] by having people do it," says Jeanne Gauna of SWOP. "People learn by watching others. So we start in pairs at first. One person handles names and calls on people. The other handles the summing-up process and keeps the meeting moving." Soon the person in the less challenging role of just calling on speakers can take on the more difficult tasks.

Team Up Newcomers with Old-Timers. Businesses, too, are learning that peer coaching works. Rather than use a training manual or have a boss serve as instructor, a company will have an experienced peer build a mentoring relationship with a new employee. W.L. Gore, maker of Gore-tex, is a good example. Gore calls his approach a "sponsor system." For each new hire, an experienced employee volunteers to be his or her starting sponsor. The sponsor, not the person in authority over you, teaches you the ropes. And it's the sponsor who decides after three months whether your contribution to the company warrants a permanent position. A second type of sponsor is the advocate sponsor, whose job it is to know your accomplishments and to speak on your behalf.[12]

Teaming up with more experienced participants in public life—whether from community organizations, churches, schools, or workplaces—helps us manage our fears, learn new skills, and grasp the context within which we are working.

We've briefly discussed ten arts of effective public life that Americans are learning in diverse settings, from the workplace to the community group. And we've woven into the entire book the suggestions of many people as to where you can practice these arts.

As we deliberately develop the arts of democratic public life, we help to reshape the institutions of everyday living—from workplaces to schools—so that their rules and practices support, instead of thwart, growth in these skills. And in the process we begin to shape the very qualities of character so needed for a living, working democracy.

12

Embracing the Democratic Self

THE ARTS OF DEMOCRACY WE TOUCHED on in this book suggest more than a distinct set of skills. They add up to a certain *quality of character.* Someone who, for example, listens actively, uses anger effectively, develops judgment through dialogue, and regularly practices reflection and evaluation is more than just highly skilled. Such a person has honed attitudes, values, habits of mind, and a temperament—that support those skills. We call the sum of these qualities of character the democratic self.

The emergence of the democratic self in a Living Democracy poses a radical challenge to long-held assumptions about the human personality.

The classical eighteenth-century liberal view of the self as a social "atom," isolated from others and driven by narrow self-interest, has been largely discredited by modern social science—even though it continues to shape our "you've got to look out for Number One" culture. That human beings are profoundly social creatures is increasingly appreciated: we become who we are through interaction with others. Abraham Maslow, one of this century's most celebrated psychologists, urged individuals to develop a wider circle of identifications...what he called the 'more inclusive Self.'

One problem blocking the emergence of Living Democracy, however, is that most popular psychology still defines quite narrowly this social aspect of the human personality. Even though it has left behind its simplistic self-fullfillment-is-all theme of the seventies and eighties, the prevailing message in popular psychology remains: we grow, we change ourselves, we find happiness by pursuing our *private* relationships. Best-selling self-help books coach us in finding ourselves through introspection—through personal journals, dream analysis, body work—and by working through issues of love and control in our intimate relationships. While many of these techniques can enhance our lives, they are simply not sufficient either to produce the individual happiness we want or the society we want.

Living Democracy—what we've found *working* in the lives of people who shaped this book—suggests that a myopic focus on self, and on intimate private relationships, ignores a huge part of the human personality. Human beings also grow, find ourselves, and find meaning as we act with others on concerns beyond ourselves. As we discover what we uniquely bring to the community in which we live. As we reshape who we are by interacting with others who are different from us..

Because the prevailing culture has so long devalued the contribution of regular citizens, too many of us have acquiesced to the notion that private life is all there is. Public life—as we discussed in Chapter Two—comes to be viewed as only what celebrities and activists have. But the effective people whom you have met in this book are teaching us something else: without rich public lives our growth remains stunted, our private lives impoverished.

Perhaps as you have read this book you have tried to imagine what some of the people are like who are doing the things we describe. Just who *are* they? Are they people like me? you might wonder.

 Four Qualities of the Democratic Self

The democratic self:

• Has patience even with oneself

• Values learning as much as winning

• Takes some discomfort in stride

• Is creative in the face of ambiguity

We believe that people who are bringing democracy to life are developing distinct qualities. A number of these qualities cluster around a common theme: the democratic self keeps the big picture in mind. Because it would take another book to explore the qualities of the democratic self in the depth they deserve, we've chosen to focus here on this cluster.

Patience, Even with Oneself

Patience as a democratic art goes much deeper than being able to wait for the bus without getting upset. It is a frame of mind—a large frame of mind.

Anyone consciously setting out to improve a human-made institution—a workplace, an organization, a bureaucratic agency, a school, any structure at all—is likely to encounter frustration, disappointment, sometimes even betrayal. Things are always more complicated than we imagine they will be. Every change creates unanticipated outcomes. Sometimes people act against even their own best interests.

When philosophers ponder this fact of inevitable disappointment, they simply call it the human condition. From Shakespeare's graceful pen, it was what occurs too often "twixt the cup and the lip." The less poetic among us simply groan, "life's tough," while the more coarse reduce it to that unlovely bumper sticker, "s—t happens."

As we develop a public life in which we work for ends we care about deeply, these painful truths—that life and social change can be deeply frustrating—require something even deeper than ordinary patience. We need an appreciation of the unevenness of human growth.

Gerald Taylor, for example, the citizen organizer with the Industrial Areas Foundation, pondered aloud how he manages to derive enormous satisfaction from his work, despite inevitable setbacks. "Philosophically I do not believe in the inevitability of progress," he said. "I only believe in change. The beauty of this work is that you are participating fully in the human condition. That means it's not linear—not a straight line going up. So I don't get upset when things don't go as planned.

"This work has taught me the meaning of real patience. Every success has seeds of new problems. I try to prepare leaders for this, so they don't get the idea that they can find *the* solution . . . To be effective, you have to be at ease with the human condition—its irrationality, its pathos."

And Carol Ford at Save Our Cumberland Mountains voiced a very similar idea: "With SOCM, I learned that you may not move a mountain in a day. You chip away at it. With that kind of thinking, things don't have to overwhelm you."

Gerald's and Carol's views were echoed by Adam Urbanski, head of Rochester's teachers' union. "Democracy means not dramatic changes but pragmatic improvements," he says. The greatest danger facing Rochester's school reform, he feels, is not from its opponents but from those supporters who expect results too soon.

The importance of cultivating the quality of patience also arose when we talked with business analysts about democratizing the workplace. Henry Sims warned, "You cannot expect people to take over new responsibilities too fast." Learning takes time. He stressed that sometimes introducing self-managed teamwork produces a "temporary fall in productivity that is difficult to accept." And he went on to emphasize that "Managers have to accept this. Persistence is needed here."

An Emphasis on Learning

Gerald's, Carol's, and Henry's comments suggest a new way of thinking about growth itself. As some wiser than we have said, it's not about solving all our problems. Growth is about moving from one set of problems to a better set of problems. In other words, as long as we can take satisfaction in our own learning, we never feel defeated. Even if we have not reached a goal, we can appreciate the capacities we've gained in the process of trying, capacities that make it possible for us to tackle new challenges.

Some Discomfort Goes with the Territory

Developing the democratic self may not always be comfortable. In fact, things can feel worse before they feel better. Learning any new skill feels awkward at first, whether it's playing tennis, mastering the piano, or learning how to make a democratic classroom work.

Remember teacher Kim Wile in Ohio, whose students became a key source of information for voters of their county? She acknowledges that "democracy can be an untidy and challenging business." Recall that she acknowledged feeling "quite comfortable in the traditional role of the directive teacher. It is far more nerve-racking to take the back seat and let the students take the reins of control." But, she adds, "watching the students' pride, excitement, and growth" made this major change worth the effort.

Similarly, corporate CEO Ralph Stayer decided to abandon authoritarian management, but that turned out to be more difficult than he'd imagined. "Initially, I had hoped the journey would be as neat and orderly as it now appears on paper. Fortunately—since original mistakes are an important part of learning—it wasn't. There were lots of obstacles and challenges, much backsliding, and myriad false starts and wrong decisions."[1]

Being Creative Despite Ambiguity

Like Gerald Taylor, Larry McNeil is an organizer with the Industrial Areas Foundation. Larry works in southern California, and he talked with us about a related quality that he feels is essential to democratic public life. "In IAF, we teach that there's tension between the world as it is and the world as you wish it to be. Sure, there's part of the world as it is that you don't want to mimic, but it's not simple. You can't live in the world as you *wish* it to be. So public life has an edge. You have to live with the tension. . . . You have to learn how to act when things aren't simple, clear-cut. You have to learn that it's possible to have core values but be flexible about how you get there. The successful people live with the tension."

The statements we've heard from Gerald, Carol, and Larry capture key qualities that can be cultivated in public life. But their words also suggest an additional dimension of the democratic personality: not simply living with ambiguity, but *being creative* in the face of ambiguity.

"I used to say apologetically that democracy is messy," Jerry Jenkins told us. She was Citizen Participation Coordinator in St. Paul for many years. "Now I've decided that I don't need to apologize for democracy. You just have to wade in. You learn the value of creative conflict. You learn how deeply interdependent we all are."

And as you've noticed throughout this book, Jerry and hundreds of other citizens have found ways to turn this "messiness" into creative solutions to the problems that disturb them. Refusing to wallow in despair, they are developing themselves and working with others to devise pragmatic approaches that build realistic hope.

Putting Insights into Practice

You've read what several successful people say about patience and the practice of Living Democracy in their lives. In the left-hand column, we've paraphrased a few of their insights. In the middle column, jot down how much you both *accept* and *practice* the insights that each of these people offer us. And include in the right column your ideas about how you can use these thoughts to improve your own life.

Insight	Extent to which I I accept it and practice it	How I can apply it to my own life
Improvements are not linear. Every success has seeds of new problems. (Gerald Taylor)		
Change comes slowly, through steady, persistent work. (Carol Ford)		
Don't expect dramatic change; work instead for pragmatic improvements. (Adam Urbanski)		
Learning is what's most important, and it takes time. (Henry Sims)		
Mistakes are an important part of learning. (Ralph Stayer)		
Building the democratic spirit in others is less comfortable, more challenging—and much more rewarding—than being directive. (Kim Wile)		
We have to live with the tension of real-world complexity. (Larry McNeil)		
Conflict and interdependence are both messy and valuable. (Jerry Jenkins)		

The democratic self doesn't express itself in only one arena of our lives. As we learn the arts of effective problem solving in, say, a democratic workplace, that learning spills over into other areas.

Recall the experiences of those in Chapter Two who described the effect of a changed workplace, or participation in a democratic community organization, on their lives outside of work. One worker in a team-run plant noted a similar spillover: "I'm in a Cub Scout organization," he said. "The meetings there used to be atrocious. [Then] I instituted an agenda system like we have at team meetings here at the plant." And a co-worker described his success in "getting more participation" in meetings of his volunteer fire department. "It *has* worked," he says.[2]

And young people we've spoken with have seen how the experience of discovering public life beyond school has altered their experience *in* school. Sixteen-year-old Kathy Rivera of Brooklyn is one. At thirteen she joined the Toxic Avengers, a group of teenagers started just months earlier from a project in a high school science class for youngsters who had dropped out of regular school. The Avengers' first big victory was forcing a glue factory in the neighborhood to stop dumping toxic wastes into the sewer. "Before I joined I was a more timid person. I kept to myself. I let people suppress my ideas," Kathy told us. "But I've learned to let people know what I believe in." She explained that now she's more motivated in school "because in the future I want to make a difference."

Formal democracy requires little of us. In formal democracy, it's the laws and institutions that count—and they're *already* established, many of them two hundred years ago. All that's really asked of us is that we pay the bill each April 15th and show up at the polls every few years.

In contrast, Living Democracy requires a great deal—not *from* us, but *of* us. Rather than being an added burden we have to bear, Living Democracy means attending energetically to the development of our democratic selves.

Embracing the Effort That Change Requires

Some popular psychology that focuses on individual fulfillment suggests that healthy gratification is effortless: "What's right is what feels good. Anything else means self-sacrifice, and that's unhealthy."

Developing Our Democratic Selves

Here we have drawn contrasts. In the left-hand column are some of the qualities that tend to thwart effectiveness. The right-hand column captures some of the qualities we find in the many effective people we're meeting. In cultivating the arts of democracy you will be developing these qualities. Circle those you think are most important for you to develop.

Pessimistic	Prudently optimistic
Easily defeated	Persevering
Despairing	Hopeful
Self-pitying	Self-respecting
Simply blaming	Accepts responsibility for action
Intolerant of uncertainty	Expects the unexpected
Fearful of embarrassment	Takes discomfort in stride
Mistrustful	Critically aware
Unthinking	Strategic
Passively frustrated	Actively engaged
Stuck	Always growing
Intolerant	Values diversity
Shut off	Seeking connection with others

The understanding of human beings that makes Living Democracy possible is based on a much older tradition. This tradition assumes that most of us naturally desire what is best for our community, even when we find it difficult to achieve. We *want* to contribute. Even when such work is challenging. Even when it doesn't offer immediate gratification. Even when it entails suffering through self-doubt and fear.[3]

The people you've met in this book confirm this view of human nature. Making a positive difference in their communities or workplaces or schools is what they genuinely want to do. Yet it obviously entails effort. They, and, we believe, most Americans, are willing—given encouragement, examples, and training—to go to a great deal of effort in order to develop the capacities they need to become effective contributors to our larger society.

Developing the democratic self takes effort, of course. But why might we bother? As we address that question, teacher Nancy Corbett comes to mind. For nineteen years she taught as a traditional stand-in-front-of-the-classroom teacher. It was comfortable. She was in control. Then she began to challenge her democratic self, and as a consequence, she writes, "I need not fear drying up (like a crinkled apple doll . . .) behind my desk, just because I have taught for so long. While projects like these [involving students in the community] will mean extra work and extra time, my own staying alive in the classroom is more than sufficient reason to adventure democratically with learners."[4]

The people we've met in writing this book are convincing: they *are* becoming more alive. They are taking charge of their lives and solving their problems. They live in hope, not despair. We hope this book can serve as *their* invitation to millions of Americans.

13

What, No Manifesto?

MOST BOOKS ABOUT SOCIAL CHANGE end with a rousing manifesto. The authors are only too eager to provide their blueprint for just how to get out of the mess we're in.

Not this book. Ending our book with a manifesto would belie its thesis. The lesson of this book is that *there is no formula*. We all must become spirited inventors. There's no single answer—not even a single starting point. Even the "teachers" in this book don't offer us the answer. They *do* offer us approaches, ways of thinking, possibilities we can adapt, and hope that might generate in us wholly new ideas.

They offer no set model but rather a stirring range of examples. They teach us to go beyond blaming. They teach us to take seriously the work necessary to become effective public people. They teach us that it is not easy, but it *is* do-able. And it is worth doing, both for ourselves and for others.

When the two of us set out to write this book, we thought we'd be lucky to find a few dozen examples that might illustrate the lessons of Living Democracy. We were wrong. Very wrong. When the book was finally finished, our offices were overflowing with hundreds of compelling stories that we couldn't squeeze into these pages.

Despite the number of examples, we can't *prove* that these stories augur more sweeping changes throughout our society. We know only that in a society that often appears overwhelmed by its problems, on the very edge of hopelessness, an extraordinarily hopeful revolution *is* under way.

It's a revolution that suggests that we Americans *can* solve our problems.

TACKLING THE CRISIS OF DEMO- CRACY

In the first chapters of this book, we spoke of the terrible public problems that bombard us daily. But we argued that they aren't the real crisis. They are solvable. And in most cases the solutions are already known.

The real crisis concerns the obstacles that prevent us from coming together to solve these problems, to act on what we know.

We call this the crisis of democracy. It is the failure of public problem solving.

Some observers see the chief barrier that prevents America from solving its problems as concentrated economic power—the fact that the top 1 percent of us receives as much income as the bottom 90 percent of us put together. Others point to a closely related barrier: the power of big money not only to influence who gets elected but to sway votes in Congress after election day.

Some cite racism, sexism, and other prejudices that keep millions of Americans from developing and contributing to their full potential. Often these are the same critics who blame "corporate-dominated" media for keeping us uninformed and isolated from one another.

Still others emphasize the fact that more and more of us are earning low wages. Add to this the rising cost of basic needs like housing, and they wonder how Americans can be expected to solve *public* problems. Surely their *private* ones are overwhelming enough.

We agree, strongly. Each of these is both a problem itself *and* a barrier to effective public problem solving.

We can't belittle these very real obstacles. Rather, we ask you to focus your attention on one key question: *How?* How can any of these problems, and the myriad of others, be addressed? How can the barriers to public problem solving be overcome?

Only by more democracy—and by a richer form of democracy. Only by people discovering that *despite* these barriers they do have sources of power to develop and use. They do have something valuable to contribute.

We're not saying that if more Americans develop their voices in public life then, automatically, our problems will be solved. We *are* saying that this shift is essential to all else that must happen. Without it, we as a society simply cannot tackle *both* the obstacles to participation and the very real economic, environmental, and social problems that beset us.

Even in a society of highly lopsided power—in companies, cities, schools, and throughout economic and political life—people can learn to find sources of power on which to build. Those who were our teachers in writing this book, those whose voices you heard here, are discovering sources of power they can develop. They are using that power to remove the barriers facing people who are usually excluded from decision making. They are addressing our society's most pressing problems. And in doing so, they are removing the barriers to Living Democracy.

If Living Democracy is not a place, not an end point, but a dynamic way of life, then we can't adopt the attitude, "well, we can't have it until we've first removed the barriers—gotten money out of politics, made the distribution of wealth more fair, and so on." The only possibility of ever bringing democracy to life is discovering that we can begin *now*. To paraphrase Gandhi, "There is no road to democracy. Democracy is the road."

We become full citizens by doing, not simply by decrying the inequities and barriers to participation. We become full citizens by engaging with others, defining our own interests while we uncover their interests. We become full citizens as we gain confidence—confidence that we *do* have something important to contribute, confidence that through vigorous public dialogue we will come to sound judgment on even the largest public issues.

BUT WHY? AND WHY NOW?

Throughout this book we've suggested some possible explanations for the emergence of Living Democracy. Not one, but many forces are converging.

First, the alarm is sounding. It gets harder and harder to block out the noise. By many measures, our society is in trouble. Homelessness has brought hunger and poverty out from behind closed doors. Mounting violence and fear grip us all. Environmental degradation assaults our senses daily. There's no longer any place to hide. Whether the problem is crime, pollution, or failing schools, more and more of us know that money alone won't buy our escape.

Second, there's the spreading realization that "those up there" who were supposed to be "taking care of business" have blown it. Could we—everyday people—do any worse? The perception that the caliber of public officials is sinking emboldens some to say, "If *he's* qualified to make public decisions, why aren't I?"

Third, a more positive note. With the fall of communism, we've lost an "opposite" to help us feel good about ourselves. A teacher acquaintance of ours asked high school students over several years in the eighties to write essays on what's good about America. Many of these teenagers responded, "What is good about America is that we're not like the Russians." But today, with the "evil empire" dissolved, we're called upon to define ourselves in positive terms—to be better, not in comparison to another failed society, but relative to our own past performance.

Finally, across many disciplines—from psychology to the natural sciences—contemporary insights ring a similar note about the interconnected nature of all life, including human beings. The dominant metaphor of our time is ecology, with its emphasis both on *relationships* and on *change*. Through awareness of the "ozone hole" and the "greenhouse effect"—to which we each contribute and from which we each will suffer—ecology's lessons of interconnectedness and change seep into popular consciousness. Living Democracy, in all its varied forms, builds on the assumption of that interconnectedness and that dynamism.

All these influences drive us to stop simply blaming and start looking for solutions.

WHAT IS DIFFERENT TODAY?

Many freedoms we now enjoy—from women's suffrage and the eight-hour day to civil rights—stem from citizen-led efforts for social progress. What we see as distinct about our current period is that change is occurring not in one sector alone, and not simply because those excluded are pushing to be included, although that is clearly central to what is happening.

Rather, changes are under way simultaneously in virtually all arenas of public life. And many initiatives for change are spurred not just by those on the "outside" but by those on the "inside" as well. It's not only the most vulnerable who know that our current assumptions and policies are failing us. Many corporate decision makers, educational bigwigs, and top-echelon human services professionals, for example, share the realization that profound rethinking is necessary. Some are even willing to risk change.

Plus, as we've underscored throughout this book, a striking feature of the upsurge in citizen engagement is that it's about much more than protesting failed policies, or even demanding redress. What characterizes many of today's initiatives is that citizens are creating an ongoing role for themselves in public decision making. This is quite different from simply overthrowing an oppressive law or instituting a needed reform.

Another way of saying what the stories in this book teach us is this: they are as much about changing the *way* decisions get made as they are about changing a given decision.

What also distinguishes the citizen empowerment of this era is that it is not a special need of a special group—activists, say, or big-shot public figures. Rather, the Americans we talk with understand that the need to contribute to that which is beyond ourselves—maybe even beyond our lifetimes—is a need that resides in almost all of us. So they don't preach to people about becoming activists for the benefit of others. Instead, they welcome others to express the deep needs they have discovered within themselves.

Another feature of today's breakthroughs is this: while many Americans grow up believing that "the good life" of material pleasures and "doing good" by serving others are opposite choices, the lives of people in this book tell a different story. Their lives are growing richer and more rewarding because they've rejected that false trade-off. They're learning that finding a place in public life need not consume them. The democratic arts they're learning in public life enrich their private lives as well. In fact, many feel that only by acting on their beliefs in public life can they be true to their commitment to their loved ones.

We hope that when you put down this book, you'll pause to ponder: just how might the lessons of those who are "living democracy," whom you've met throughout this book, apply to relationships in the public world that you already have, be they at work, your school, or in your community?

And we hope that you'll want to pick up your pen or telephone to reach some of the many resources we've included in the pages that follow, or explore similar opportunities in your own community.

We also welcome you to write to us. Please share your ideas, and find out about resources at the Center for Living Democracy that might help answer your questions.

Finally, thank you for joining us on this journey. And thanks once more to all those who so generously shared their experiences to make this book—and the promise of Living Democracy—possible.

Resources For Building a Living Democracy

HERE ARE ONLY A HANDFUL of the thousands of organizations nationwide that are making our democracy come alive to solve real problems. Because the number of such groups far exceeds what we can include here, we've listed only those organizations highlighted in the book, with a few exceptions. Please write to us if you want additional suggestions. Many of these organizations have newsletters and other publications from which you can learn. Some have training programs. Get in touch!

Organizations

National Multi-Issue Citizen Organizations

Association of Community Organizations for
Reform Now (ACORN)
Organizing and Support Center
1024 Elysian Fields Avenue
New Orleans, LA 70117
504-943-0044 FAX: 504-944-7078
National Office
730 8th Street SE
Washington, D.C. 20003
202-547-9292 FAX: 202-546-2483
Newsletter: *U.S.A. of ACORN*

Industrial Areas Foundation (IAF)
Ed Chambers, Executive Director
36 New Hyde Park
Franklyn Square, NY 11011
516-354-1076

National People's Action (NPA)—
National Training and Information Center
Gale Cincotta, Chairperson
810 North Milwaukee Avenue
Chicago, IL 60622
312-243-3035
Newsletter: *Disclosure*

Pacific Institute for Community Organizations
(PICO)
John Bauman
171 Santa Rosa Avenue
Oakland, CA 94610
510-655-2801

Regional and Citywide Multi-Issue Citizen Organizations

East

Brockton Interfaith Community
Scott Spencer, Director
65 West Elm Street,
Brockton, MA 02401

Hartford Areas Rally Together (HART)
Jane Boucher, Executive Director
660 Park Street
Hartford, CT 06106
203-525-3449
Newsletter: *HART Beat*

Merrimack Valley Project (MVP)
Ken Galdston, Director
198 South Broadway
Lawrence, MA 01843
508-686-0650

Naugatuck Valley Project (NVP)
Susan Wefald, Director
47 Central Avenue
Waterbury, CT 06702
203-574-2410

Midwest

Interfaith Organizing Project
Ed Shurna, Director
1617 West Washington
Chicago, IL 60612
312-243-3328

Joint Ministry Project
John Norton, Director
P.O. Box 14626
Minneapolis, MN 55414-0626
612-645-2754

South

Kentuckians for the Commonwealth
P.O. Box 864
Prestonburg, KY 41653
606-886-0043
Newsletter: *Balancing the Scales*

Kentucky Local Governance Project
c/o MACED
433 Chestnut Street
Berea, KY 40403

Newsletter: *Local Voices: Building Community Through Grassroots Democracy*
Save Our Cumberland Mountains (SOCM)
P.O. Box 479
Lake City, TN 37769

West

Southwest Organizing Project (SWOP)
Louis Head
211 Tenth Street SW
Albuquerque, NM 87102
505-247-8832, 505-243-4116

Organizations Affiliated with the Industrial Areas Foundation

Allied Communities of Tarrant (ACT)
P.O. Box 3565
Fort Worth, TX 76113
817-332-1830

Communities Organized for Public Service (COPS)
P.O. Box 830355
San Antonio, TX 78283
512-222-2367

East Valleys Organization (EVO)
899 West Foothill Boulevard, Suite 1,
Monrovia, CA 91016
818-301-9633

The Metropolitan Organization (TMO)
202 North Loop West, Suite 221
Houston, TX 78203
713-868-1429

Shelby County Interfaith (SCI)
491 East McLemore
Memphis, TN 38106
901-722-5561

Sonoma County Faith-Based Community
Organizing Project
430 Murphy Avenue
Sebastopol, CA 95472
707-829-8961

South Central Organizing Committee (SCOC)
2186 West 31st Street
Los Angeles, CA 90018
213-731-8464

United Neighborhoods Organization (UNO)
3763 East 4th Street
Los Angeles, CA 90063
213-266-0577

Valley Interfaith
P.O. Box 1616
Weslaco, TX 78596
512-565-6316

Single-Issue Citizen Organizations

National

National Association of Resident Management
Associations (NARMA)
Gail Sivels, Associate Director
4524 Douglas Street NE
Washington, D.C. 20019
202-397-7002

National Low-Income Housing Coalition
1012 Fourteenth Street NW
Washington, D.C. 20005
202-662-1530

Local/Regional

Heal the Bay
Dorothy Green, Founding President
1640 Fifth Street, No. 112
Santa Monica, CA 90401
310-394-4552, 310-270-4151

Pennsylvania Environmental Network
Charles Leiden
306 Coleridge Avenue
Altoona, PA 16602
814-946-9291

Organizations Working for a More Democratic Economy and Workplaces (Chapter Five)

National

Center for Ethics and Economic Policy
2512 9th Street, No. 3
Berkeley, CA 94710-2542
510-549-9931

Federation for Industrial Retention and Renewal
(FIRR)
Jim Benn, Executive Director
3411 West Diversey Avenue, No. 10
Chicago, IL 60647
312-252-7676

Institute for Community Economics (ICE)
57 School Street
Springfield, MA 01105-1331
413-746-8660 FAX: 413-746-8862
Newsletter: *Community Economics*

National Center for Employee Ownership
Corey Rosen, Executive Director
2201 Broadway, Suite 807
Oakland, CA 94612
510-272-9461
Newsletter: *Employee Ownership Report*

Southern Finance Project
329 Rensselaer
Charlotte, NC 28203
704-372-7073

East

Burlington Community Land Trust
Brenda Torpy, Director
P.O. Box 523
Burlington, VT 05402
802-862-6244

Cooperative Home Care Associates (CHCA)
Rick Surpin, President
349 East 149th Street
Bronx, NY 10451
212-993-7104

Steel Valley Authority (SVA)
Robert Erickson
120 East Ninth Avenue
Homestead, PA 15120
412-462-8408

Midwest

Appalachian Center for Economic Networks
(ACEnet) (Formerly Worker-Owned Network)
94 Columbus Road
Athens, OH 45701
614-592-3854
Newsletter: *Network News*

CAN-DO
343 South Dearborn Avenue, Suite 910
Chicago, IL 60606
312-939-7171

Chicago Focus
Dan Broughton
6 North Michigan Avenue, Suite 1516
Chicago, IL 60602
312-332-5100

Congress for a Working America
Chris Crawley, Executive Director
731 West Washington Street
Milwaukee, WI 53204
414-225-6200

Institute for Social Justice
Elena Hanggi
523 West 15th
Little Rock, AR 72202
504-376-2528

Midwest Center for Employee Ownership
Dan Swinney
3411 West Diversey Avenue, Room 10
Chicago, IL 60647
312-278-5418 FAX: 312-278-5918

Midwest Center for Labor Research/
Early Warning Network
3411 West Diversey Avenue, Room 10
Chicago, IL 60647
312-278-5418 FAX: 312-278-5918
Publication: *Labor Research Review*

South Shore Bank and Shorebank Corporation
7054 South Jeffery Boulevard
Chicago, IL 60649-2096
312-288-1000 or 1-800-NOW-SSBK
FAX: 312-493-6609

South
Center for Community Self-Help
413 East Chapel Hill Street
Durham, NC 27701
919-683-9686
Newsletter: *Self-Help*

Organizations Helping Citizens Reclaim the Media (Chapter Six)

Center for Integration and Improvement of Journalism
Jon Funabiki, Director
San Francisco State University
1600 Holloway Avenue
San Francisco, CA 94132
415-338-7434

Center for Media and Values
1962 South Shenandoah Street
Los Angeles, CA 90034
310-559-2944
Publication: *Media and Values*

Fairness and Accuracy in Reporting (FAIR)
Jeff Cohen
130 West 25th Street
New York, NY 10001
212-633-6700
Newsletter: *Extra!*

Institute for Global Communications
Jillaine Smith
18 De Boom Street
San Francisco, CA 94107
415-442-0220

Media Network
39 West 14th Street, Suite 403
New York, NY 10011
212-929-2663

National Alliance for Media Arts and Culture
1212 Broadway, Suite 816
Oakland, CA 94612
510-451-2717

National Federation of Community Broadcasters
666 11th Street NW, Suite 805
Washington, D.C. 20001
202-393-2355

National Federation of Local Cable Programmers
P.O. Box 27290
Washington, D.C. 20038-7290
202-829-7186

National Video Resources
73 Spring Street, Suite 606
New York, NY 10012
212-274-8080

NYU Interactive Telecommunications
Program
Alternate Media Center
Ms. Red Burns, Director
New York University
Tisch School of the Arts
721 Broadway, 4th Floor
New York, NY 10003
212-998-1888

Old Colorado City Communications
Dave Hughes
2502 West Colorado Avenue, No. 203
Colorado Springs, CO 80904
719-632-4848

Open Public Events Network
(Open/Net)
Lee Wing, Director
116 West Jones Street
Raleigh, NC 27611
919-733-6341

Public Electronic Net (PEN)
City of Santa Monica
Ken Phillips
1685 Main Street, Room 110
Santa Monica, CA 90407
310-458-8383

Public Interest Video Network
1642 R Street NW
Washington, D.C. 20009
202-797-8997

The Video Project
5332 College Avenue, Suite 101
Oakland, CA 94618
510-655-9050

Media Outlets Practicing Living Democracy (Chapter Six)

Austin Community Television (ACTV)
Melissa Hield
1143 North Avenue
Austin, TX 78702
512-478-8600

Berks Community Television (BCTV)
Ann Sheehan
645 Penn Street
Reading, PA 19601
215-374-3065

Community Reporter
Kathy Vadnais
233 Banfil Street
St. Paul, MN 55102
612-224-0845

Deep Dish TV
Center for New Television
1440 North Dayton Street
Chicago, IL 60622
312-951-6868

Indian Country Today
Tim Giago
P.O Box 2180
Rapid City, SD 57709
605-341-0011

KNON
Mark McNeil, Station Manager
4415 San Jacinto
Dallas, TX 75204
214-828-9500

KVI
Mike Siegel
200 Tower Building
Seattle, WA 98101
206-223-5700

National Public Radio
2025 M Street NW
Washington, D.C. 20036
202-822-2346

Tualatin Valley Community Access Channels
(TVCA)
Paula Manley
1815 169th Place, Suite 6020
Beaverton, OR 97006
503-629-8534

Wichita Eagle
Davis (Buzz) Merritt, Jr., Editor
Steve Smith, Managing Editor
825 East Douglas, P.O. Box 820
Wichita, KS 67201-0820
316-268-6405

Organizations Promoting a Participatory Model of Human Services (Chapter Seven)

American Health Decisions
Citizens' Committee on Ethics
Mary Strong, President
Oakes Outreach Center
120 Morris Avenue
Summit, NJ 07901-3948
908-277-3858

Behavioral Science Institute
Homebuilders Division
Daniel Johnson, Associate Director
34004 Ninth Avenue South, Suite 8
Federal Way, WA 58003-6796
206-927-1550

Center for Medical Consumers
237 Thompson Street
New York, NY 10012
212-674-7105

Center for Urban Affairs and Policy Research
Northwestern University
2030 Sheridan Road
Evanston, IL 60201
708-491-3995

The Connecticut Union of Disability Action
Groups (CUDAG)
Shelley Teed-Wargo
30 Jordan Lane
Wethersfield, CT 06109
203-257-4371

Family Preservation—Families First
Susan Kelly, Director
235 South Grand, Suite 411
Lansing, MI 48909
517-373-3465

Mountain States Health Corporation
Paul McGinnis, Project Director
1193 Royvonne Avenue SE, No. 14
Salem, OR 97302
503-378-1764/8

National Citizen's Coalition for Nursing Home
Reform
Elma Holder, Executive Director
Barbara Frank, Associate Director
1224 M Street NW, Suite 301
Washington, D.C. 20005
202-393-2018

National Council of Independent Living
Troy Atrium, Fourth and Broadway
Troy, NY 12180
518-274-1979

National Mental Health Consumers Association
P.O. Box 1166
Madison, WI 53701-1166
608-256-4060

National Self-Help Clearinghouse
Frank Riessman, Director
25 West 43rd Street
New York, NY 10036
212-642-2944

On Our Own of Montgomery County
Ryan Disher, Executive Director
213 Monroe Street
Rockville, MD 20850
301-251-3734

Oregon Health Decisions
921 S.W. Washington Street, No. 723
Portland, OR 97205
503-241-0744

Y-ME
Sharon Green, Executive Director
18220 Harwood Avenue
Homewood, IL 60430
708-799-8338 FAX: 708-799-5937

Other Organizations Highlighted in Chapter Seven

Homestead-Gardens Public Housing Project
Dr. Roger C. Mills
1103 Gulf Way
St. Petersburg Beach, FL 33706
601-869-4859

Kenilworth-Parkside Resident Management
Corporation
450 Quarles Street NE
Washington, D.C. 20019
202-396-2327

Organizations Facilitating Collaborative Problem Solving (Chapter Eight)

National

Center for Community Change
1000 Wisconsin Avenue NW
Washington, D.C. 20007
202-342-0519
Newsletter: *Community Change*

Community Design Exchange
923 23rd Avenue East
Seattle, WA 98112
206-329-2919 FAX: 206-720-6201

Maverick Institute
P.O. Box 2723
Tucson, AZ 85702-2723
602-629-0929

National Civic League
1445 Market Street, Suite 300
Denver, CO 80202-1728
303-571-4343
Publication: *National Civic Review*

National League of Cities
1301 Pennsylvania Ave. NW
Washington, D.C. 20004
202-783-2961

Local/Regional

Chattanooga Venture
Eleanor Cooper, Executive Director
506 Broad Street
Chattanooga, TN 37402
615-267-8687

Community Forum
(Formerly Futures Forum)
1515 East Osborn
Phoenix, AZ 85014
602-263-8853

Roanoke Neighborhood Partnership
Room 355, Municipal Building
215 Church Avenue SW
Roanoke, VA 24011
703-345-8250

City Offices Promoting Citizen Participation (Chapter Eight)

Citizen Advisory Board/Office of the Mayor
Benjamin Greene, Assistant to the Mayor
710 North 20th Street
Birmingham, AL 35203
205-254-2277

Citizen Participation Coordinator
City of St. Paul, Department of Planning and
Economic Development
Ann Copeland
25 West Fourth Street
St. Paul, MN 55102
612-266-6595

City of Seattle Department of Neighborhoods
Jim Diers, Director
Arctic Building, Room 400
700 Third Avenue
Seattle, WA 98104
206-684-0464

Division of Neighborhood Affairs
City of Dayton, Department of Human and
Neighborhood Resources
Cilla Bosnak, Superintendent
101 West 3rd Street
Dayton, OH 45402
513-443-3775

Office of Neighborhood Associations
Diane M. Linn, Director
1220 S.W. 5th, Room 204
Portland, OR 97204
503-823-4519

Other Organizations Mentioned in Chapter Eight

Dayton Neighborhood Development
Dean Lovelace, Director
909 Irving Avenue
Dayton, OH 45469-2510
513-229-4641

North Seattle's Family Center
Ellen Stewart
13540 Lake City Way NE
Seattle, WA 98125
206-364-7930

Organizations Furthering Education for Living Democracy (Chapter Nine)

Center for Collaborative Education
Heather Lewis and Priscilla Ellington,
Co-Directors
1573 Madison Avenue, Room 201
New York, NY 10029
212-348-7821

Center for Educational Renewal
Miller Hall DQ-12, University of Washington
Seattle, WA 98195
206-543-6230

Citywide Coalition for School Reform
South Wacker Drive, Suite 1100
Chicago, IL 60606
312-592-6105

Coalition of Essential Schools
Prof. Theodore Sizer, Director
Brown University, 1 Davol Square
Providence, RI 02903
401-863-3384
Newsletter: *Horace*

Cooperative Learning Center
Dr. David Johnson and Dr. Roger Johnson
College of Education, University of Minnesota
202 Pattee Hall, 150 Pillsbury Drive SE
Minneapolis, MN 55455-0298
612-624-7031

Designs for Change
220 South State Street
Chicago, IL 60604
312-922-0317

Educational Resources Information Center
(ERIC)
U.S. Department of Education
Office of Educational Research and Improvement
Washington, D.C. 20208-1235
1-800-USE-ERIC

Educators for Social Responsibility (ESR)
Larry Dieringer, Executive Director
23 Garden Street
Cambridge, MA 02138
617-492-1764

Foxfire Fund Inc.
Hilton Smith
P.O. Box B
Rabun Gap, GA 30568
706-746-5318, 706-746-5828
FAX: 706-746-5829

Institute for Democracy and Education (IDE)
Dr. George Wood, Director
119 McCracken Hall
Ohio University
Athens, OH 45701-2979
614-593-4531

Kentucky Education Reform Task Force
Office of Communications
Kentucky Department of Education
Capital Plaza Tower
Frankfort, KY 40601

National Clearinghouse on School-Based
Management
P.O. Box 948
Westbury, NY 11590

National Coalition of Education Activists
(NCEA)
Debi Duke
P.O. Box 405
Rosendale, NY 12472
914-658-8115

National Committee for Citizens in Education
(NCCE)
900 2nd Street NE, Suite 8
Washington, D.C. 20002-3557
202-408-0447, 1-800-NETWORK (English),
1-800-LE AYUDA (en español)
This group also operates ACCESS, a computer-
ized information bank.

National Society for Experiential Education
3509 Haworth Drive, Suite 207
Raleigh, NC 27609-7229
919-787-3263

Parents' Institute for Quality Education
Dr. Alberto Ochoa
Policy Studies in Language and Cross-Cultural
Education
San Diego State University
San Diego, CA 92182-0137
619-594-5155

Quality School Consortium—Institute for Reality
Therapy
William Glasser, Founder
7301 Medical Center Drive, Suite 104
Canoga Park, CA 91307
818-888-0688

Rethinking Schools
Bob Peterson and David Levine
1001 East Keefe Avenue
Milwaukee, WI 53212
414-964-9646

Rochester Teachers' Association
Adam Urbanski, President
277 Alexander Street
Rochester, NY 14607
716-546-2681

School Development Project
Comer Project for Change in Education
Dr. Edward T. Joyner, Director
55 College Street
New Haven, CT 06511
203-737-4000

The Urban Network: A Program in Urban Design
for Elementary and Urban School Children
Dr. Sharon Sutton
College of Architecture and Urban Planning
2000 Bonisteel Boulevard, Room 3120
The University of Michigan, Ann Arbor, MI
48109-2069

Walt Whitman Center for the Culture and
Politics of Democracy
Dr. Benjamin Barber, Director
Department of Political Science
Hickman Hall, Douglass Campus
Rutgers University
New Brunswick, NJ 08903
908-932-6861

Yale University Child Study Center
Dr. James P. Comer, Director
230 South Frontage Road, P.O. Box 3333
New Haven, CT 06510-8009
203-785-2548

Schools Highlighted in This Book
The Alternative Community School (ACS)
David Lehman, Principal
111 Chestnut Street, Ithaca, NY 14850
607-274-2183

Central Park East Secondary School (CPESS)
Deborah Meier and Paul Schwarz, Co-Directors
1573 Madison Avenue
New York, NY 10029

Organizations Involving Youth in Democratic Living and Learning (Chapters Seven and Nine)

The GREEN Project—Global Rivers
Environmental Network
School of Natural Resources
University of Michigan
Ann Arbor, MI 48109-1115
617-764-6453

Kids Against Crime
Linda Warsaw, Founder
P.O. Box 22004
San Bernardino, CA 92406
714-882-1344

KIDS Consortium (Kids Involved Doing Service)
Marvin Rosenblum, Executive Director
P.O. Box 27
East Boothbay, ME 14544
207-633-3152
For their newsletter, please write to:
State House Station 130, Augusta, ME 04333

The Monday Group Environmental Education
Seminar
Bill Hammond, Director
Lee County School District
Environmental Education Department
2055 Central Avenue
Fort Myers, FL 33901
813-275-3033

National Youth Leadership Council
Jim Kielsmeier
1910 West County Road B, Room 216
Roseville, MN 55113
612-631-3672 or 1-800-366-6952
Newsletter: *The Generator*

Project Public Life—Public Achievement
147 Humphrey Center
301 19th Avenue South Minneapolis, MN 55455
612-625-0142

Youth Action Program (YAP)
Sonia Bu, Director
1280 Fifth Avenue
New York, NY 10029
212-860-8170

YouthBuild
55 Day Street
West Somerville, MA 02144
617-623-9900
National organization that grew out of Youth
Action Program.

Organizations Promoting Public Dialogue (Chapters Ten and Eleven)

Catholics for a Free Choice (CFFC)
1436 U Street NW, Suite 301
Washington, D.C. 20009-3916
202-986-6093
Serves as a clearinghouse for dialogue on abortion.

Jefferson Center for New Democratic Processes
364 Century Plaza
1111 Third Avenue South
Minneapolis, MN 55404-1007
612-333-5300 FAX: 612-344-1766

Kettering Foundation—National Issues Forum
200 Commons Road
Dayton, OH 45459-2799
800-221-3657, 513-434-7300

National Issues Forum
Carl W. Eschels, Director
116 Somerset Drive NE
Grand Rapids, MI 49503
616-451-0478

Study Circles Resource Center
Paul Aicher, Chairman
Phyllis Emigh, Director
P.O. Box 203, Route 169
Pomfret, CT 06258
203-928-2616 FAX: 203-928-3713

Utne Reader Neighborhood Salon Association
Griff Wigley
1624 Harmon Place
Minneapolis, MN 55403
613-338-5040

Training Resources for Democratic Living

The following organizations offer training for communities, community organizations, and individuals.

Appalachian Center at the University of Kentucky
The Commonwealth Fellowship Program
Lance Brunner, Director
Appalachian Center, 641 South Limestone
University of Kentucky
Lexington, KY 40506-0333
606-257-8264

Association of Community Organizations for
Reform Now (ACORN)
1026 Elysian Fields Avenue
New Orleans, LA 70017
504-943-0044
Aside from its head office in New Orleans, ACORN has active organizations throughout the country. Citizens who get involved in their communities through ACORN acquire training in a learning-through-doing approach. ACORN also operates a training center in the Midwest, located at 410 South Michigan Avenue, 4th Floor Annex, Chicago, IL 60605. Call 312-939-7488.

Community Boards of San Francisco
1540 Market Street, Room 490
San Francisco, CA 94102
415-863-6100
Publication: *Dispute Resolution Access: A Guide to Current Research and Information* (first issue free)
Community Boards conducts conflict management trainings nationwide in three areas: (1) they train educators and/or students to implement peer mediation in schools; (2) they train educators how to institute conflict resolution curricula in classrooms; (3) they train communities to begin neighborhood justice systems and train volunteers as mediators. In San Francisco, free neighborhood dispute resolution is also offered.

Gameliel Foundation
220 South State Street
Chicago, IL 60604
312-427-4616
Three week-long training sessions take place at Gameliel each year during March, July, and November. The experiential, interactive training is conducted by a multiethnic staff of organizers.

Grassroots Leadership Training Programs
Michelle Handler, Director of Education
Tema Okun, Director of Training
1300 Baxter Street, Suite 200
P.O. Box 36006
Charlotte, NC 28236
704-332-3090
Grassroots Leadership teaches organizations how to strategize and educate people about their concerns and goals.

Growing Community Associates
P.O. Box 5415
Berkeley, CA 94705
510-869-4878
Co-founders Carolyn Shaffer and Sandra Lewis and associates offer workshops, trainings, and consulting services to the general public and to groups and organizations. Growing Community teaches community-building skills and helps groups navigate the phases of community life.

Highlander Research and Education Center
1959 Highlander Way
New Market, TN 37820
615-933-3444
Highlander's training programs are more specialized and oriented toward organizers who have submitted applications for admission into the adult or youth weekend workshops. There are also limited programs in environmental issues and "economy schools," which guide small-scale community development.

Industrial Areas Foundation
36 New Hyde Park
Franklyn Square, NY 11011
516-354-1076
Anyone interested in community organizing (specifically revitalizing and rebuilding cities) can apply for training.

Iowa Peace Institute
917 Tenth Avenue, Box 480
Grinnell, IA 50112
515-236-4880 FAX: 515-236-6905
The Institute teaches conflict resolution to schools
(two to three times a year) and the general public.

Midwest Academy
225 West Ohio, Suite 100
Chicago, IL 60610
312-645-6010
The Academy conducts six to eight week-long
training sessions every year and offers ongoing
consulting and training for a limited number of
organizers and organizations.

National Training and Information Center
810 North Milwaukee Avenue
Chicago, IL 60622
312-243-3035
The Center provides training to nonprofit organizations in areas such as leadership development,
fundraising, and long-range planning. (Trainings
are designed according to the needs of an organization.)

Organize Training Center
442A Vicksburg
San Francisco, CA 94114
415-821-6180 FAX: 415-821-1631
The Center offers an array of training services
ranging from a guided-reading tutorial for individuals to on-site workshops for organizations across
the country. Phone consultations are also available.

Western States Center
522 S.W. Fifth, Suite 1390
Portland, OR 97204
503-228-8866
The Center offers grassroots training once a year
to people in the Northwest involved in citizen
organizations.

Resource and Information Centers
Center for Policy Alternatives
1875 Connecticut Avenue, NW, Suite 710
Washington, D.C. 20009
202-387-6030 FAX: 202-986-2539
Promotes state and local policy innovations
involving citizen participation.

Citizens for Tax Justice
1311 L Street NW, Suite 400
Washington, D.C. 20005
202-626-3780
A good source for facts on tax policy and its
impact on citizens.

World Hunger Year/Reinvesting in America
Robin Garr, Field Coordinator
505 8th Avenue, 21st Floor
New York, NY 10018
212-629-8850
A clearinghouse for information on successful
projects addressing poverty, hunger, and homelessness.

Periodicals
City Limits
40 Prince Street
New York, NY 10012
New York's community affairs news magazine.

Co-op America
2100 M Street NW, Suite 403
Washington, D.C. 20037
800-424-2667, 202-872-5307
Linking responsible businesses that believe in the
values of cooperation, community, and environmental health with consumers in a national network, a new "alternative marketplace."

GEO, Grassroots Economic Organizing Newsletter
P.O. Box 5065
New Haven, CT 06525
203-389-6194
Covers developments in worker ownership and
workplace democracy.

In Context
P.O. Box 11470
Bainbridge Island, WA 98110
206-842-0216
Focuses on community-based initiatives with emphasis on ecological and social sustainability.

Kettering Review
200 Commons Road
Dayton, OH 45459
800-221-3657, 513-434-7300
Reflective, provocative essays on citizens' role in democratic public life.

Neighborhood Works
Center for Neighborhood Technology
2125 West North Avenue
Chicago, IL 60647
Focuses on urban, citizen-led economic and social development and related national policy.

Organize Training Center Mailer
442A Vicksburg
San Francisco, CA 94114
415-821-6180 FAX: 415-821-1631
A quarterly collection of newspaper and magazine articles from all over the country dealing with citizen empowerment.

Shelterforce
National Housing Institute
439 Main Street
Orange, NJ 07050
201-678-3110
The latest strategies for meeting America's housing crisis, from a non-profit organization building a national network of tenant and housing groups.

Social Policy
Room 1212, 33 West 42nd Street
New York, NY 10036
Readable essays on self-help and people-centered politics.

Utne Reader
c/o LENS Publishing Co., Inc.
1624 Harmon Place, Suite 330
Minneapolis, MN 55403
613-338-5040
Selections from the best of the alternative press.

Directories of Citizen Organizations

Walls, David, *Activist's Almanac: The Concerned Citizen's Guide to the Leading Advocacy Organizations in America* (New York: Fireside, 1993).

Brockway, Sandi, ed., *Macrocosm USA: An Environmental, Political, and Social Solutions Handbook with Directories* (Cambria, California: Macrocosm USA, Inc., 1992).

Notes

Chapter One: A Powerful New Concept For Effective Living

1. Jason Deparle, "The Problems of the Ghetto," *New York Times*, May 17, 1992, Week in Review section.

Chapter Three: Claiming Our Self-Interest (It's Not Selfishness)

1. Allan Luks with Peggy Payne, "Helper's High: The First Phase," in *The Healing Power of Doing Good* (New York: Ballantine Books, 1992).

Chapter Four: Discovering Power (It's Not a Dirty Word)

1. Seth Kreisberg, *Transforming Power* (Albany, N.Y.: SUNY Press, 1992), 29.
2. Virginia Sherry, "Heroes for Hard Times," *Mother Jones*, Jan. 1988, 25–33.
3. "Shared Decision Making at the School Site: Moving Toward a Professional Model," *American Educator*, Spring 1987, 16.
4. "Shared Decision Making at the School Site: Moving Toward a Professional Model," 17.
5. M. C. Rist, "Here's What Empowerment Will Mean for Your Schools," *Executive Educator*, Aug. 1989, 19.
6. Thomas A. Stewart, "New Ways to Exercise Power," *Fortune*, Nov. 6, 1989, 52, quoting Reuben Mark at Colgate.
7. Texas IAF Network, *Vision, Values, Action*, 38.
8. *Washington Post*, Oct. 21, 1991.
9. Dorothy Stoneman, "Leadership Development," *A Handbook from the Youth Action Program of the East Harlem Block Schools*, Youth Action Program, 1280 Fifth Avenue, New York, N.Y. 10029, 161–162.
10. R'Moshe ben Asher, "Community Organizing in Orange County, California," *Organizing*, Fall–Winter 1992, 33.

Chapter Five: Our Jobs, Our Economy, and Our Lives

1. "The Wealth Grab," *Dollars and Sense*, Oct. 1992, 23. See also: "The 1980's: A Very Good Time for the Very Rich," *New York Times*, Mar. 5, 1993, 1.

2. For help in making consumer choices based on corporate policies, contact the Council on Economic Priorities, 30 Irving Place, New York, N.Y. 10003. For a comprehensive list of socially responsible investment opportunities, see Co-op America's *National Green Pages*, 1850 M Street NW, Suite 700, Washington, D.C. 20036. Or write to Social Investment Forum, 711 Atlantic Avenue, Boston, Mass. 02111.

3. Gerald Epstein, "Mortgaging America," *World Policy Journal*, vol. 8, no. 1, Winter 1990–91, 35, 38.

4. Jeremy Brecher and Tim Costello, eds., *Building Bridges: The Emerging Grassroots Coalition of Labor and Community* (New York: Monthly Review Press, 1990), 28.

5. For a useful analysis of the labor economy and the impact of Reagan's policy on labor and unions during the 1980s, see Bennett Harrison and Barry Bluestone, *The Great U-Turn: Corporate Restructuring and the Polarizing of America* (New York: Basic Books, 1988).

6. "Trapped in the Impoverished Middle Class," *New York Times*, Nov. 17, 1991, Business section, 10.

7. "Executive Pay: The Party Ain't Over Yet," *Business Week*, Apr. 26, 1993, 57.

8. Myron Magnet, "The Truth About the American Worker," *Fortune*, May 4, 1992, 57–58.

9. Robert Levering, Milton Moskowitz, and Michael Katz, *The 100 Best Companies to Work for in America* (Reading, Mass.: Addison-Wesley, 1989 revised, 1992).

10. *Newsweek*, Dec. 12, 1991, 46.

11. Quoted in "Money Best," *Marin Independent Journal*, May 11, 1992, B6.

12. Ralph Stayer, "How I Learned to Let My Workers Lead," *Harvard Business Review*, Nov.–Dec. 1990, 8.

13. John Naisbitt and Patricia Aburdene, *Reinventing the Corporation* (New York: Warner Books, 1985), 93, citing a Yankelovich, Skelly, and White source.

14. *Dallasite*, Dec. 1991.

15. *Newsweek*, Dec. 16, 1991, 46.

16. *Employee Ownership Report*, vol. 11, no. 6, Nov.–Dec. 1991, 5.

17. Quote used with permission from the research of Robert Levering for the revised edition of *The 100 Best Companies to Work for in America*.

18. "Report Seeks to Bridge Schools, Jobs," *AFL-CIO Newsletter*, Apr. 27, 1992, 2.

19. *AFL-CIO Reviews the Issues*, Report No. 61, July 1992, 3.

20. Magnet, "The Truth About the American Worker," 64.

21. Anne Donnellon, *The Meaning of Teamwork* (forthcoming).

22. Stayer, "How I Learned to Let My Workers Lead," 7, 9.

23. Susan G. Cohen and Gerald E. Ledford, Jr., *The Effectiveness of Self-Managing Teams: A Quasi-Experiment*, Center for Effective Organization, University of Southern California, 1992, 5–6. (CEO G 91-6 [191])

24. Edward E. Lawler III, *High-Involvement Management: Participative Strategies for Improving Organizational Performance* (San Francisco: Jossey-Bass, 1986), 223.

25. Donald E. Petersen and John Hallkirk, *A Better Idea: Redefining the Way Americans Work* (Boston: Houghton Mifflin, 1991), 46.

26. Corey Rosen and Karen M. Young, eds., *Understanding Employee Ownership* (Ithaca, N.Y.: ILR Press, 1991), 8.

27. Rosen and Young, *Understanding Employee Ownership*, 2–3.

28. Rosen and Young, *Understanding Employee Ownership*, 10–11.

29. Dan Swinney, *Towards a New Vision of Community Economic Development*, unpublished paper, Midwest Center for Labor Research, Apr. 1991, 7. Please see Resources p. 306 for more information on the center.

30. "15 Employee Owned Companies on List of Top 400 Private Firms," *Employee Ownership Report*, vol. 12, no. 1, Jan.–Feb. 1992, 6.

31. Joseph Blasi, Douglas Kruse, and Michael Conte, comps., *Employee Ownership Index*, press release by Rutgers University, May 1993.

32. Rosen and Young, *Understanding Employee Ownership*, 10–11.

33. Rosen and Young, *Understanding Employee Ownership*, 15.

34. Rosen and Young, *Understanding Employee Ownership*, 3.

35. Rosen and Young, *Understanding Employee Ownership*, 127.

36. Jonathan Rowe, "Workers Run Home-Care Business," *The Christian Science Monitor*, Aug. 6, 1990, 12.

37. The Financial Democracy Campaign states that the Savings and Loan bailout will cost the United States $1.2 trillion, including interest. Typically, estimates of the cost do not include interest, which will ultimately account for about two-thirds of the total. The Financial Democracy Campaign charges that the method chosen by the government to deal with the bailout—thirty- to forty-year bank bonds—has added this interest burden. Its estimate is taken from a report coauthored by Dan Brumbaugh, former chief economist for the Federal Home Loan Bank Board. See James R. Barth and R. Dan Brumbaugh, Jr., *Stanford Law and Policy Review*, vol. 2, no. 1, 1990, 58–67.

38. Estimate from Citizens for Tax Justice, Washington, D.C.

39. *AFL-CIO News*, Apr. 27, 1992, 10, citing the Children's Defense Fund.

40. For general background about the topic, see: Donald L. Barlett and James B. Steele, *America: What Went Wrong?* (Kansas City, Mo.: Andrews and McMeel, 1992).

41. Margie Romero, "Making Bread from Scratch," *In Pittsburgh*, Nov. 13–19, 1991. See also: Tom Croft, "Achieving City Pride," *Labor Research Review*, no. 19, 1992, 10.

42. For more information, write to the Midwest Center for Labor Research. For their address, see Resources p. 306.

43. Alison Jones, "Bonnie Wright, Profile," *News and Observer*, Jan. 4, 1990.

44. For more information, write to the Center for Community Self-Help. The address appears in Resources p. 306.

45. For this and other data about the Community Land Trust approach, write to the Institute for Community Economics (ICE). See Resources p. 305. for its address.

46. "'Partner' Helps Buyers Grab a First Rung on Housing Ladder," *Los Angeles Times*, Jan. 28, 1992, A5.

47. Interview with Chuck Matthei, June 1992.

48. Jeremy Brecher, "If All the People Are Banded Together: The Naugatuck Valley Project," in *Building Bridges: The Emerging Grassroots Coalition of Labor and Community*, 1990, 93–105. Additional material about the project comes from the Naugatuck Valley Project. For their address, see Resources p. 304.

Chapter Six: Making the Media Our Voice

1. Ben H. Bagdikian, *The Media Monopoly*, 3rd ed. (Boston: Beacon Press, 1990), 21.

2. David K. Dunaway, "Save Our Stations," *New York Times*, May 23, 1992, opinion page. The number of radio stations permitted to one owner rose from twenty-four to sixty; the number of TV stations rose from twelve to twenty-four.

3. David Rynecki, "How Are We Doing?" *Columbia Journalism Review*, Jan.–Feb. 1992, 5, citing Times Mirror-Gallup polls.

4. Strategies for Media Literacy, San Francisco, California. These and related data can be found in its newsletter, *Strategies*, vol. 4, no. 4.

5. Ben H. Bagdikian, "A Modern Morality Play in Manteca," *San Francisco Bay Guardian*, July 17, 1991.

6. Mike Feinsilber, "Something's Missing in One-Paper Towns," *Washington Times*, Dec. 7, 1991.

7. Donald L. Barlett and James B. Steele, *America: What Went Wrong?* (Kansas City, Mo.: Andrews and McMeel, 1992).

8. Tim Giago, Rapid City, South Dakota, from an interview with researcher Tamara Gould, Jan. 27, 1992.

9. "Paper Gives a Voice to Plains Indians," *New York Times*, Sept. 19, 1991.

10. "Paper Gives a Voice to Plains Indians."

11. Pat Aufderheide and Jeffrey Chester, *Talk Radio* (New York: Benton Foundation, 1990), 6, citing Radio Advertising Bureau data. *Talk Radio* is available from 1710 Rhode Island Avenue, Washington, D.C. 20036.

12. Aufderheide and Chester, *Talk Radio*, 7–8.

13. National Issues Forum address: 200 Commons Road, Dayton, Ohio 45459-2799, 513-434-7300.

14. Our thanks to research intern Kate Melby and researcher-writer Trena Cleland for their assistance in gathering this information on Paso del Norte.

15. Red Burns, "Beyond Statistics," in Martin C. J. Elton, William A. Lucas, and David W. Conrath, eds., *Evaluating New Telecommunications Services* (New York: Plenum, 1978). Burns is director of the Alternate Media Center, Tisch School of the Arts, New York University. Please see Resources p. 307 for the complete address.

16. Red Burns, "Cultural Identity and Integration in the New Media World," paper presented at the University of Industrial Arts, Helsinki, 1991.

17. Red Burns, "Beyond Statistics." Italics added.

18. Jennifer Stearns, *A Short Course in Cable, How UAW Members Can Use TV More Effectively*, United Auto Workers, Washington, D.C., 1982.

19. Don Rittner, *Ecolinking* (Berkeley: Peachpit Press, 1992).

20. Dave Hughes, from an interview with researcher-writer Trena Cleland.

21. Dorothy Green, from an interview with researcher-writer Trena Cleland.

22. Andrew Hay, "Using Video: Make Television Work for You," *Neighborhood Works*, June–July 1992, 16–19.

23. Ted Koppel, "Nightline," Sept. 27, 1989.

24. Jay Davis, adjunct staff, Center for Media and Values, Los Angeles, Calif., and Atlanta, Ga., Dec. 1991. From an interview with researcher-writer Trena Cleland. Italics added.

25. Bruce Campbell, from an interview with researcher-writer Trena Cleland.

Chapter Seven: From Client to Citizen

1. The Youth Action Program is a youth-oriented group that engages young people in community improvement projects, leadership development opportunities, and cultural awareness. It has also spawned a national program called YouthBuild. For their address, see Resources p. 312.

2. David Grossman and Geraldine Smolka, "New York City's Poverty Budget," Community Service Society of New York, 1984; Diane Kallenback and Arthur Lyons, "Government Spending for the Poor in Cook County, Illinois: Can We Do Better?" Center for Urban Affairs and Policy Research, 1989. For their address, please see Resources p. 308.

3 Martin E. P. Seligman, *Learned Optimism* (New York: Pocket Books, 1990), 87–88. Italics added.

4. From an interview with Susan Baird Kanaan, independent researcher, Chevy Chase, Md., 1991.

5. Frank Riessman, "The Self-Help World View," unpublished paper, *National Self-Help Clearing House*. See also Frank Riessman and Audrey Gartner, "The Surgeon General and the Self-Help Ethos," *Social Policy*, Fall 1987.

6. *Self-Helper*, vol. 7, no. 1, Winter 1992, 2.

7. Frank Riessman, "Restructuring Help: A Human Services Paradigm for the 1990s," *American Journal of Community Psychology*, vol. 18, no., 2, 1990, 229.

8. P. S. Jensen, "Risk, Protective Factors and Supportive Interventions in Chronic Airway Obstruction," *Archives of General Psychiatry*, vol. 40, no. 11, 1983. This is only one of many examples compiled by Louis J. Medvene, Associate Professor of Psychology, Claremont Graduate School, Benezet Psychology Building, 241 East 11th Street, Claremont, Calif. 91711-6175.

9. Our appreciation to researcher-writer Trena Cleland for providing the case study for this section on Kids Against Crime.

10. David Osborne and Ted Gaebler, *Reinventing Government* (Reading, Mass.: Addison-Wesley, 1992), 60.

11. Osborne and Gaebler, *Reinventing Government*, 62.

12. Robert L. Woodson, *Washington Post*, Nov. 12, 1988, letter to the editor.

13. Osborne and Gaebler, *Reinventing Government*, 64.

14. "A Ten-Point Agenda For Change," *Shelterforce*, Nov.–Dec. 1992, no. 66, 14.

15. Sarah Griffen and Chris Tilly, "Rocking the House: Public Tenants Hold Jack Kemp to His Word," *Dollars and Sense*, Dec. 1991, 12–15.

16. D. Speigel, H. C. Kramer, J. R. Bloom, and E. Gottheil, "Effect of Treatment on Survival of Patients with Metastatic Breast Cancer," *The Lancet, 8668,* 1989, 888–891.

17. *Utne Reader*, Jan.–Feb. 1992, 94.

18. Dr. Roger C. Mills, "The Psychology of Mind Applied to Substance Abuse, Drop-out and Delinquency Prevention, The Modello-Homestead Gardens (Public Housing) Intervention Project," paper presented at the Florida Alcohol and Drug Abuse Association Annual Conference, Orlando, Fla., Apr. 1991, 11, 14, 22. Also, untitled video about Modello-Homestead Gardens produced by the Metro-Dade Police Department and Informed Families, 1991.

19. "Fostering the Family," *Newsweek*, June 22, 1992, 64.

20. Joan Barthel, *For Children's Sake: The Promise of Family Preservation*, Edna McConnell Clark Foundation, 250 Park Avenue, New York, N.Y. 10177-0026, 1992. An excellent introduction to family preservation programs.

21. Frank Riessman, "Self-Help-Mutual Aid and Social Change," *Perception, Canada's Social Development Magazine*, vols. 15-4–16-1, Fall–Winter 1992, 56.

22. Riessman, "Self-Help-Mutual Aid and Social Change," 57.

Chapter Eight: Governing "By the People"

1. Our thanks to researcher-writer Trena Cleland for developing the case study from which this is drawn. For a complete case study, please contact the Center for Living Democracy. The address is at the end of this book.

2. Phillip M. Stern, *The Best Congress Money Can Buy* (New York: Pantheon Books, 1988).

3. From Common Cause, Washington, D.C.

4. *Citizens and Politics: A View from Main Street America.* Prepared for the Kettering Foundation by the Harwood Group, June 1991, v. For the address of the Kettering Foundation, please see Resources p. 312.

5. *Citizens and Politics: A View from Main Street America*, 37.

6. Amitai Etzioni, "A New Community of Thinkers, Both Liberal and Conservative," *Wall Street Journal*, Oct. 8, 1991.

7. For the address of the Community Design Exchange, please see Resources p. 309.

8. John Stuart Hall and Louis F. Weschler, "The Phoenix Futures Forum: Creating Vision, Implanting Community," *National Civic Review*, Spring 1991, 135.

9. For the address of American Health Decisions, please see Resources p. 308.

10. Northwest Area Foundation, *Newsletter of the Northwest Area Foundation*, no. 12, Mar. 1992, 8.

11. *Seattle Times*, June 3, 1991.

12. For more information about a model citizen-led program for community policing, contact: Safe Streets Now! a division of the Drug Abatement Institute, 1221 Broadway, Plaza Level, Suite 13, Oakland, CA 94612, 510-846-4622.

13. Cornelius J. Behan, "Coping with Fear," *Public Management*, Jan. 1986, 5.

14. James Bennet, "New York, Saying Crime Figures Distort Reality, Asks Public to Help Rate the Police," *New York Times*, Aug. 16, 1992, 22.

15. Joseph N. Boyce, "Softer Style of Policing Takes Hold in Cities Like Tacoma Park, Md.," *Wall Street Journal*, Aug. 5, 1992, A7; Behan, 3.

Chapter Nine: Educating Real-World Problem Solvers

1. Many of the initiatives cited in this chapter draw on the work of philosopher John Dewey. For a persuasive argument for democratic education written almost forty-five years ago, see L. Stiles and M. Dorsey, *Democratic Teaching in Secondary Schools* (New York: Lippincott, 1950).

2. Deborah W. Meier, "Schools and Democracy: Choice Can Save Public Education," *The Nation*, Mar. 4, 1991.

3. There are, for example, three hundred schools in the Coalition of Essential Schools network, based at Brown University; two thousand teachers linked through the Fox-fire network, centered in Georgia; one hundred schools applying the James Comer model, centered in New Haven; fifty chapters of Educators for Social Responsibility, headquartered in Cambridge; dozens of schools in William Glasser's Quality Schools movement; and dozens of chapters of the Institute for Democracy in Education, based at Ohio University. You'll find their addresses in Resources p. 310.

4. *Institute for Democracy in Education Reports*, Jan.–Feb. 1991. For the Institute's address, please see Resources p. 310.

5. Bill Elasky, "Becoming," *Democracy & Education*, vol. 4, no. 4, Summer 1990, 20.

6. Kim Wile, "Voter Information Persons," in *Students Writing About Community Affairs: Teachers Working with Students to Make a Difference Now, Not in Some Far-Off Future.* Occasional Paper no. 3, Institute for Democracy in Education, 1989, 16–19.

7. Nancy Corbett, "Magic Moments," *Democracy & Education*, vol. 4, no. 2, Winter 1989, 10, 13.

8. Bill Hammond, "The Monday Group: From Awareness to Action," *Secondary Schools Activity Guide*, Project WILD, Salina Star Route, Boulder, Colo. 80302, 1983, 267.

9. *The Generator, National Journal of Service Leadership*, vol. 11, no. 3, Winter 1991.

10. David W. Johnson, Roger T. Johnson, Edythe Johnson Holubec, and Patricia Roy, *Circles of Learning*, Association for Supervision and Curriculum Development, Alexandria, Va., 1984, 7. These authors have created a wealth of teaching tools to further cooperative learning. For more information, contact the Cooperative Learning Center, College of Education, University of Minnesota, 150 Pillsbury Drive SE, Minneapolis, Minn. 55455-0298.

11. David W. Johnson and Roger T. Johnson, *Cooperation and Competition: Theory and Research* (Edina, Minn.: Interaction, 1989).

12. David W. Johnson and Roger T. Johnson, "Cooperative Learning and Achievement," in Shlomo Sharan, ed., *Cooperative Learning: Theory and Research* (New York: Praeger, 1990), 22–37.

13. Johnson, Johnson, Holubec, and Roy, *Circles of Learning*, 50.

14. Ruth Sidney Charney, *Teaching Children to Care*, Northeast Foundation for Children, 1992, 10.

15. JoAnn Shaheen, "Democratic Discipline, Democratic Lives," *Democracy & Education*, vol. 3, no. 2, Winter 1988, 5. Shaheen has also produced a curriculum for creating a democratic elementary school classroom. The curriculum, *Free to Teach, Free to Learn*, is available from the Master Teacher, Inc., Leadership Lane, P.O. Box 1207, Manhattan, Kans. 66502, 1-800-669-9633.

16. "Teachers Alter Roles in Spanish," *New York Times*, Apr. 16, 1992, A17.

17. Elasky, "Becoming," 20.

18. Contract between the Denver Public Schools and the Denver Classroom Teachers Association, Jan. 1, 1991, to Aug. 31, 1994. Executive Summary.

19. From an interview with former CDL Associate Director, Molly Hamaker.

20. Edward B. Fiske, *Smart Schools, Smart Kids: Why Do Some Schools Work?* (New York: Simon & Schuster, 1991).

21. *KIDS: The newsletter for people involved in getting children involved*, Spring 1992. Please see Resources p. 312 for the address of KIDS.

22. "True Service Can't be Coerced," *New York Times*, Aug. 2, 1992, editorial page.

23. "School Faces Suit on Volunteerism," *New York Times*, Sept. 23, 1990, A22.

24. "History of the West Philadelphia Improvement Corps," Ira Harkavy, Director, Penn Program for Public Service, University of Pennsylvania, 3440 Market Street, Philadelphia, Pa. 19104. Quotations are from Ira Harkavy's testimony before the House Education and Labor Committee, June 28, 1989.

25. Polaroid's 1991 Annual Report, 23.

26. The Greater Baltimore Committee, 111 South Calvert Street, Suite 1500, Baltimore, Md. 21202.

27. "After Two Tough Years, Reformers Look to Future," *Education Week*, vol. 9, no. 7, Oct. 18, 1989, 10.

28. Kim Wile, *Students Writing About Community Affairs: Teachers Working with Students to Make a Difference Now, Not in Some Far-Off Future*, 19.

29. Wile, *Students Writing About Community Affairs: Teachers Working with Students to Make a Difference Now, Not in Some Far-Off Future*, 49.

Chapter Ten: Mastering the Arts of Democracy: One-on-One Skills

1. Write to the Center for Living Democracy for more about the "Believing Game." The address is at the end of this book.

2. The Listening Project, Rural Southern Voice for Peace, 1898 Hannah Ranch Road, Burnsville, N.C. 28714.

3. Roger Fisher, William Ury, and Bruce Patton, *Getting to Yes: Negotiating Agreement Without Giving In*, 2nd ed. (New York: Penguin Books, 1991).

4. Parker J. Palmer, "Community, Conflict and Ways of Knowing: Ways to Deepen Our Educational Agenda," in *Combining Service and Learning: A Resource Book for Community and Public Service*, vol. 1, National Society for Experiential Education, 111–112. For more information, write or call the society. The address is in Resources p. 311.

5. A clearinghouse for such "common ground" groups is being set up by Catholics for a Free Choice; for more information, call 202-986-6093. The address is in Resources p. 312.

6. We thank researcher-writer Trena Cleland for her case study of Community Boards, from which these quotations are drawn.

7. David Singer, "Teaching Alternative Dispute Resolution to America's School Children," *Arbitration Journal*, Dec. 1991, 33.

8. For a useful comparison of seven conflict resolution programs and their training materials, order *Fostering Peace* from the Iowa Peace Institute. For the address, please see Resources p. 314.

9. Deborah Prothrow-Stith with Michaele Weissman, *Deadly Consequences: How Violence Is Destroying Our Teenage Population and a Plan to Begin Solving the Problem* (New York: HarperCollins, 1991), 175.

10. Singer, "Teaching Alternative Dispute Resolution to America's School Children," 34.

11. "Beyond Adversity: The Value of Collective Bargaining in a Free Society (A Conversation with W. J. 'Bill' Usery, Jr.)," *Labor Relations Today*, U.S. Dept. of Labor, Bureau of Labor-Management Relations and Cooperative Programs, Nov.–Dec. 1987, 4.

Chapter Eleven: Mastering the Arts of Democracy: Group Skills

1. Colman McCarthy, *Washington Post* columnist, quoting from Peter Kropotkin's *Mutual Aid: A Factor in Evolution* (Concord, Mass.: Paul & Co. 1988).

2. Benjamin J. Barber, "Public Talk and Civic Action: Education for Participation in a Strong Democracy," *Social Education*, vol. 53, no. 6, Oct. 1989.

3. Susan Campbell, "Reviving Discourse as a Citizen's Art," *Hartford Courant*, Nov. 16, 1991.

4. Len Oliver, *Study Circles: Coming Together for Personal Growth and Social Change* (Cabin John, Md.: Seven Locks Press), xv.

5. *Focus on Study Circles*, the Newsletter of the Study Circles Resource Center, Winter 1992. For their address, please see Resources p. 312.

6. Thanks to Center for Living Democracy former Associate Director Molly Hamaker for this interview.

7. Daniel Yankelovitch, *Coming to Public Judgment* (Syracuse, N.Y.: Syracuse University Press, 1991), 24.

8. "Directions, Policy Choices Made by Arizona's Youth on AIDS, Employment, Water, Arizona Extension 4-H, and the Maverick Institute," 1988. For the address of the Maverick Institute, see Resources p. 309.

9. Roberto Suro, "Toward Deeper Debates of the Public Agenda, " *New York Times*, July 19, 1992, Week in Review section, 18. Ned Crosby heads the Jefferson Center. Please see Resources p. 312 for the Center's address.

10. Melanie A. Zuercher, *Making History: The First Ten Years of KFTC* (Prestonburg, Ky.: Kentuckians for the Commonwealth, 1991). For KFTC's address, see Resources p. 304.

11. Cooperative Home Care Associates planning document, 1992, 10. For CHCA's address, see Resources p. 305.

12. John Naisbitt and Patricia Aburdene, *Reinventing the Corporation* (New York: Warner Books, 1985), 44.

Chapter Twelve: Embracing the Democratic Self

1. Ralph Stayer, "How I Learned to Let My Workers Lead," *Harvard Business Review*, Nov.–Dec. 1990, 8.

2. Ann C. Crouter, "Participative Work as an Influence on Human Development," *Journal of Applied Developmental Psychology*, vol. 5, 1984, 84.

3. Michael and Lise Wallach, "Virtue Desired," *Rethinking Goodness* (Albany, N.Y.: SUNY Press, 1990).

4. *Democracy & Education*, Winter 1989, vol. 4, no. 2, 13.

Index

The Authors

HUSBAND-AND-WIFE TEAM **Frances Moore Lappé** and **Paul Martin Du Bois** direct the Center for Living Democracy in Brattleboro, Vermont. Both are best-selling authors with decades of hands-on leadership in social change organizations.

FRANCES MOORE LAPPÉ created a nutrition revolution in 1971 with her *Diet for a Small Planet*, which has sold more than three million copies in six languages. In 1975, she co-founded the Institute for Food and Development Policy, described by the *New York Times* as one of the nation's most respected food think tanks. Lappé has authored or coauthored eleven books, from *Food First: Beyond the Myth of Scarcity* (1977) to *Rediscovering America's Values* (1989). They have been used in a broad array of college courses—including economics, nutrition, and sociology—in hundreds of U.S. colleges and universities. They have also been translated into twenty-two languages and used in over fifty countries. Her articles have appeared in publications as diverse as the *New York Times, Reader's Digest, Journal of Nutrition Education, Los Angeles Times, Tikkun, Utne Reader,* and *Harpers.*

Lappé has received numerous awards for her work. In Sweden in 1987, she became the fourth American to receive the Right Livelihood Award, sometimes called the "alternative Nobel," for her "vision and work healing our planet and uplifting humanity."

PAUL MARTIN DU BOIS founded a community newspaper, a rape crisis center, and an inner-city printing company during the early 1970s in Rochester, New York. He also served as executive director of FIGHT (Freedom, Independence, God, Honor, Today), at that time New York State's largest African-American community organization, developing city-wide programs in education, employment, and housing.

As a tenured professor at the University of Tennessee and Tennessee State University in the late 1970s, Du Bois taught graduate courses while hosting regular radio and television programs on public policy. He served as president of Planned Parenthood of Nashville and consulted on leadership issues in state governments, minority training programs, human service agencies, and professional associations.

In the 1980s, Du Bois served as director of the public policy program and vice president of the College of the Atlantic in Maine, and then as vice president of Cambridge College in Massachusetts. In 1985, he became executive director of the Association of Humanistic Psychology. In addition, he has served in many important volunteer positions, including president of a NOW (National Organization for Women) chapter, and board member of a Native American economic development corporation and RAN, the Rainforest Action Network.

Du Bois also has received numerous honors, travel awards, and research grants. In 1979, he wrote *Modern Administrative Practices*, a textbook on leadership in human services that has been widely used in graduate courses. His writings also include a book on health care policy and hospices as well as over thirty articles.

Du Bois and Lappé founded the Center for Living Democracy to put the message of *The Quickening of America* into action. Through workshops and other training programs, extensive public speaking, publications, and the distribution of citizen learning tools, the Center enables Americans to discover the rewards of public engagement.

Please Let Us Hear From You

If you have been moved by this book, please let us know. Tell us:

What you agree with in this book or find most helpful—its strengths—and what you disagree with—its weaknesses:

_____

_____

_____

Whether you'd like us to send information about the Center for Living Democracy. (We offer workshops and many other presentations on Living Democracy, and we distribute a wide array of learning tools to help you put this book to use. We also have a volunteer program.): Yes ☐   No ☐

Other people (or organizations) you think we should reach with the message of this book—and any suggestions you have for contacting them:

_____

_____

Thank you!

Your name _____

Address_____

Telephone Number _____

Detach or copy and send to:

Center for Living Democracy
RR#1 Black Fox Road
Brattleboro, VT 05301
Phone: (802) 254-4331
Fax: (802) 254-1227